The Spirit of the Old Testament

Journal of Pentecostal Theology
Supplement Series

35

General Editor

John Christopher Thomas

ISSN 0966 7393

Deo Publishing

The SPIRIT *of the* OLD TESTAMENT

Rickie D. Moore

deo
PUBLISHING

BLANDFORD FORUM

Journal of Pentecostal Theology Supplement Series, 35
ISSN 0966 7393

Printed by Henry Ling Ltd, at the Dorset Press, Dorchester, DT1 1HD, UK

British Library Cataloguing-in-Publication data
A catalogue record for this book is available from the British Library

ISBN 978-1-905679-11-9

Contents

Preface

This collection of a number of my Old Testament studies is diverse in terms of both the range of biblical materials covered (focusing on books from all three parts of the Hebrew canon) and the span of times during which the separate articles were composed (coming from all phases of my 25-year stint, so far, of teaching and studying the Old Testament). Yet alongside this diversity there is, I believe, a detectable unity that runs through these pieces. It is a commonality that emerges in large part from the sustained communal context of worship and work that has been the locus and stimulus for most of these writings – the Church of God Theological Seminary. It is a coherence that stems even more particularly from the calling that I took up early on within the heart of the Seminary's corporate mission – a call to pursue an approach to Old Testament interpretation that refused the dichotomy between academic scholarship and Pentecostal spirituality and sought instead to re-fuse the connection between the sacred Scriptures and the Holy Spirit. The opening chapter of this volume is something of a testimony of how my journey in this calling unfolded, and it has been written presently to serve as an introduction and preview to the articles that follow.

All of these articles (or earlier versions of them), except those appearing in Chapters 1 and 6, have been published before in a number of venues that are specified in the acknowledgements below. I am most grateful for the publishers' permissions that allow so many of my dispersed works to come together now in a way that will facilitate ease of use, especially for my students, whose needs and interests have been the generating motivation for this present project. Yet as these works come together, gratitude must now be dispersed, for in traversing such a broad range of topics and times, I have many to thank, and I regret that this brief preface can in no way do justice to them all. Still I would venture to point to several whose help looms large across the span of this corpus.

First of all, I want to thank my Seminary elders, colleagues, and students, whose fellowship in our high calling these many years has provided much of the instigation and inspiration for this work. Robert Crick has been an especially important elder, who has played a pivotal role in helping me come to know my identity and calling before God within the church and the academy. Steven Land has been a formative and faithful mentor to me, particularly in the fusion of Pentecostal spirituality and scholarship, which he has so prophetically pioneered for us all. Chris Thomas has been a choice brother and chosen partner to me, especially in answering and attending to the call to 'write down the vision', so that those who come after us 'may run with it' (Hab. 2.2). I am amazed and grateful for the fruit of this partnership with Chris, beginning with the visionary venture of the *Journal of Pentecostal Theology,* which we founded together, and continuing right up to this present volume, which by Chris's own instigation and urging appears as a companion to his volume, *The Spirit of the New Testament.* The two can now stand together as a fitting testimony to the Spirit who spans every gap (intertestamental and otherwise) between us. In the Spirit, I can only believe for much more fruit to come.

I also want to express gratitude for those who have contributed to my writing in a less direct, though still vital way. This would include the wider community of biblical and theological scholars whom I first encountered in my esteemed teachers at Lee University and then Vanderbilt University. I am particularly appreciative of my Vanderbilt mentor, James L. Crenshaw, and his rigorous commitment to careful literary study and the artful articulation of it. My first professional publication, which is now presented in Chapter 11 of this volume, was first written as paper for a course I took with him in my second year of graduate school. His example raised a high standard that has never left me. Another important mentor for me from the wider academy, as my footnotes amply show, has been Old Testament theologian, Walter Brueggemann. Through his prolific writings and more recently through his generous friendship to me, he has opened more vistas and engendered more encouragement to chart new paths than he will ever know.

My own tribe within the academy has been the Society for Pentecostal Studies. My many friends and colleagues in this vibrant fellowship have contributed vital stimulus and support to me through the years in pursuing the paths of study represented in this volume. With gratitude, I now hope these collected writings will offer to this special community something beneficial in return.

Closer to home, I would finally acknowledge with profound thanksgiving those in my local church communion with whom I regularly worship, minister, and pray – and also my extended and imme-diate family members, most especially my wife, Jean, and our children, Hannah and Emily & Matthew, in whose companionship I find the cup of life and daily bread. The lives of all of these are alive in all my writing, even where they do not appear in the footnotes. They are bound to it as they are bound to me by the same Spirit whom I have discovered in the disparate pages of the Old Testament, the same Spirit who is ever striving to make all of our lives of a piece, all the disparate pages of our vocational life, church life, and family life – a living testi-mony that is singular and pure and whole.

Rickie D. Moore
January 1, 2008

Acknowledgments

The publishers and journals whose names appear below have kindly granted permission to include versions of the following articles in this volume:

'Canon and Charisma in the Book of Deuteronomy', *Journal of Pentecostal Theology* 1 (1992), pp. 75-92.

'Deuteronomy and the Fire of God', *Journal of Pentecostal Theology* 7 (October 1995), pp. 11-33.

'The Prophetic Calling: An Old Testament Profile and Its Relevance for Today', *Journal of the European Theological Association* 24 (2004), pp. 16-29.

'The Prophet as Mentor: A Crucial Facet of the Biblical Presentation of Moses, Elijah, and Isaiah', *Journal of Pentecostal Theology* 15.2 (April 2007), pp. 155-73.

'"And Also Much Cattle?!": Prophetic Passions and the End of Jonah', *Journal of Pentecostal Theology* 11 (October 1997), pp. 35-48.

'The Prophetic Path from Lament to Praise: Tracking the Burden of Habakkuk', *The Living Pulpit* 11.4 (October-December, 2002), pp. 26-27.

'Futile Labor vs Fertile Labor: Observing the Sabbath in Psalm 127', *The Living Pulpit* 7.2 (April-June, 1998), pp. 24-25.

'A Home for the Alien: Worldly Wisdom and Covenantal Confession in Proverbs 30:1-9', *Zeitschrift für die alttestamentliche Wissenschaft* 106 (1994), pp. 96-107.

'The Integrity of Job', *Catholic Biblical Quarterly* 45.1 (January 1983), pp. 17-31.

'Raw Prayer and Refined Theology: "You have not spoken straight to me, as my servant Job has" ', in Terry L. Cross and Emerson B. Powery, eds., *The Spirit and the Mind: Essays in Informed Pentecostalism* (In Honor of Donald N. Bowdle) (Lanham, MD: University Press of America, 2000), pp. 35-48.

Abbreviations

AncB	Anchor Bible
Bib	*Biblica*
BDB	*A Hebrew and English Lexicon of the Old Testament*, ed. F. Brown, S.R. Driver, and C.A. Briggs (Oxford: Clarendon Press, 1907)
BZAW	Beihefte zur Zeitschrift für die alttestamentliche Wissenschaft
CBQ	*Catholic Biblical Quarterly*
CBQMS	Catholic Biblical Quarterly Monograph Series
EPTA	European Pentecostal Theological Association
EvTh	*Evangelische Theologie*
FthSt	Freiburger theologische Studien
HKAT	Handkommentar zum Alten Testament
IB	Interpreter's Bible
ICC	International Critical Commentary
Int	*Interpretation*
JAAR	*Journal of the American Academy of Religion*
JBL	*Journal of Biblical Literature*
JNSL	*Journal of Northwest Semitic Languages*
JPS	Jewish Publication Society Translation (1955)
JPT	*Journal of Pentecostal Theology*
JPTSup	Journal of Pentecostal Theology Supplement Series
JSOT	*Journal for the Study of the Old Testament*
JSOTSup	Journal for the Study of the Old Testament Supplement Series
JTS	*Journal of Theological Studies*
KJV	King James Version
LXX	Septuagint
MT	Masoretic Text
NAB	New American Bible
NASB	New American Standard Bible
NEB	New English Bible
NICOT	New International Commentary on the Old Testament

NIV	New International Version
NJPS	New Jewish Publication Society Translation (1999)
NRSV	New Revised Standard Version
OTL	Old Testament Library
RB	*Revue Biblique*
RSV	Revised Standard Version
SBLDS	Society of Biblical Literature Dissertation Series
SBLMS	Society of Biblical Literature Monograph Series
VT	*Vetus Testamentum*
VTSup	Vetus Testamentum Supplement Series
ZAW	*Zeitschrift für die Alttestamentliche Wissenschaft*

1

A Pentecostal Approach to Teaching Old Testament

Finally there comes a time for summing things up. I have now taught Old Testament at a Pentecostal seminary, namely, the Church of God Theological Seminary, for a quarter of a century, and if I am not yet quite to the place of offering a total summation, I feel I can at least see it from here. It does not seem at all too early to do some subtotaling. There is a desire that can begin to stir in someone my age that, more and more these days, I take to be a worthy desire – one that the Old Testament (OT) itself would seem to commend and reinforce – and that is the desire to pass on one's deepest, most passionately held disco-veries and deposits to the next generation.[1] This is the spirit in which I wish to offer this presentation, and it goes along with the context in which I wish to offer it. Specifically, I want to give to those who would come after me in my extended Pentecostal family, particularly those in the vocation of studying and teaching Scripture and even more particularly in teaching the OT, something of my experience, my exploration, and my experimentation in pursuing, as I have done these last 25 years, a distinctly Pentecostal approach to the OT. And I want to do this in order to help and to instigate, if not inspire, others to find their own way forward, rather than someone else's.

When I began teaching the OT in 1982 I had to find my way be-tween two very separate worlds: (1) a North American classical Pente-costal church world that constituted the primary background of my engagement with the OT and (2) a late modern Western academic world that posed the primary foreground – the foreground especially insofar as I had yet, at that time, to finish my Vanderbilt PhD disserta-tion, and so the academy loomed large before me as the context in which I would have to prove myself as a scholar and a teacher. I say that I had to find my way *between* these two worlds, because, although I was deeply owing to them both, I was at rest in neither. Yet I had the growing sense, quite vague at first, that I must somehow not only

---

[1] See e.g. Ps. 78.1-8; Deut. 6.4-9.

navigate but also chart the uncharted territory between them, at least in my assigned province of OT study.

Early on I found two OT texts (or did they find me?) that gave me important bearings on my context – texts that in fact became defining paradigms for helping me to locate my place in the midst of these two vastly different worlds. The first was the story found in 2 Kings 22–23 of King Josiah and his reform that yielded the discovery of the book of the *torah* in the Jerusalem temple. This story helped me find myself particularly in relation to my North American Pentecostal background. The second was the story found in Daniel 1 where Daniel and the 'three Hebrew children' had to confront King Nebuchadnezzar's program of assimilation into the Babylonian empire and culture. This story helped me find my standpoint particularly in relation to the modern Western academy. These two OT stories came into view for me early in the development of my introductory OT course[2] and from then on shaped the course of my development.

In the Josiah narrative, Judah's neglect and loss of an older portion of canonical Scripture posed for me an extreme biblical example of the kind of problem I faced in my own Pentecostal context. The old covenant, in some seriously questionable ways, had been eclipsed by the new. For Judah in the 8th century BCE, the people had fallen under the sway of a kind of ancient dispensationalism wherein the gospel of the Davidic covenant had come to be taken in a way that dispensed with the *torah* of the Mosaic covenant. To lose the *torah* within the very midst of the temple well symbolized how the latter covenant tradition, even without any direct or official dismissal or displacement of the former, had been allowed to bury and banish the old covenant for

---

[2] The course title, as I inherited it in 1982, was simply 'Introduction to the Old Testament'. Several years ago during a time of seminary-wide curriculum review, the title was changed, in line with the way I had developed the course in the meantime, to 'Pentecostal Explorations of the Old Testament'. A parallel change was also made for our seminary's NT introductory course, 'Pentecostal Explorations of the New Testament', taught by my NT colleague, John Christopher Thomas, whose own distinctive Pentecostal directions are laid out in his 1998 Society for Pentecostal Studies presidential address, 'Pentecostal Theology in the Twenty-First Century', *Pneuma: The Journal of the Society for Pentecostal Studies* 20.1 (Spring 1998), pp. 3-19; esp. 13-16; now reprinted in John Christopher Thomas, *The Spirit of the New Testament* (Leiden/Blandford Forum: Deo Publishing, 2005), ch. 1. It was about this time that I began to team teach my introductory course, every other time it was offered, with Lee Roy Martin, my former student become colleague, who has been a valuable collaborative partner in my OT teaching ever since.

all practical (or *praxis*) purposes.[3] For Pentecostalism in the late 20th century, I sensed how the church had similarly fallen under the sway of popular dispensational approaches to the OT,[4] which had pushed this part of the canon increasingly into the background of our praxis and unto the margins of our faith. I did not have it all figured out, but I sensed somehow at the time that, as grandiose as it might sound, *the OT needed in some sense to be recovered or re-discovered within Pentecostalism* and that this was somehow at the heart of what I was being called upon to do or at least to pursue.

Furthermore, the story of Josiah, as I began to appropriate it for my situation, soon seemed to offer me a decisive clue as to how this task of recovering or re-discovering the OT was to unfold in my context. When Josiah first received the lost book that had been found, he immediately sought a word of the LORD concerning this book from the prophetess, Huldah (2 Kgs 22.11-14), whereupon Huldah promptly breaks forth with a prophetic word confirming and validating this written word of God. The Evangelical hermeneutical models that for such a long time had been informing (or was it conforming?) my Pentecostal tradition, especially in its more formal educational programs and processes, had taught me never to expect such a thing – a prophecy validating Scripture! Wasn't it supposed to go only the other way? At the very least, this story began to point me toward more dynamic ways of seeing the Word of God and the coming together and ongoing lively interplay between God's Scripture and God's Spirit. Thus I began to sense from Scripture itself that *a larger place needed to be acknowledged and allowed for the role of the Spirit in approaching and interpreting Scripture* and in our stated hermeneutical models and methods for biblical study.[5]

---

[3] Indeed the so-called Temple Sermon of Jeremiah, which came on the heels of Josiah's Reform (Jer. 7.1-15; cf. 26.1-9), clearly shows how the people were chanting a doctrine of eternal security in 'the temple of the LORD, the temple of the LORD' (7.4) to the complete disregard of the ethical demands of the Decalogue (7.9-10 – 'Will you steal, murder, commit adultery, swear falsely, burn incense to Baal and walk after other gods whom you do not know, and then come and stand before me in this house, which is called by my name and say, "We are saved to do all these abominations"?'). Jeremiah here thunders against this positional soteriology of cheap grace or, in his terms, 'trust in … this place, which I gave to you and your fathers' (7.14) with no commitment to *torah* 'ways' (7.3-5). Translations of Scripture in this volume are my own, unless otherwise noted.

[4] See Gerald T. Sheppard. 'Pentecostals and the Hermeneutics of Dispensationalism: The Anatomy of an Uneasy Relationship,' *Pneuma* 6.2 (Fall 1984), pp. 5-33.

[5] I remember how I was soon encouraged in this very direction from one voice that arose from within the ranks of Evangelicalism itself, Clark Pinnock,

And so the story of Josiah's revival posed a powerful biblical paradigm for my own sense of call to bring into the light the book of the old covenant in connection with the present voice of the Spirit, against dispensational approaches that had diminished the place of this ancient book and Evangelical hermeneutical perspectives that had diminished any place for this present voice.

It was not long after this that the story of Daniel 1 came into view as another passage of paradigmatic import for me as a Pentecostal OT teacher, helping me specifically with my relationship to the modern Western academy. I connected with this story at many points. The modern Western academy was not my native country; like Daniel and his compatriots in the first chapter of Daniel, I was an exile in a foreign land. Yet I could accept this as something brought about similarly by God's sovereign purpose and action. As Dan. 1.2 declares, exile to Babylon came because 'God *gave* ... Judah ... into the hand' of Nebuchadnezzar. Western modernity, like ancient Babylon, was a human dominion, and the clear implication of Daniel is that all human dominions arise only because God raises them. As Dan. 2.21 declares, God 'changes times and seasons; he removes kings and sets up kings'.

It was important for me to see that God had raised up Western modernity and that he had made me subject to it. And like Daniel and the three Hebrew children, I had been subjected in particular with respect to an educational program, which was, as it was in their case, coincidentally, a three-year program (Dan. 1.5) – a program with a surface agenda to teach me 'the language and the letters' of this alien dominion (Dan. 1.4) but also having a deeper aim to effect a more fundamental change of identity – in my case, this would be registered by the addition of a three-letter suffix, 'PhD'; in their case a more obvious re-identification with new alien names that bore witness to the gods of the Empire replacing native names that testified to a faith and an inheritance in Yahweh (Dan. 1.7).

Yet as this story highlights, Yahweh has his own agenda that is not subject to any human dominion, whether ancient and Middle Eastern or modern and Western. And so when 'Daniel resolves' (1.8 – and notice the text here uses not his newly given Babylonian name, Belteshazzar, but rather '*Daniel* resolves') to resist swallowing all of Babylon's agenda, the same God who '*gave*' the Hebrews 'into the hand' of Babylon (1.2) promptly acts to '*give* Daniel favor' with the Babylonians

The Scripture Principle (San Francisco, CA: Harper & Row, 1984), who offered here a daring revision of Evangelical doctrine on Scripture by means of what he described as a more Trinitarian model that particularly recognized a greater place for the Holy Spirit in all aspects of the production and processes of Scripture, from inspiration to interpretation to application.

(handwritten marginal notes:) we have done what Judah did ?! (Pentecostals)

(1.9), enough for him and his fellow Hebrews to pass a ten-day test ('better and healthier … than all … who ate the king's portion' – 1.15) – a surpassing grade that pre-figures their passing of the third-year test, their oral comps, if you will ('ten times better … in all matters of wisdom and understanding' – 1.20), all because, as the text says, 'God *gave* (the verb נתן [*nathan*] for the third time in the story) these four young men knowledge and skill in all literature and wisdom; and Daniel had discernment in all visions and dreams' (1.17). Thus, God's agenda involved giving something more than Babylon was capable of giving. Babylon, like the modern Western academy, can provide a formidable education in 'knowledge and skill in all literature', but God alone can give 'ten times more' and even more than that – something qualitatively and not just quantitatively more, namely, 'discernment in all visions and dreams'.

It was this last phrase in Dan. 1.17 that particularly caught my attention, for it points to a charismatic kind of knowledge coming together with an academic kind of knowledge, a knowing that is at home in the kingdoms of this world being augmented by a knowing that comes from beyond this world as something alien to it and yet now imported into it. When I saw these two modes of knowledge coming together in this single verse and in the person of Daniel, it was as if I was seeing for the first time with biblical clarity and authority the kind of agenda and aim that God had for me and for our Pentecostal seminary. Like a biblically grounded course objective and program goal, what I saw this verse illuminating was God's desire for my students, our graduates, to have 'knowledge and skill in all literature' but also at the same time and in juxtaposed contact with this, a divinely endowed gift of discernment in divine revelation.

Don't get me wrong; I did not take this as a mandate to start a charismatic clinic on dream interpretation. What I saw in Daniel was divine revelation coming into view in a way that, rather than elevating human understanding to absolute mastery, humbled all human understanding before God's unspeakable mystery. Again and again in the rest of the book I could see Daniel himself laid low before God's apocalyptic revelations – visions of the end that reveal the limits and spell the end of Daniel's own capacity to know and to interpret,[6] even as they pose 'the handwriting on the wall' for all Babylonian claims for ultimate knowledge and control (see Dan. 5).

In this too I could see a compelling paradigmatic insight for where I found myself in relation to the academy of Western modernity. In the humbling light, and at times even stunning radiance, of the apocalyptic

---

[6] See Dan. 2.16-23; 24-28; 4.18-19; 7.15-16; 8.15-17, 27; 9.2-23; 10.1-19; 12.8.

vision of my own Pentecostal heritage and experience, I, like Daniel, could see the end – the end of me and of my claims regarding the Master of Divinity and the end of Western modernity with all of its claims to possess ultimate knowledge and ultimate control through all of its institutions and methodologies, including its academic ones. Like Daniel, I came to see the handwriting on the wall. As in his case, others had seen it before I arrived on the scene. By the end of the 20th century many people had noticed the handwriting on the wall of modernity with more and more talk of *post*-modernity. I was summoned in to take a look after the party had already begun to break down. Yet I believe that through the apocalyptically conditioned eyes of my Pentecostalism[7] I was helped to see that there was more behind this handwriting than just 'the hand of a man' (Dan. 5.5). The seismic shift from modernity to post-modernity was not merely the doing of human cultural forces and developments, but it was also an *un*doing wrought by the hand of the God who not only sets up kingdoms but also brings them down.

Thus, I was given a new grasp on the story of my own context in late Western modernity through this old text from the book of Daniel that had now grasped me. I could see my place within modern biblical criticism by way of a much larger perspective. I was witnessing the fall of the dominance of a human system. I was living through a 'changing of times and seasons' – a changing behind which God's hand and God's vision could be seen coming to interpret, to critique, indeed to judge all things. As the Hebrew meaning of the name Daniel attests, 'God judges'. The book of Daniel, then, in its vision of the downfall of all human systems, which would include those of the modern Western academy, suggested to me grounds for a kind of *biblical criticism of modern biblical criticism*. Yet there was no room here for me to become elevated in this realization, for God alone appeared as the ultimate critic whose criticism was bringing me to the ground (like Daniel in 10.9!) along with everything else.

So how, then, was I to teach the OT in view of the paradigms that these two OT stories of Josiah and Daniel had opened to me? I have spent a good part of my years since then trying to respond to this question, and I still have not arrived at a complete and final answer. Yet I will now offer what I can up to this point.

First, I was led to focus on the importance of story as a literary form for the OT. The significance I found in the two biblical narratives

---

[7] See Steven J. Land, *Pentecostal Spirituality: A Passion for the Kingdom* (JPTSup 1; Sheffield: Sheffield Academic Press, 1993), whose groundbreaking study elaborates Pentecostal theology's grounding in a distinctive convergence of apocalyptic vision and passions.

noted above encouraged me to see and to pursue the significance of the place of narrative itself in relation to both Pentecostalism and the whole of Scripture, even as post-modern approaches had begun to shift attention from historiography to story.[8] Narrative, in terms of testimony and narrative preaching, had clearly been Pentecostalism's prime mode of discourse from the beginning, long before it had become trendy.[9] Yet the post-modern shift in this direction provided fresh impetus to appreciate and to re-appropriate Pentecostalism's native narrative orientation and to see how well it connects with the emphasis given to narrative in Scripture, particularly in the OT.

Introducing Torah as the Hebrew canon's primary meta-narrative gave me good opportunity to begin elaborating this emphasis and exploring this connection. The leading role of narrative in Scripture parallels the primary place of testimony in Pentecostalism. From this significant starting point there was plenty of ground to explore. Some of the paths I took were simply a matter of course. I gave prime attention to the narrative shape of the Torah as well as to each of its five books. I did the same for the Former Prophets collectively and for each of its books individually.[10] I tried to highlight important qualities and characteristics of Hebrew narrative, always with an eye to those things

[8] For an accessible early overview of this development in theology, see George W. Stroup, *The Promise of Narrative Theology* (Atlanta, GA: John Knox Press, 1981).

[9] See Michael Dowd, 'Contours of a Narrative Pentecostal Theology and Practice' (paper presented to the 15th Annual Meeting of the Society for Pentecostal Studies, 1985). For a more detailed elaboration of these and other aspects of early Pentecostal hermeneutics of Scripture, see Kenneth J. Archer, *A Pentecostal Hermeneutic for the Twenty-First Century: Spirit, Scripture, and Community* (JPTSup 28; Sheffield: T. & T. Clark, 2004), chs. 3–4, esp. pp. 118-20.

[10] Space constraints in my introductory course kept me from doing the same for the narrative books of the Hebrew canon's third division, the Writings, but I did treat these materials (viz. Chronicles, Ezra, and Nehemiah, as well as Ruth and Esther) as a grouping under the rubric of 'Narrative' (alongside three other groupings for the other books of the 'Writings': (1) 'Poetry' [Psalms, Lamentations, and Song of Songs], (2) 'Wisdom' [Proverbs, Job, and Ecclesiastes], and (3) 'Apocalyptic' [Daniel]), and I drew attention to some of the narrative distinctives of Chronicles, Ezra, and Nehemiah and to the ways that the small narrative books of Ruth and Esther reflect striking literary-theological parallels to Israel's macro-narratives (e.g., Ruth to the story of Abraham in Gen. 12–21 and Esther to the story of Joseph in Gen. 37–50) – a canonical patterning that accords with our seminary program's emphasis on having each student, as a part of their orientation course and final MDiv project, tell their 'own story' in the light of the 'Christian story'.

that might relate to Pentecostal inclinations and concerns,[11] like the
open-ended conclusions so prominent in OT narrative books (as seen
in Genesis) and canonical divisions (as seen at the close of both the
Torah and the Former Prophets) – open endings that reflect a
worldview set ajar by the already-but-not-yet promise of divine intervention and impending encounter. Modern biblical criticism, coming
from modernity's closed worldview of naturalistic cause and effect, was
inclined toward the kind of interpretive moves that would look past
and override such things as the unresolved ending of the Pentateuch in
favor of an hypothesized Hexateuch that would offer settlement and
resolution to Torah's hanging conclusion.[12] Thus, a closed story was
postulated that better suited modernity's own closed worldview.[13]

[11] I chose as a supplementary textbook for the introductory course, Walter
Brueggemann's *The Creative Word: Canon as a Model for Biblical Education* (Philadelphia, PA: Fortress Press, 1982), which devotes an important section of its
chapter on Torah to the distinctive narrative features and dynamics of Israel's
most important story, highlighting such things as (1) the *particularity* of Israel's
story, (2) *flexibility* rather than rigidity of form in telling and re-telling the story,
(3) the *imagination-evoking freedom* left to the listener to be engaged with the
story, (4) an *experiential focus* that is communal and inter-generational rather than
just private and individualistic, and (5) *daring, bottom-line trust* in the story that
refuses to seek for deeper grounding and validation in some other epistemology,
rationale or canon of authority (pp. 23-27). The parallels found here with Pentecostal testimony appeared altogether striking to me.

[12] I point here to Gerhard von Rad's famous argument that Israel's canon
originated as a Hexateuch (Gen.–Josh.) rather than as a Pentateuch, on the assumption that the Hebrews' initial and foundational canonical corpus could not
have developed without the closure of Israel's settlement of the land. G. von
Rad, 'The Form-Critical Problem of the Hexateuch', in *The Problem of the Hexateuch and Other Essays* (New York: McGraw-Hill, 1966), pp. 1-78. It was Martin Noth, of course, who argued that the account of Israel's exile from the land
forms a corresponding closure at the end of Israel's next major canonical division, the Former Prophets, as he interpreted this collection in the context of and
in terms of an hypothesized 'Deuteronomistic History' seen to be artificially
redacted to move from Deuteronomy's 'prophecy' of exile to 2 Kings fulfillment of it. M. Noth, *Überlieferungsgeschichtliche Studien*, 2nd ed. (Tübingen:
Niemeyer, 1957), pp.1-110, translated into English under the title, *The Deuteronomistic History* (Sheffield: JSOT Press, 1981). Ironically, it was von Rad himself
who later challenged Noth's view of complete closure of the end of 2 Kings
with his brilliant comment on 2 Kings' final paragraph, where he suggested that
the final note on Babylonian goodwill shown to Judah's exiled king signals a
deliberate and highly pregnant theological move 'not to close the door of history, but to leave it open,' *Old Testament Theology*, vol. I (trans. D.M.G. Stalker;
New York: Harper & Row, 1962), p. 343 n. 22.

[13] For a similar point involving Hebrew Scripture that ranges beyond narrative materials, see Walter Brueggemann, *Abiding Astonishment: Psalms, Modernity,*

However, in the light of Pentecostalism's view of reality,[14] I could see how Torah's open-ended story reflected and issued from Israel's open worldview. It is simply the kind of story that gets generated when a living God comes and then *becomes* the main character.

In a similar way, I was able to notice and to appreciate the prophetic character and agenda of the narratives that constitute the books of Joshua, Judges, Samuel and Kings against modern historical critical approaches that stressed only historiography and data for the history of Israel rather than recognizing a literary agenda that centered on Yahweh and the open-ended, forward-focused outworking of Yahweh's prophetic word.[15] In this light, the narrative nature and shape of these books could be seen to accord with their original Hebrew canonical categorization as the 'Former *Prophets'* much more than with their later

and the Making of History (Louisville, KY: Westminster/John Knox Press, 1991). In this remarkable discussion of the so-called historical Psalms (Pss 78, 105, 106, 136) Brueggemann lays out a set of contrasts between modern modes of representing the past and those that prevailed in ancient Israel through these Psalms and the canonical narratives that stand behind them, and he does so in order to argue that critical approaches committed to the modern modes are conditioned to miss, dismiss, and misunderstand the profound counter-criticism carried in the ancient modes. In his words, 'Modern, critical reconstructions are based on a series of choices which value a) *writing,* b) *state-story,* c) *fact,* d) *control,* and e) *cause and effect,* and conversely, which disregard an alternatives of a) *oral testimony,* b) *clan-story,* c) *miracle,* d) *gift,* and e) *slippage* (Brueggemann's term for "mystery")' (p. 40). The correspondences between these latter values of OT narrative and those of Pentecostal testimony are striking and suggest Pentecostalism's remarkable potential for resonating with and opening up fresh interpretive insight into the elements and ethos of OT literature.

[14] See Jackie David Johns, 'Pentecostalism and the Post-Modern Worldview' *JPT* 7 (1995), pp. 73-96.

[15] For example, the book of Joshua, when it is interpreted as an attempt at historiographical reportage, can appear only as a primitive, romanticized, anachronistic and flawed chronicle – an account riddled with inconsistencies particularly in relation to its emphasis on the completeness of the conquest, and especially so when viewed over against the picture of *in*completeness that so prominently appears in the book of Judges. However, when one attends to the narrative's prophetic agenda of testifying to the faithfulness of God to his promise, despite but not completely and unendingly oblivious to the contingencies of Israel's response, a literary theological work of nuance, dramatic tension, and profound depth comes into view. See e.g. L. Daniel Hawk, *Every Promise Fulfilled: Contesting Plots in Joshua* (Literary Currents in Biblical Interpretation; Louisville, KY: Westminster/John Knox Press, 1991). Also see the profound theological interpretation that my colleague Lee Roy Martin derives through a Pentecostal approach to the narrative of Judges: *The Unheard Voice of God: A Pentecostal Hearing of the Book of Judges* (Blandford Forum: Deo, 2008).

re-categorization as '*Historical* Books'. And in this, Pentecostal interpretive impulses could find much with which to resonate and to relate.

Yet what really began to inform and even transform my approach to teaching the OT was what I began to see in the book of Deuteronomy. This book was not merely another narrative of the Torah; it was a narrative about how Moses re-presented or interpreted the previously given Torah narrative to the new generation. Simply put, it appears as *the first instance and leading example within Scripture* of the *interpretation of Scripture*. It could be described as the Bible's own paradigm for biblical hermeneutics.[16] To a certain extent, what Moses here does with the children of Israel he charges the parents and the elders of all succeeding generations of Israel to do. So what does Moses here do? In the terms of Deuteronomy's own introduction, he begins 'to *expound* this *torah*' (Deut. 1.5), by speaking 'according to all that Yahweh had commanded him unto them' (Deut. 1.3). Significantly, in speaking '*according to all Yahweh had commanded him*' Moses is seen to be responding and attending not only to the written word but also to the spoken word, to a voice as well as a text,[17] or in terms that lie closer to our Pentecostal categories, to canon *and charisma*, indeed to Scripture *and Spirit*.[18] And even as he is responding and attending to both, he is calling God's people into a process and a practice of responding and attending to both of these divine aspects of revelation 'here and now this day' (5.3) – to a *torah so righteous* and to a *God so near,* as he puts it in 4.7-8.

Thus, I found in Deuteronomy the OT's own grand example of teaching the old testament, of renewing the old covenant, of bringing

---

[16] I make this point in my study, 'Deuteronomy and the Fire of God: A Critical Charismatic Interpretation' (see Chapter 3 below), where the subtitle refers not only to my interpretation but also to Deuteronomy's own essential character as an act of interpretation. Recently, this point has been made and developed in a related though somewhat different way by another Pentecostal scholar, Randall J. Pannell, *Those Alive Here Today: The "Day of Horeb" and Deuteronomy's Hermeneutical Locus of Revelation* (Longwood, FL: Xulon Press, 2004). See my review of this book in *Pneuma* 8.1 (Spring 2006), pp. 159-62.

[17] See my study, 'Canon and Charisma in the Book of Deuteronomy' (Chapter 2 below). Also see how Lee Roy Martin has now pushed forward the discussion of Pentecostal biblical hermeneutics from the concept of *reading the text*, which has become the terminology so prominent in post-modern hermeneutics, to the more biblically grounded concept and dynamic of *hearing the voice of the text*; on this, see especially Chapter 3 of his monograph, *The Unheard Voice of God*, cited above.

[18] I elaborate this dual emphasis throughout the book of Deuteronomy in my study, 'Canon and Charisma in the Book of Deuteronomy', presented in Chapter 2 of this volume.

forth the old, just like in the Josiah story, not merely as a word of the past to be studied for antiquarian interest but as a word with which *a God so near* is still speaking through living prophetic presence and authority 'right now to all of us who are alive here today' (5.3)! Even as I had recognized this living voice coming forward to me from Moses in Deuteronomy, Moses in Deuteronomy recognized this voice coming forward to him and all the children of Israel from that primal theophanic encounter with God at Sinai (or Horeb, as Deut. prefers to call it) where God's word was both written and spoken 'out of the midst of the fire' (see Deut. 5; esp. vv. 2-5 and 22-24), thus coming forth, one could say, both canonically and charismatically at once.[19] And now Deuteronomy itself could be seen as a new word on the old, likewise coming forth canonically and charismatically at once. It was thus not just a remembering but a re-experiencing of the same hermeneutical fusion found in the theophany of Sinai – that preeminent revelatory event in the OT that came to be remembered precisely in the feast of Pentecost. Yet when the *Day* of Pentecost was fully come, it became clear once again that merely remembering this event was not enough. For, the book of Acts recapitulates Deuteronomy in its insistence that 'this was that' which was meant to be re-experienced with newness and 'now-ness' by each and every new generation of the people of God.[20]

Still, I could see that remembering itself was an important first step in the hermeneutic of Deuteronomy. Moses begins 'to expound *torah*' precisely by first remembering. He recalls and retells the Torah story (Deut. 1-4). Thus I could see the significance of narrative for the OT being heightened here in this move to re-tell the story that Torah had already told. Moses expounds the narrative in a narrative way. But even more than that, going one step further, he emphatically calls God's people to take up the remembering and the retelling of the story as part of their own covenantal and hermeneutical practice with their children who come after them.[21]

[19] See my discussion on this point as well in 'Canon and Charisma in the Book of Deuteronomy' and 'Deuteronomy and the Fire of God' (Chapters 2 and 3 below).

[20] In the words of Deuteronomy, 'this covenant is ... with the one who stands here with us today before Yahweh our God, and also with the one who is not (yet) here with us today' (Deut. 29.14-15; vv. 13-14 in the Hebrew). In the words of the book of Acts, this 'promise is to you and to your children, and to all that are afar off, *even* as many as the Lord our God shall call' (Acts 2.39).

[21] See the especially forthright calls in Deut. 4, 6, and 8, and for a full treatment of the theme throughout the book of Deuteronomy, see the study of Edward P. Blair, 'An Appeal to Remembrance: The Memory Motif in Deuteronomy', *Int* 15 (1961), pp. 41-47.

I noticed two other things that were particularly suggestive to me in the way Moses modeled and commended the telling of the story in Deuteronomy. 1. He uplifted the corporate story of all the people, but included parts of his own personal story as well. 2. Moses stressed the importance of remembering *all the way* that God had led them. After giving the explicit charge to 'remember ... all the way' in Deut. 8.2 and as if to illustrate its implications, Moses immediately proceeded to specify some humbling and unflattering details from the past – the sort of details that folks might like to excise from their story, were they not being specifically required to remember *all* the way. Here and elsewhere throughout Deuteronomy, Moses thus told a story that is not romanticized public relations but critical interpretation and self-analysis, both in its corporate and personal dimensions.[22] In other words, Moses testified forthrightly to Israel's failures and also to his own. I remember how it dawned on me that I was seeing here a remarkable example of critical analysis, indeed the Bible's own biblical criticism – criticism that was in fact more profoundly critical than anything I had ever encountered in modern academic criticism, where the critical canon always seems to be aimed at something or someone else, never going *all the way* in its critical scrutiny to face serious criticism of self. Yet the latter is unavoidable for any who would be encountered by the face of God, for there we would meet something far more critical and infinitely higher than higher criticism.[23]

All of this led me, as a Pentecostal, to a new, critical, and biblically informed definition of testimony: *Testimony is the story we tell when God gets us told.* And this further led me to a new, critical, and biblically informed teaching practice: *To teach the biblical narrative narratively and critically* in line with Moses' hermeneutical lead in attempting to tell the next generation more than simply how to interpret our Scriptures but also to offer critical testimony as to how God's word interprets us,

_____

[22] See Deut. 2–3 and 9–10, esp. 3.23-28 for Moses' inclusion of testimony of his own failure and consequent debarment from the promised land (cf. also 32.48-52).

[23] I remember hearing many years ago my esteemed mentor and colleague Steven J. Land remark that 'the holiness of God is the ultimate critical principle.' I find something akin to this remarkable statement in the title and thrust of the book by Jürgen Moltmann, *The Crucified God: The Cross of Christ As the Foundation and Criticism of Christian Theology* (New York, NY: Harper & Row, 1974). Along this line, I have come to see the Cross of Christ as the consummate theophany, and thus the ultimate criticism, the final judgment, and the radical end of all our human constructions and systems. Thus, the Cross turns out to be the true *post* in post-modernism and finally in *all* of our 'isms', even our 'Pentecostal*ism*'.

tell the whole story

self criticism

including something of the story of how God's word, to the point of humbling self criticism, has personally interpreted me.

As far as the component of my own personal story was concerned, in time this took form in two articles that I incorporated into the curriculum of my introductory Old Testament course. One was the study cited earlier and now featured as Chapter 3 in this volume, 'Deuteronomy and the Fire of God: A Critical Charismatic Interpretation' – a study that embodied a triple meaning in its subtitle. Not only did I propose (1) a critical and charismatic interpretation of Deuteronomy and at the same time argue that (2) Deuteronomy itself was a critical and charismatic act of interpretation, I also narrated as a part of this argument how Deuteronomy had functioned to render (3) a critical and charismatic interpretation of my own life, particularly of my journey through the wilderness of my graduate study.[24]

The other article was an unpublished paper entitled, 'The Church of God Commitment to "The Whole Bible Rightly Divided"'. Here is the beginning of the testimony it presents:

> The first teaching of the Church of God, as recorded in the denomination's official *Minutes*, reads, 'The Church of God stands for the whole Bible rightly divided. The New Testament is the only rule for government and discipline.' The first statement in this teaching is drawn directly from Paul's word to young Timothy in 2 Timothy 2.15: 'Study to show yourself approved unto God, a worker that needs not to be ashamed, *rightly dividing the word of truth.*'
> The second statement in our teaching is not drawn directly from any Scripture. In fact, our statement on the New Testament as the 'only rule for government and discipline' clashes in a most disturbing way with what Paul writes Timothy in the very next chapter: '*All Scripture is given by inspiration of God, and is profitable for doctrine, for reproof, for correction, and for instruction (or discipline, so NEB) in righteousness*' (2 Timothy 3:16). As one who has been called specifically to study and to teach Old Testament Scripture in the Church of God, I have found this clash between Paul's statement ('*All Scripture ... is profitable for discipline*') and our statement ('*the New Testament is the only rule for government and discipline*') to be a very difficult problem for this young 'workman'! And this problem is not unrelated to an earlier, even much more profound problem I had with 'the whole Bible rightly divided.' Let me tell you a little about how my struggle with the Word of God unfolded.
> I came out of my Old Testament graduate program at Vanderbilt University a withered soul. There I learned to survive among teachers who conveyed almost nothing of the faith Paul had in God's Word or the spiritual devotion he had for his students. Even as I had no Paul in the

---

[24] See the second section of 'Deuteronomy and the Fire of God' (presented in Chapter 3 of this volume), entitled, 'A Journey in the Study of Deuteronomy'.

university, in the church I had no Paul; that is, some elder who supe-
rintended my calling with passion, discernment, and godly authority.
Although I am sure I would have confessed at any point along the way
that I believed in 'the whole Bible rightly divided', the deepest com-
mitments of my heart were becoming wrongly divided, and they were
taking me further and further from any real, operative authority of
God's Word in my life. The Bible, whether at church or at the university, became more and more a passive object of study and less and less a
medium of God's living voice. Bible study became more and more a
self-serving career and less and less a corporately attested calling. No
elder, such as Paul was to Timothy, ever addressed these crucial issues
in me, not until I met Steve Land at the 1980 Church of God General
Assembly. He spoke of his scholarship and mine as a sacred trust and
ministry that belong to the church. This was a word unfamiliar to my
ears, but it was a word of God to this young Timothy, and it threw an
uncomfortable shaft of light upon my divided heart. [25]

The point of including such testimony is not to replace critical study
with personal confessions, but rather it is to take seriously, indeed canonically, the critical implications of Scripture's own hermeneutical
model and methods and claims. It is to recognize in the light of these
claims that 'critical study' in its modern modes has not been nearly
critical enough. [26] It is to take the first feeble, faltering, and risking steps
toward our own post-modern children, who, for a while now, have
been waiting for us and even dying for us to get real with them and to
tell them *the real story* or *testimony* behind our purportedly 'critical'
work. I submit that it is not about how confessional we should be in
our classrooms, but rather about how *critical* we are willing to be, for
God's sake, and about how critical, for our children's sake, we see the
current situation to be.

In this way the story of Scripture has functioned to open up my
own story and from there the larger story of how we have come to our
current situation in the church and in the academy. This larger story,
the beginnings of which can be seen in the excerpts of my personal
story, as noted above, was something I began to perceive and to pursue
in earnest several years ago when I revised (or re-envisioned) my lecture on the history of modern biblical criticism. Using the story line of
Babylon presented in the OT meta-narrative as a hermeneutical key,
especially as it is represented and concentrated in the book of Daniel, I
re-framed this lecture as 'The Story of the Rise and Fall of Modern
Biblical Criticism'. Even here I saw that a narrative approach, follow-

[25] Rickie D. Moore, 'The Church of God Commitment to "The Whole Bible Rightly Divided"' (unpublished paper, pp. 1-2).
[26] See my discussion of this point in 'Deuteronomy and the Fire of God',
presented in Chapter 3 of this volume.

[handwritten margin notes:] Many people have warned me of this!

Find this and read it.

ing the authoritative lead of the biblical narrative, was appropriate and also critical – critical in a manner that cut both ways. For Babylon was providentially and magnificently raised up as an instrument to judge and to humble God's own people before it was itself weighed and found wanting. And I found this to be the same story for the Western Enlightenment academy and the church.

Along this line, I have proceeded to lay out the story of modern biblical criticism in terms of three phases. The phases are familiar to students of the history of biblical scholarship, even if the particular terms of the story line wherein I place them might not be. First, the rise unfolds as the Enlightenment project of building a tower of scho-①larship by means of historical criticism, specifically as it develops its source-critical, form-critical, and tradition-critical methods – all focused on the history of the biblical text's formation or, as is now often said, the *author behind the text*. Second, a decisive shift is registered in ② the last third of the twentieth century with the advent of literary approaches that shake this tower by suddenly moving the focal point from the biblical text's formation to its final form, that is, from the author behind the text to *the text in front of the reader*. However, this is a shift that does not stop and thus quickly brings on the third phase ③ wherein the tower of modern biblical criticism begins to fall as the focal point moves all the way to *the reader in front of the text* with hermeneutical approaches first constructed by and for social groups but then giving way more and more to what can be constructed and *even deconstructed* by the individual reader's response. Hence, modern interpretation, once a monolith like Babylon, has thus fallen more and more into an anarchy of scattered voices, like Babel.

Yet Pentecost is Scripture's answer to Babel. And in this light, Pentecostalism should be about pursuing an approach that, while attentive to the text, the author, and the reader, is above all focused on *the Spirit of the text, the Spirit behind the author, the Spirit above the reader, and the Spirit within the unfolding story, from Scripture to now, that binds all of these together **in the Spirit.*** This yields a hermeneutical method that is less about the politics of constructing and de-constructing and more about submitting to **being** *de-constructed* and then *re-constructed* like Israel was in Babylon and like the disciples were at Pentecost, which is precisely where Peter finally found his hermeneutic for understanding the OT, as attested in his Pentecost message (Acts 2). What opened the way to *understanding the Scripture* was *standing under the Spirit* outpoured. This was good for Paul and Silas, the Pentecostal preacher in me wants to add right about now, and it's good enough for me.

Yet I want to be clear here, that I am not advocating a retreat into the past or into some sectarian ghetto of interpretation that is cut off from the wider world. This is not where the Spirit led Daniel in Baby-

Read Acts 2

lon or Paul after Pentecost, and I do not believe that is where the Spirit is leading us now in our current situation. I believe that, just like Paul and Daniel, we are being led to respond respectfully but critically to the 'isms' of our context.

In the context of my OT introductory course this includes historical criticism and its sub-sets. Thus, I respect *source* criticism and its many insights into the literary tensions and complexities that reflect the evident, though elusive, activities of human sources behind the biblical documents, while I also remain open to seeing remarkable connections that can point to *a source behind and beyond* what source criticism has considered, such as I see being done in the amazing article of my Pentecostal colleague and team-teaching partner, Lee Roy Martin, 'Where are the Descendants of Abraham: Finding the Source of a Missing Link in Genesis'.[27]

And I similarly respect *form* criticism and its capacity to detect and delineate specific ancient literary patterns and conventions, while I remain ready, at the same time, to see how the richness of my own Pentecostal *Sitz im Leben* and Pentecostal modes of discourse might relate to, resonate with, and even better identify and explicate certain forms and patterns in Scripture, such as can be seen, for example, in the proposal that I offer in my treatment of Deuteronomy to understand this book's form-critical classification in terms, quite literally, of a *camp meeting*, or in my proposal to see the book of Job in terms of a

---

[27] Lee Roy Martin, 'Where are the Descendants of Abraham: Finding the Source of a Missing Link in Genesis', in Terry L. Cross and Emerson B. Powery, eds., *The Spirit and the Mind: Essays in Informed Pentecostalism* (In Honor of Donald N. Bowdle) (Lanham, MD: University Press of America, 2000), pp. 23-34. I would even describe this article as a kind of neo-source-critical study. Here Martin recognizes an anomaly that has been completely overlooked in biblical scholarship. Why does Genesis, after the first chapter, begin every new section of the book with the patriarchal *Toledoth* formula, affixed to the name of a patriarch ('These are the descendants of so and so'), except in the case of the most clearly demarcated new section, beginning at Gen. 12.1, and the most famously 'patriarchal' of all the patriarchs, Abraham, whose very name defines him as 'father of many nations'. Martin proceeds to argue that the source of this missing *Toledoth* reference for Abraham is to be found in the fact that the book of Genesis is here reflecting the effects of God being the source and creator of Abraham's 'family' in a manner that has only one parallel in the book: God's creation of the world in Genesis 1, which is the only other major section of the book to begin without the *Toledoth* formula. Genesis 12.1, then, begins a new account of divine creation, not just another *Toledoth* of human *procreation*. Martin develops this argument with a number of striking connections between Gen. 12 and Gen. 1, on the one hand, and between Gen. 12 and the Abrahamic tradition that extends forward into the New Testament, on the other.

paradigm for 'praying through',[28] or in my relating of the praise and lament of Psalms to the extremities of Pentecostal spirituality from ecstatic shouts to 'sighs too deep for words'.

I likewise respect *tradition* criticism and its potential for insights into the human ways and means by which different and even competing ideas, terms, themes, and beliefs are developed, altered, augmented and passed on through time and human communities and generations, while I yet remain open, and especially so in my treatment of the Hebrew prophets and prophetic books,[29] to that which goes beyond the merely human factor in holding together within a unitary canonical corpus and spiritual vision the otherwise irreconcilable *di*visions between 'this and that' datum or school of tradition and between 'then and now'. Such a striking unity in diversity is a compelling sign, to those who have eyes to see and ears to hear, of the presence of a holy, prophetically attested center of gravity beneath it all and beneath us all.

I have already indicated the respect and even priority I give to literary criticism, which only accords with the priority I give to the biblical text itself as received in its final form. And I have also already registered something of my regard for post-modern criticism as a providential means by which the hubris and hegemony of Western Enlightenment interpretation has been humbled, deconstructed, and judged. In this I recognize a striking parallel with the Solomonic paradigm in ancient Israel, represented in both the narrative of Kings and the wisdom of Proverbs, specifically in the way this Solomonic Enlightenment, so called, is shown to have been judged at the end of Kings and deconstructed in Ecclesiastes – a book that forcefully registers, to my mind, the Solomonic *Post*-Enlightenment.

Yet the Old Testament goes a step further than contemporary post-Enlightenment criticism by grasping (or being grasped by) the revelation of apocalyptic – a vision of the end of a human system, be it Solomonic or Babylonian, that discloses the End of *all* human systems. The last verse of the epilogue of Ecclesiastes takes note of this apocalyptic end (12.14) and most of the latter prophets and especially Daniel

---

[28] See the discussion of this point in my study, 'Raw Prayer and Refined Theology: "You have not spoken straight to me, as my servant Job has",' which appears below as Chapter 12 of this volume. I highlight in my OT course how this pattern of 'praying through' is well represented in a number of the lament Psalms and also in the book of Habakkuk (see my short study on Habakkuk in Chapter 8 of this volume).

[29] See my studies in Chapters 4 and 5 of this volume: 'The Prophetic Calling: An Old Testament Profile and its Relevance for Today' and 'The Prophet as Mentor: A Crucial Facet of the Biblical Presentations of Moses, Elijah, and Isaiah'.

bear crucial and intense witness to it. They were into deconstruction long before our day. In fact, they saw the deconstruction of our day from a long way off, but they realized, unlike so many post-modern voices of today, that this is not just a time for *our* voices to be heard, but rather for the one who has ears to hear to heed what the Spirit is saying to the churches. Without this apocalyptic vision, so inherent in our own Pentecostal spirituality and heritage, the hermeneutics of our Pentecostalism will only add to the cacophony of Babel. On the other hand, as Daniel shows us, in the light of the vision of the End a wholly new interpretation can be given, for God's sake, even in the midst of Babylon.

This overview of the development of my introductory Old Testament course has now become a fitting preview for this collection of studies. I would bring this overview and preview to an end in the same way that I end my course, with Daniel. I find in the last words of his book a personally fitting wish and an appropriately open-ended way for me to close this introductory chapter:

> But as for you, go your way till the end; for you shall lay down but then rise up to your inheritance at the end of the days (Dan. 12.13).

2

Canon and Charisma in the Book of Deuteronomy[*]

As everyone knows, biblical study is experiencing a revolution. Interpretation has been thrown wide open as new voices have entered the
discussion and new eyes have encountered the text, as the historical-
critical establishment and its rationalist-fundamentalist counterpart have
increasingly given way to the recognition that what is brought to the
text makes a decisive difference in what is found there.[1] The shifting
methodological landscape is no doubt unsettling for many of us, even
for those of us representing new perspectives. One might well wonder
what gaining a voice means if the polity is to be anarchy. Yet amidst
such humbling uncertainty there arises still the hope that a new voice

process

[*] First published in *Journal of Pentecostal Theology* 1 (1992), pp. 75-92.

[1] Of course there are those who would go further and say that what is brought to
the text makes *all* of the difference – that interpretation, after all, is essentially the
'creating' of meaning. This brings us to the vast chasm of hermeneutical debate which
has opened in our time. While I am not prepared here to take on such expansive
matters, I would say that Pentecostals would seem to have a unique vantage point to
bring to the discussion. To put the issue somewhat, perhaps even too, simplistically, it
seems to me that Pentecostals, in their claims for a substantive ongoing revelatory role
for the Holy Spirit, find themselves located in the crossfire between, for want of better
terms, the liberal-critical tradition of biblical interpretation and the conservative Evangelical tradition. It seems that both of these traditions approach interpretation as a
matter which is essentially limited to the reader and the text. Whereas the former
tradition sees this finally in terms of an open and merely human process, whether
focusing on the text or, as is more common nowadays, on the reader, the latter sees
everything finally in terms of a closed divine deposit. Pentecostals, on the other hand,
would want to approach interpretation as a matter of the text, the community, and also
the ongoing voice of the Holy Spirit. And this opens up a view of interpretation which
can appreciate both the necessary place of human subjectivity in a dynamic process
(seen to be at work in the interpreting community *and* in the biblical text), as well as
the place of the final authority of God manifested in and through the process (see the
overview of F.L. Arrington, 'Hermeneutics, Historical Perspectives on Pentecostal and
Charismatic,' in *Dictionary of Pentecostal and Charismatic Movements* [ed. S.M. Burgess,
G.B. McGee and P.H. Alexander; Grand Rapids, MI: Zondervan, 1988], pp. 376-89).
Such an approach draws dismissals from both sides – as a relativizing of divine authority
from the conservative Evangelical side and as an absolutizing of human process from
the liberal-critical side.

will be heard – a voice from the text which will be much better than our own.

I approach this study as a Pentecostal and as one who is consciously attempting to integrate my Pentecostal vocation and perspective with critical Old Testament scholarship. Such integration is not easy for me, for I spent many years learning to keep these things mostly separate from one another. And now that I feel the need to pursue this inter-face, the way ahead is far from clear. In terms of examples, there is little for one to follow.[2] Thus the present effort is of necessity explora-tory and experimental.

I propose here to look at the way in which the book of Deuteron-omy sets forth the place and role of both inscripturated word and pro-phetic utterance. Not only does Deuteronomy evidence repeated emphasis on the establishment of each of these revelatory dimensions, but in chs. 4 and 5 there is seen sustained reflection, I would suggest, on the dialectical and complementary relationship between canonical word and what I would term charismatic revelation.

My Pentecostal perspective (or testimony) on Spirit and Word ob-viously parallels and is certainly informing my perceptions on the Deu-teronomy passages. Yet these perceptions, it seems to me, surface elements in the text that have been hidden and suppressed by other perspectives of long standing. Briefly stated, the noticing of such di-alectical possibilities in Israel's testimony of revelation has not been served by a historical-critical tradition that has legitimated the attribu-tion of any tension or shift in emphasis to different literary sources or redactional layers.[3] Moreover, discernment of these possibilities has

---

[2] Yet I would note John W. McKay, 'The Old Testament and Christian Charismatic /Prophetic Literature,' in *Scripture: Meaning and Method. Essays Presented to Anthony Tyrrell Hanson for his Seventieth Birthday* (ed. B.P. Thompson; Hull: University of Hull Press, 1987), pp. 200-17; and 'The Experience of Dereliction and of God's Presence in Psalms: An Exercise in Old Testament Exegesis in the Light of Renewal Theology,' in *Faces of Renewal: Studies in Honor of Stanley M. Horton* (ed. P. Elbert; Peabody, MA: Hendrickson, 1988), pp. 3-13. Since I first published this study on 'Canon and Cha-risma' in 1992, there have been quite a number of studies that opened up the field of Pentecostal biblical hermeneutics. For an important recent overview, see Kenneth J. Archer, *A Pentecostal Hermeneutic for the Twenty-First Century: Spirit, Scripture, and Com-munity* (JPTSup 28; Sheffield: T. & T. Clark, 2004).

[3] Interestingly, a similar point has been made in certain quarters of Jewish biblical scholarship, which appreciates the dialectical dimensions of revelation in a way that is different, albeit not entirely unrelated, to my own. Note the following comment of S. Talmon, 'Revelation in Biblical Times,' *Hebrew Studies* 26 (1985), p. 60: "Such a separation of the sources in biblical literature [with respect to revelatory notions] is entirely unacceptable not only to Jewish exegetes who are considered 'pre-critical,' such as S.D. Luzatto and D. Hoffmann – not to speak of the medieval commentators. Scholars trained in critical method such as Benno Jacob, Umberto Cassuto and M.H. Segal also categorically refuse to divide the concepts of the biblical belief in God and

Charisma - divinely conferred power or talent

been equally impeded among conservative Evangelical scholars, the primary opponents of the historical-critical mainstream, insofar as they have been committed to a larger theological scheme that sees a radical and dispensational break between charismatic utterance and completed canon.[4]

My treatment approaches Deuteronomy in its final form – a course that needs little justification in this day of crumbling consensus.[5] Of course, I realize that where so little justification is needed, little justification can be claimed.[6] For the moment, any deeper justification will have to wait, perhaps for all of us.

The starting point for this treatment of revelation in Deuteronomy is 18.9-22. This text sets forth the office of the prophet in ancient Israel, with the words,

> Yahweh, your God will raise up for you a prophet like me from your midst, from among your kindred; him you shall heed (v.15).[7]

Peter's Pentecost sermon in Acts 3, of course, takes this passage as a prophetic reference to Jesus (v. 22) – an eschatological move that Deu-

revelation into the particular formulations of the Elohistic, Jahwistic, Priestly, Deuteronomistic, Prophetic or Chronistic schools. The various names and epithets of God and the various forms of divine revelation and their multifarious content are regarded not as expressions of different concepts of Deity but as manifestations of the sole and only God who reacts to man's deeds in many different ways and allows himself to be perceived by men in sundry modes of revelation." For a prime example of the more typical way that historical criticism has been applied in this area, and one involving one of the passages on which I will focus, see A. Rofé, 'The Monotheistic Argumentation in Deuteronomy IV 32-40: Contents, Composition and Text,' *VT* 35 (1985), pp. 434-45.

[4] This relates primarily to the doctrine of the cessation of the *charismata* after the completion of the New Testament canon, as developed by Benjamin B. Warfield, but the doctrine has implications for the broader view of biblical revelation. This point has been developed more fully in an earlier version of this paper which I presented at the 20th Annual Meeting of the Society for Pentecostal Studies, 1990. For an extended biblical and theological challenge of Warfiedian cessationism, see J. Ruthven, *On the Cessation of the Charismata: A Critique of the Protestant Polemic on Post-Biblical Miracles* (JPTSup 3; Sheffield: JSOT Press, 1996).

[5] See e.g. J.G. McConville, *Law and Theology in Deuteronomy* (JSOTSup 33; Sheffield: JSOT Press, 1984), who challenges Pentateuchal criticism on a position no less central and pivotal than the linkage between Deuteronomy and Josiah's reformation. The call to shift focus to the final form of the text – in large part because of historical-critical scholarship's incapacity to sustain consensus on the prior compositional history of the text – was, of course, sounded first and most influentially by B.S. Childs, *Biblical Theology in Crisis* (Philadelphia, PA: Westminster Press, 1970); and his, *Introduction to the Old Testament as Scripture* (Philadelphia: Fortress Press, 1979). See also D.J.A. Clines, *The Theme of the Pentateuch* (JSOTSup 10; Sheffield: JSOT Press, 1978).

[6] Put differently, where any reading can be justified, *no* reading can be justified. And does this not bring us precisely to deconstructionism?

[7] Translations of the Hebrew in this chapter are my own.

teronomy itself sets up by its closing acknowledgement that 'a prophet like Moses' had not yet arisen in Israel (34.10).[8] Still the reference clearly points in the first place to an ongoing succession of prophets, situated as it is beside the other laws concerning the continuing leadership institutions of ancient Israel.[9]

Deuteronomy not only sets forth the prophetic office as a continuing medium of charismatic revelation but also explicitly sets forth the abiding place of the written canon in Israel. We see this establishment of canon in the leadership section just mentioned:

> When he (the king) sits on the throne of his kingdom, he shall write for himself in a book a copy of this law, obtained from the Levitical priests. It is to be with him, and he should read it all the days of his life (17.18-19).

We see this again in the summary section of the book:

> Moses wrote this law and gave it to the priests, the sons of Levi, who carried the ark of the covenant of Yahweh, and to all the elders of Israel. Moses then commanded them, 'At the end of every seven years, at the observance of the year of release, at the feast of booths, when all Israel comes to appear before Yahweh your God at the place he will choose, you shall read this law before all Israel in their hearing' (31.9-11).

Thus the two revelatory channels, those of canonical writing and charismatic speech, are both explicitly set forth in the book of Deuteronomy and projected forward into Israel's future life. Moreover, a rather close relationship is suggested when the stated effects, which Deuteronomy posits for these two modes of revelation, are compared.

The continuing impact of written revelation is spelled out clearly in ch. 31.

> When all Israel comes to appear before Yahweh your God at the place he will choose, you shall read this law before all Israel in their hearing ... that they may heed and learn to fear Yahweh your God, and that they may be careful to do all the words of this law. Their children, who have not known it, should then heed and learn to fear Yahweh your God all the days you live in the land that you are crossing the Jordan to possess (31.11-13).

And this echoes the role seen for written revelation in the law of the king.

---

[8] This point is perceptively made by P.D. Miller, '"Moses My Servant": The Deuteronomic Portrait of Moses,' *Int* 41 (1987), pp. 245-55 (p. 249).

[9] See the summary argument of M.G. Kline, *Treaty of the Great King* (Grand Rapids, MI: Eerdmans, 1963), p. 101.

He should read it all the days of his life, that he may learn to fear Yah-weh his God, by keeping and doing all the words of this law and these statutes (17.19).

These same themes of heeding God's word and fearing him are likewise evident in the passage that introduces the office of prophecy. 'Whoever does not heed my words which he (the prophet) shall speak in my name, I myself will require it of him' (18.19). The intended goal of heeding God's words is presupposed here by this solemn warning against failure to do so. Similarly the expectation of responding to the true prophet with solemn fear is presupposed by the concluding dis-claimer that the disproven prophet need not evoke such fear (v. 22).[10]

This equivalence of canon and prophecy in their stated goals of en-gendering fear of and obedience to God suggests a close linkage. Con-versely, the distinction between canon and charismatic utterance would seem to presuppose that each revelational medium would have its own respective function. Perhaps Deuteronomy could be seen addressing this implicitly in the way it accentuates the *enduring* character of the written word, while indicating the *occasional* nature of the prophetic word. Thus, the written law must be read 'every seven years' and passed on to the children 'as long as you live in the land' (31.10, 13). By contrast, the prophet is someone whom God 'will raise up for you' (18.15). The expression 'raise up' is plainly linked in biblical usage to the transitory and timely responsiveness of God, as becomes clear in the book of Judges (see 2.16, 18; 3.9, 15).

Of course, as soon as the contrast between written revelation and prophecy is drawn in terms of permanent vs. occasional, some might be inclined to conclude from this that prophecy was understood here in Deuteronomy as nothing other than temporary revelation on its way to becoming permanent written revelation.[11] Yet Deuteronomy offers nothing in explicit support of this view, nor does the view seem to square with presentations of the prophetic tradition in other parts of the OT. While it is true that there is much prophetic utterance which

---

[10] It is true that the root גּוּר (*gur*) is used instead of the more common word for fear, יָרֵא (*yara*), yet 33.8 parallels these two roots in a couplet. One might argue that the object of fear in Deut. 18.22 is the prophet rather than, as elsewhere, God. However, the Hebrew syntax is ambiguous, using (after the verb) the preposition מִן (*min*) with the third masculine singular suffix, for which NEB proposes the translation, 'it,' in reference apparently to the word spoken. But could the suffix not also refer to God? Or, rendering *min* differently, could not the entire phrase be translated, 'You shall not fear *because of* him [i.e. the prophet]'?

[11] This would follow from the assumptions of those who would see the New Tes-tament *charismata* as being limited to the revelatory function that led to and was ec-lipsed by the written canon.

eventuates in written canon,[12] it is also clear that the OT bears witness to a number of manifestations of divinely inspired prophetic speech that do not eventuate in the canonical recording of the verbal content. Indeed we see this even within the traditions of Moses. We read in Num. 11.25, 'Yahweh came down in a cloud and spoke to him (Moses), and took some of the spirit that was upon him and placed it upon the seventy elders; and when the spirit rested upon them, they prophesied.' Then, after this act of prophesying, *for which no record of contents is given*, there follows the 'unrecorded' prophesying of Eldad and Medad, the two men upon whom 'the spirit rested' after the rest of the elders had departed. And with memorable words, Moses checks the intent of his follower to discredit this prophesying that took place outside of his presence, 'Would that all Yahweh's people were prophets; that Yahweh would place his spirit upon them!' (11.29).

Other examples of 'unrecorded' prophetic utterance[13] include the two occasions when Saul encounters prophetic bands and begins prophesying among them (1 Sam. 10.10-13 and 19.20-24).[14] The second occasion is actually a succession of three episodes in which two groups of messengers precede Saul in encountering the prophets and prophesying. Then there are the one hundred 'prophets of Yahweh' whom Obadiah hid from Jezebel and Ahab (1 Kgs 18.3-4), presumably to silence their prophesying. Here again, we encounter evidence of inspired utterance, which finds no record in the canonical writings.[15]

---

[12] Indeed, a consensus of modern scholarship on OT prophecy is that most of the prophetic 'writings' originated as speech and not as literature. See the review article by W.E. March, 'Prophecy,' in *Old Testament Form Criticism* (ed. J.H. Hayes; San Antonio, TX: Trinity University Press, 1974), pp. 141-77. See also C. Westermann, *Basic Forms of Prophetic Speech* (trans. H.C. White; Philadelphia, PA: Westminster Press, 1967).

[13] Some helpful insights on this subject were provided by my colleague, John Christopher Thomas, who has taught a section on the Holy Spirit in the OT as part of his seminary course, 'Theology of the Holy Spirit.'

[14] While my interest here is the theology within, rather than the history behind, the text, I would, nevertheless, note in passing that the conventional move to relate these references to an ecstatic (typically Canaanite) tradition of prophecy, disassociated from classical Israelite prophecy, so-called (see the classic statements S. Mowinckel, '"The Spirit" and "Word" in the Pre-exilic Reforming Prophets,' *JBL* 53 [1934], pp. 199-227), is undoubtedly informed by the same presuppositions which have left modern scholarship so ill-prepared to perceive the integration here noted between canon and charisma. For a recent historical reconstruction of Israelite prophecy which stresses the continuity of a charismatic dimension, see K. van der Toorn, 'From Patriarchs to Prophets: A Reappraisal of Charismatic Leadership in Ancient Israel,' *JNSL* 13 (1987), pp. 191-218.

[15] Perhaps the 'sons of the prophets,' mentioned throughout the Elisha cycle (2 Kgs 2.3; 4.1; 5.22; 6.1; 9.1), should be seen as another biblical testimony to prophesying which does not eventuate in recorded revelation, especially in view of the strong

In addition to all of this evidence against the idea that prophetic speech was ever seen as only a phase in a revelatory process which ended with inscripturated canon, there is the story in 2 Kings 22-23. Here, the prophetess Huldah is called upon to confirm that the law book found in the temple is indeed the word of God (22.14-20). It is remarkable how that in this instance, what could be regarded as an already canonized revelation is seen to depend in some sense upon a subsequent charismatic revelation.

All of these examples serve to strengthen the impression that prophetic utterance, in addition to its role in generating certain portions of the written canon, was seen to have a place and function in Israel's revelatory experience that stood on its own alongside that of inscripturated revelation. Thus we come back again to this issue of Israel's theology of revelation, and there seems to be good reason to look once again to the book of Deuteronomy, where, as was previously noted, the place of written canon and the office of charismatic utterance are explicitly and emphatically set forth. Moreover it seems promising to look in particular to Deuteronomy's sustained reflection upon the theophany of Yahweh at Horeb (Deut. 4 and 5), since this is the decisive moment from which Deuteronomy is careful to trace both of these revelatory provisions.[16] So in reference to God's institution of prophecy we read,

> you asked of Yahweh your God at Horeb on the day of the assembly, 'Let me not hear again the voice of Yahweh my God, or see this great fire any more, so that I will not die.' Then Yahweh said to me, 'What they have spoken is good. I will raise up for them a prophet like you from among their kindred; I will put my words in his mouth, and he shall speak to them all that I command him' (18.16-18).

And in reference to Israel's canonical origins we read,

> On the day you stood before Yahweh your God at Horeb ... he announced to you his covenant, which he commanded you to perform, that is, the ten words; and he wrote them upon two stone tablets (4.10a, 13).

Thus it is perhaps appropriate to find light on the complementary relationship between prophecy and canon in Deuteronomy's extended

---

probability that the term 'sons' here denotes representatives of the prophetic vocation and not mere followers of a prophet. See J.R. Porter, 'בני הנבאים' *JTS* 32 (1981), pp. 324-29.

[16] Whereas S. Talmon ('Revelation in Biblical Times,' pp. 55, 65) has recently stressed that nowhere in 'ancient Hebrew literature does one find either a systematic or a comprehensive description of "revelation,"' he goes on to argue forcefully that the 'Sinai Theophany is the foundation upon which rests the subsequent biblical concept of revelation'.

reflection upon the revelation at Horeb, which is presented in chs. 4 and 5. I would suggest that this is precisely what we begin to find as we look to the passage that leads into the Horeb testimony. Moses says,

> See, I have taught you statutes and ordinances as Yahweh my God commanded me, to do accordingly in the land that you are entering to possess. Keep them and do them, for that is your wisdom and your understanding in the eyes of the peoples, who will hear of all these statutes and say, 'Surely this great people is a wise and understanding nation.' For what great nation is there that has a god so near to it as Yahweh our God is to us whenever we call to him? And what great nation is there that has statutes and ordinances so righteous as all this law that I am placing before you today? (4.5-8).

The last two verses in this passage seem especially significant. Verse 8 most emphatically points to the vital and incomparable character of Israel's *canon*, which is denoted here by the words 'statutes and ordinances so righteous.' Yet v. 7, with parallel wording, points to the equally vital and incomparable endowment of having 'a god so near.' And this latter phrase, I would suggest, relates implicitly to *prophecy*, for it is precisely this matter of divine nearness that Deuteronomy uses to characterize the nature and origin of prophetic revelation.[17] For ch. 4 moves quickly from here to recall when Israel '*came near* and stood' before Yahweh at Horeb (v. 11), where Yahweh, Moses reminds them, 'spoke to you out of the midst of the fire' (v. 12). Then ch. 5 quickly takes up Israel's initial reaction to the ensuing experience of divine nearness. Expressing to Moses their extreme fear of being consumed by the divine presence, the Israelites say to Moses, 'You *go near* and hear all that Yahweh our God will say, then you yourself can speak to us all that Yahweh our God will speak to you; and we will heed and do it' (5.27). This is, of course the precise moment that 18.16-17 recalls as the originative point of Moses' prophetic role and also of Israel's

[handwritten marginalia: Deut = # god so near]

---

[17] See L. Boadt, *Jeremiah 1–25* (Wilmington, DE: Michael Glazier, 1982), pp. 190-91, who is one scholar to recognize prophecy's central concern with divine nearness. Broadt links Deut. 4.7 with Jer. 23.23, which reads, 'Am I a God at hand, says Yahweh, and not a God afar off?' This latter verse falls within an extended discussion of prophecy. Here the fundamental association of prophecy with divine nearness is assumed, even while Jeremiah is wanting to uplift Yahweh's transcendence as well. Broadt goes on to point out the emphasis among Israelite prophets on divine nearness through the frequently used phrase, 'Yahweh is with us' (Isa. 7.14; Hos. 11.9; Amos 5.14). I am indebted to my graduate assistant, Marcia Anderson, for sharing this reference with me. P.D. Miller (*Deuteronomy* [Interpretation; Louisville, KY: John Knox, 1990], pp. 56-57), however, argues that divine nearness in Deut. 4.7 is identified with God's law, drawing support from Deut. 30.11-14. However, contra Miller, the nearness stressed in this latter passage seems to depend upon the immediacy of Moses' role of speaking 'to you this day' (v. 11).

prophetic office. Thus Deuteronomy grounds prophecy in this concern for an ongoing revelatory manifestation of divine nearness.

By lifting up the unique phenomenon of Yahweh's nearness, Deut. 4.7 not only points in the direction of prophetic utterance but also begins to illuminate its distinctive role in Israel's revelatory experience. The occasional and responsive nature of prophetic revelation, which I noted earlier in connection with the verb 'raise up' and which is here reflected in the phrase, 'whenever we call to him',[18] is now shown to be vitally significant for its role in manifesting 'a god so near.'

Deuteronomy 4.7-8, then, seems to constitute an important testimony to the complementary relationship of written word and charismatic word. God's people are called here to recognize and to hold together the law 'so righteous,' which is firmly and *continuously* manifest in their written canon, and the God 'so near,' which is dynamically and *continually* manifest in Yahweh's prophetic revelation.[19]

This dialectic, I would propose, is a primary focus of ch. 4, which elaborates a call for Israel to remember the revelation of Horeb (vv. 9-40), for this is precisely where the *law so righteous* and the *God so near,* indeed where written word and charismatic word, were first experienced *together* by Israel. Attention is called to this union right away in v. 13, which says, 'He [Yahweh] announced to you his covenant, which he commanded you to perform, that is, the ten words; and he wrote them upon two stone tablets.' This *declaring* and *writing* of Yahweh, which would later give way to the *declaring* and the *writing* of Moses and those who would follow after him, clearly represent the written word and the charismatic word and the fact that they were seen to be held together from this foundational moment of Israel's covenant. Furthermore, the hortatory force of the entire recollection of Horeb in Deut. 4 and 5 reflects the concern to continue to hold

aiming to exhort

---

[18] The 'occasional' force of 'whenever' is generated in Hebrew, of course, by the temporal use of the preposition before the infinitive construct. See BDB, p. 91. Whereas it is common to think of prophecy more in terms of a unilateral divine initiative than a divine response to Israel's call, it is important to realize that God's prophetic initiative through Moses, which is the very one emphasized in the book of Deuteronomy, comes as a response to the people's request. Furthermore divine responsiveness to Israel seems inherent in the usage of 'raise up' (e.g. Judg. 3.15) and in the whole context of the law setting forth prophecy in Deut. 18, since it is preceded by the prohibition of seeking the help of pagan mediaries. A later explicit example of God sending a prophet in response to Israel's cry can be seen in Judg. 6.7-8, 'When the people of Israel cried to Yahweh ... Yahweh sent a prophet to the people of Israel.'

[19] See W. Brueggemann, *Creative Word: Canon as a Model for Biblical Education* (Philadelphia, PA: Fortress Press, 1982), pp. 113-17, who appreciates the dialectical relation of these verses along other lines of emphases, yet lines which do not seem irrelevant to the interplay that I have noted between canonical and charismatic revelation. I will comment on this later.

together these revelatory aspects against what seems to be considered the primary threat and tendency of Israel to displace or diminish the *God-so-near* (the charismatic-word) side of the dialectic.

Thus v. 12, after recalling that, 'Yahweh spoke to you out of the midst of the fire,' emphasizes, 'you were hearing (שמע, *shama*) the sound (קוֹל, *qol*) of words[20] but saw no form, there was only a voice (קוֹל).' Verses 15-24 then go on to develop an extended warning against Israel's choosing a form (i.e. an idol) to the neglect of the voice of God. Here the idolatrous form is contrasted with Yahweh's word, the dynamism and untamed nearness of which is represented and manifest in the fire.[21] This section begins,

> Take heed to yourselves, for you saw no form on the day Yahweh spoke to you out of the midst of the fire, beware lest you ... make a graven image for yourselves, in the form of any figure ... (vv. 15-16).

Similarly, the section ends,

> Take heed to yourselves, lest ... you make a graven image in the form of anything which Yahweh your God has forbidden you. For Yahweh your God is a devouring fire (vv. 23-24).

Against Israel's temptation to displace Yahweh's lively presence with a lifeless form, this passage insists upon heeding Yahweh's word as manifested in the fire. For the second time we hear, 'You saw no form' (cf. v. 12), but, as v. 36 will later summarize the counterpoint, 'He let you see his great fire, and you heard his words out of the midst of the fire.'

It is important how that the next section (vv. 25-31) extends this same struggle between static form and dynamic word into the context of Israel's future history, where Yahweh's dynamic word, we know, was to be manifest through the institution of prophecy rather than direct theophany. In the future, we are told, Israel will face the same temptation. And if Israel makes 'a graven image in the form of anything' (v. 25), Yahweh promises to scatter Israel and make them 'serve gods of wood and stone, the work of men's hands, that neither see, nor

---

[20] My translation here accentuates the presence of the participle. The emphasis upon *hearing*, not only here but throughout chs. 4 and 5 (e.g. 4.1; 5.1), reminds one of Samuel Terrien's argument for the oracular orientation of Israelite faith (*The Elusive Presence* [New York: Harper & Row, 1978], pp. 112, 121, 172, 182, 201, 279) – an orientation which has also been noted in Pentecostalism. See M.B. Dowd, 'Contours of a Narrative Pentecostal Theology' (paper presented to the 15th Annual Meeting of the Society for Pentecostal Studies, 1985).

[21] One is reminded here of Jeremiah's later appropriation of this same imagery of fire to characterize the overpowering immanence of the prophetic word within himself (Jer. 20.8; also 23.29). One might also be reminded of the fire of Acts 2.

[Marginal handwritten note: God did not reveal himself physically. So any physical representation created was an idol – not the true God –]

hear' (vv. 26-27). While Yahweh was earlier seen representing his covenant in tablets of stone (v. 12), the people of Israel are here shown the bankruptcy of any attempt on their part ever to reduce divine revelation to stone or any other static form. Yet if the Israelites, after experiencing this bankruptcy, then seek Yahweh 'with all (their) heart and with all (their) souls,' Yahweh promises (in line with 4.7 – 'whenever we call upon him') that Israel can 'return unto (עַל, *al*) Yahweh and hear (שָׁמַע, *shama*) his voice (קוֹל, *qol*)' (vv. 29-30).[22] With parallel wording, the hearing of the voice here is linked to the hearing of the voice at Horeb (v. 12). And the 'God so near' at Horeb parallels the restoration to Yahweh's presence here. Quite appropriately, then, the ending of this section grammatically parallels the ending of the previous section on Horeb. The earlier conclusion declared, 'Yahweh your God is a devouring fire' (v. 24), while v. 31 concludes, 'Yahweh your God is a merciful God.'

The summary section which now follows (vv. 32-40) immediately brings together these elements of devouring fire and divine mercy: 'Did any people ever hear the voice of a god speaking out of the midst of the fire, as you have heard, and still live?' (v. 33). This statement is especially significant for the way it seems intentionally and once again to link the divine voice, which the preceding section had just projected into Israel's future, with the divine voice at Horeb. The inference is registered that through future prophetic word, as through past theophanic word, Israel is mercifully kept alive.

The summary pushes on to the decisive point that Israel's hearing (from heaven) and seeing (upon earth)[23] of Yahweh's words and deeds[24]

---

[22] My translation here brings out the important parallel with 4.12.

[23] 4.36 reads, '*Out of heaven* ... he let you *hear* his voice ... and *on earth* he let you *see* his great fire ...'

[24] Both word and deed, which significantly are held together in the Hebrew term, דָּבָר (*davar*, cf. Deut. 8.3), are stressed in this section. We see this in the appeal to both the voice, which is heard, and the fire, which is seen, at Horeb (see 4.36). Moreover, the 'fire which is seen' is augmented in this section with the 'signs and wonders' that Israel 'was shown' (vv. 34-35) in the exodus and that Israel *will see* in the future conquest of Canaan (v. 38). All of this suggests that Israel's hearing and seeing, and that Yahweh's dynamic word, are not being relegated to past history. In addition to this passage, Deut. 34.10-11 also makes a strong linkage between 'signs and wonders' and prophecy. Discussing all of the occurrences of the phrase 'signs and wonders' in the Hebrew Bible and pointing up the phrase's connection to prophecy is D.N. Fewell, *Circle of Sovereignty: A Story of Stories in Daniel 1–6* (Sheffield: Almond Press, 1988). That miraculous signs as well as words belonged to prophetic ministry is abundantly clear throughout the OT, especially in the Elijah and Elisha stories. See my study, *God Saves: Lessons from the Elisha Stories* (JSOTSup 95; Sheffield: JSOT Press, 1990).

have been provided *'in order that you might know* that Yahweh is God,[25] there is no other besides him' (v. 35). The point is repeated with imperative force and with accent on the present, post-Horeb moment:[26] 'Know therefore this day, and lay it to your heart that Yahweh is God in heaven above and on the earth beneath; there is no other' (v. 39). Here again, Moses is setting the revelation of Yahweh's dynamic word over against Israel's temptation to idolatry. Throughout the chapter we have seen how Israel is warned against substituting forms from earth and/or heaven (cf. vv. 17-19) for the living voice of God, substituting artificial 'gods so near,' as it were, for the true manifestation of Yahweh's nearness. Now God's living word, which Israel hears and sees, is given as the basis of the revelation which rules out all of these other gods 'in heaven above and on the earth beneath.'[27]

Having affirmed the 'God-so-near' aspect of Yahweh's revelation against being displaced by a static form, this chapter concludes with a verse that turns attention to the other aspect of Yahweh's revelation, the 'law so righteous' (cf. vv. 7-8):

> Therefore you shall keep his statutes and his commandments, which I command you this day (v. 40).

Interestingly, this statement turns our attention to the *past* words of God but does so in relation to the *present* words of (the prophet) Moses. 'This day' involves emphasis upon the present moment, especially since it has just been heard in v. 39. It is as if the *nearness* of divine revelation needs to be reinforced even with respect to the 'law so righteous'. A look at ch. 5 would indicate that this suggestion is on target.

Chapter 5, which is well known for its presentation of the core text of Israel's 'law so righteous,' the decalogue, surrounds this core text with special stress on the fact that these *written words* (cf. 5.22) were originally given and are now continuing to be given in relation to *spoken words* which address Israel in the present. The section preceding the decalogue (vv. 1-5) is especially concerned that the written word not be left in the past. Moses says,

---

[25] Cf. the comments on 'a biblical way of knowing' offered by J.D. Johns and C.B. Johns, 'Yielding to the Spirit: A Pentecostal Approach to Bible Study,' *JPT* 1 (1992), pp. 109-34.

[26] It is not insignificant that this point directly follows a reference to *still future* manifestations of divine revelation in the conquest (v. 38). This post-Horeb generation is made responsible for what Israel has seen and heard in the past, because Israel is presently seeing and hearing, and will continue to see and hear, the same living word of Yahweh.

[27] In making this point, I am struck by how 1 John begins with emphasis upon the living word that has been heard and seen (1.3; cf. 2.27) and ends with a call to renounce idolatry. Is it possible that this oft-puzzling ending of 1 John is to be illuminated by the same theological move as we see in Deut. 4?

(they lost faith?) and substituting things they can touch for the thing that pushes them

> *Hear*, O Israel, *the statutes and the ordinances* that I *speak in your hearing this day*, ... Yahweh our God made a covenant[28] with *us* in Horeb. Not with our fathers did Yahweh make this covenant, *but with us*, who are *all of us here alive this day* (vv. 1-3, emphasis mine).

The section following the decalogue (vv. 22-33) is especially concerned with future revelation beyond this initial giving of the written word. Moses recalls,

> These words Yahweh spoke to all your assembly at the mountain out of the midst of the fire, the cloud, and the thick darkness, with a loud voice; and he added no more. And he wrote them upon two stone tablets and gave them to me ... and you said ... if we hear the voice of Yahweh our God any longer, we shall die ... Go near, and hear all that Yahweh our God says; and speak to us all that Yahweh our God speaks to you (vv. 22, 25, 27).

God's positive response to Israel's specific request here opens the way for further revelation, not only through Moses' prophetic role at Horeb (v. 31) but also through the ongoing prophetic institution that stems from this moment, as seen in 18.15-18. In this latter part of ch. 5, concern for the future is registered especially in God's express desire that Israel's initial fear at hearing his spoken word (vv. 23-26) would continue.

> Oh that they had such a mind as this *always*, to fear me and keep all my commandments, that it might go well with them and with their children forever! (v. 29).

Thus, Israel's fearing before Yahweh's revelation here in ch. 5 (see also v. 5) parallels Israel's hearing and seeing of Yahweh's revelation in ch. 4. Each of these responses to God's *dynamic* word are made crucial for keeping God's *enduring* word.

In summarizing our look at the Horeb testimony of Deuteronomy 4–5, it is clear that Israel's having of a 'god so near' (as Yahweh is through his ongoing, dynamic prophetic utterance) is an urgent theological concern in Deuteronomy. Chapter 4 shows this revelatory provision to be crucial in resisting the temptation to *draw near* to idolatrous images of stone. And ch. 5 shows this provision to be crucial in resisting the tendency for Israel to *draw away* from God's word, reducing it to past inscriptions of stone, which do not continue to live in Israel's present or future.

Charismatic word is thus shown here to have a vital, ongoing role alongside written word. Deuteronomy here seems to see the essential and distinct contribution of charismatic revelation in terms of the ma-

---

[28] Here the 'covenant,' as in 4.13, is used specifically to introduce the decalogue.

nifesting of God's nearness in a way that counters an idolatrous manu-
facturing of divine presence, on the one hand, and a legalistic distanc-
ing of divine word, on the other. Thus, without charismatic revelation,
Israel is prone both to violate Yahweh's first word[29] and to antiquate his
entire word.

In the light of the foregoing considerations, I would suggest some
broader implications. The concerns I have traced in chs. 4 and 5 would
seem to be significantly related to the thrust of Deuteronomy as a
whole. In this pivotal book, Moses addresses his last words to the new
generation. He is concerned that God's word, which had been given
and heard *before*, be heard, seen and kept *now* – and not just now but
on and on into Israel's future. Deuteronomy, it could perhaps be said,
is itself a prophetic word on Israel's canon – a word through which
God makes himself and his canon present to the new generation. Thus,
Deuteronomy *remembers* the paradigmatic revelatory moment of Horeb
where God both wrote and spoke his word, in order for this same
revelatory synergism to be *manifest in the present and carried forward into
the future*. Is it too much, then, to say that Deuteronomy in general and
chs. 4 and 5 in particular offer a *past basis, present model and future projection of the complementary relationship* between written word and charismatic word in the Old Testament?

Reinforcement for this last point could perhaps be found in the very
terminology by which Israel expressed some of its primary epistemological and revelatory concepts. I would offer here a couple of sugges-
tions that might merit further exploration. An especially important
term for God's revelation is דבר (*davar*). While this is commonly translated as 'word,' it is well known that it expresses much more than our
term 'word,' often requiring the translation 'event.' This vocabulary
would accord with the argument above for seeing divine revelation as
bringing closely together the notions of written word, spoken word,
even manifested or embodied word. Complementing this, an important term for Israel's knowing is ידע (*yada*). Here again, the common
translation, 'to know,' falls short of the Hebrew notion, for our term
'know' points to the conceptualization of an object, whereas the Hebrew term resists such a subject–object dichotomy and points more to
the actualization of a relationship between knower and known.[30] Again
the Hebrew terminology seems to correspond in a striking way to the

---

[29] I refer here, of course, to the decalogue's command against idolatry, which is
surely the *first command*, even though it is possible to be understood as the *second word*,
the first being, 'I am Yahweh your God who brought you out of the land of Egypt,
out of the house of bondage' (5.6). See W. Harrelson, *The Ten Commandments and
Human Right* (Philadelphia, PA: Fortress Press, 1980), p. 7.

[30] See Johns and Johns, 'Yielding to the Spirit.'

foregoing case for seeing Israel's apprehension of divine revelation as including ongoing relationship to the manifest presence of God. Thus God's word (דבר) and Israel's knowing (ידע), terms which come together in Deut. 4.35, are terms which appear to correspond profoundly to one another and to the dynamic, integrative paradigm of revelation pointed to above.

A few concluding remarks are now offered. I have sought to show that Deuteronomy exhibits an urgent concern to observe a dynamic integration of canon and charisma in Israel's ongoing revelatory experience – a concern developed in Deuteronomy 4 and 5 and expressed most succinctly in the theological juxtaposing of 'a god so near' and 'a law so righteous.' Walter Brueggemann, as noted earlier, has appreciated the dialectical relation between these theological affirmations in Deut. 4.7-8. He sees this reference holding together a 'delicate and difficult balance' that rejects a 'God-less Torah (legalism),' on the one hand, and a 'Torah-less God (romanticism)' on the other.[31] In view of the foregoing discussion, I would suggest that the tension be posed in terms of a Spirit-less Word (rationalism), on the one hand, and a Word-less Spirit (subjectivism), on the other. This may bring matters closer to home in seeing what is at stake in holding together the canonical-charismatic revelatory paradigm heretofore considered.[32] Obviously, to put the issue this way is to point forward from the text of Deuteronomy to the theological and hermeneutical concerns of Pentecostalism – a move which may not appear to be so overdrawn when one considers the historical and theological connections between the Sinai event (the Horeb theophany) in the Old Testament and the Pentecost event in the New Testament.[33]

Within this tension of canon and charisma – a tension that the hermeneutical traditions of modern Western theology have found ways to eliminate – Pentecostals must find their way. This tension will provide no easy place to stand – Sinai didn't either – but it just may provide the way for a new voice to be heard, one that we all need to hear.

I return at last to my starting point, where I suggested that my look at the final form of the text needed little justification in this day when longstanding formulations and the forms of study which they have

---

[31] Brueggemann, *Creative Word*, pp. 113-17.

[32] I would add that the dialectical relation between canon and charisma, between prescribed righteousness and divine nearness, and between Torah and God, suggests an interpenetration rather than a dichotomization of terms, so that, for example, canon can be seen to manifest divine nearness (cf. Deut. 30.11-14) and charismatic revelation can be seen to manifest prescribed righteousness (cf. 2 Kgs 22.15-17), but only as each is inseparably related to the other.

[33] On this see R. Stronstad, *The Charismatic Theology of St. Luke* (Peabody, MA: Hendrickson, 1984), pp. 58-62.

represented have lost their absolute sway. We talk of paradigm shifts, but the biblical texts that we study would undoubtedly pose such a matter in terms of idolatry. Aren't we now witnessing the crumbling of our idols? And I refer not just to the canons of historical criticism but even to our claims upon the *final form* of the text. Would not Moses warn us against even these, when he says, 'Take heed to yourselves, since you saw no form on the day that Yahweh spoke to you at Horeb out of the midst of the fire' (Deut. 4:15)?

While some would want to read our present hermeneutical revolution in terms of the triumph of deconstructionism, the biblical texts which we study would bear witness to the ultimate deconstructionist, Yahweh, whose word (דבר) deconstructs *all* of our 'final' forms – even the enterprise of deconstruction itself, which makes an idol of the smashing of idols (cf. Jehu in 2 Kgs 10). Could all the deconstructing which is going on in contemporary Western hermeneutics be a disclosure of what we are essentially and finally capable of doing apart from a word which truly comes forth from the mouth of a living God? Unfortunately, this question of our deconstructive potential has implications not just for our literature but also for our politics. Within this context, I would want to approach the final form of the text, but in the light of the consuming fire. Let every reader[34] decide for him- or herself whence this fire comes.[35]

---

[34] In place of 'reader' I could have put 'worshipper,' for aren't we all? And hasn't the time come for us all to be more honest about what it is or who it is that we are worshipping in our reading and in our writing?

[35] I gratefully acknowledge the help of my colleagues in the preparation of this study, especially John Christopher Thomas, Cheryl Bridges Johns, Steven J. Land and James M. Beaty for their theological insight and their spiritual discernment and support.

3

Deuteronomy and the Fire of God: A Critical Charismatic Interpretation[*]

This study proposes a fresh approach toward something scarcely seen in biblical scholarship until recently – a literary theological reading of the entire book of Deuteronomy.[1] My treatment finds the theme of the fiery revelation of God at Horeb at the heart of the book, something which modern biblical scholarship heretofore has hardly noticed.[2]

My subtitle has double meaning. On the one hand, I am offering and urging an approach to the biblical text that is critical and at the same time charismatic, in the sense of its self-conscious commitment to read the biblical text through the lens of Pentecostal experience and confession. On the other hand, I want to say that the book of Deuteronomy is itself an act of interpretation that is, in a similar way, both charismatic and critical. Indeed Deuteronomy is the biblical canon's first programmatic attempt to re-read or interpret the canonical tradition previously given,[3] and it surely must be seen as a remarkably critical attempt, if criticism has anything at all to do with being rigorously

---

[*] First published in *Journal of Pentecostal Theology* 7 (October 1995), pp. 11-33.
[1] Literary treatment of the whole of Deuteronomy in its final form was scarcely attempted in academic scholarship until Robert Polzin's *Moses and the Deuteronomist* (New York: Seabury, 1980), but Dennis T. Olson, *Deuteronomy and the Death of Moses: A Theological Reading* (Minneapolis, MN: Augsburg Fortress, 1994), offered the first full-scale literary *theological* treatment. Olson acknowledges the scarcity of attempts to approach Deuteronomy in this manner, drawing attention to the mixture of genres and particularly its casting in terms of a speech, which make Deuteronomy less inviting to literary approaches than, say, the narrative materials of books like Genesis or Samuel (see Olson, p. 2).
[2] While it has been common to see the content of the decalogue, and particularly the first commandment as represented in the Shema, at the center of the book (see P.D. Miller, *Deuteronomy*, Interpretation Series [Louisville, KY: John Knox Press, 1990], pp. 14-15), this has not done justice to Deuteronomy's fuller emphasis upon the theophanic dimension of the Horeb revelation.
[3] The clearest acknowlegement of this point that I know is Walter Brueggemann, 'The Case for an Alternative Reading,' *Theological Education* 23 (1987), p. 96: 'The primal script is the Mosaic event and the Mosaic narrative of Exodus and Sinai. Deuteronomy is a rereading of this ancient script, a second reading (cf. Deut. 17.18), from whence comes the name Deuteronomy, a derivative reading which is done with authority and imagination.'

open to perspectives which stand over against one's own standpoint, to
voices which intrude, as it were, from the margin.

A self-consciously Pentecostal perspective comes to the table of
modern biblical scholarship as a voice from the margin. Perhaps for this
reason it is better prepared to see the starkly marginal location of Deuteronomy's own word, a context no less marginal than the wilderness
and yet ultimately even more marginal than that. It is a word that
comes, so Deuteronomy claims, from out of the midst of the fire of
God. This claim may be more relevant to a critical understanding of
Deuteronomy, and perhaps even to the dynamic of critical interpretation itself, than 'critical' scholarship has yet dared to entertain. I hope
to show in this paper how I, at least, have come to believe so. Such an
effort has prompted me to begin, like the book of Deuteronomy, with
a story. It is a story that leads to my interpretation of Deuteronomy
that I will then set within the context of current Deuteronomy scholarship. Yet it is a story that tells not only how I have come to interpret
Deuteronomy but also how Deuteronomy has come to interpret me.

A Journey in the Study of Deuteronomy
I have been a student of the book of Deuteronomy for a long time. As
a child growing up in a Pentecostal denomination, it was natural for
me to take the first words of Deuteronomy, 'These are the words of
Moses to all Israel', as a personal invitation to draw near and to listen
with all God's people to this one who had stood before the very fire of
God on the holy mountain. I had never seen this fire, but this old
man's words were not difficult for me to trust, perhaps because of the
elders gathered around me, whose faces at times seemed to reflect what
I took to be the light from that same fire. I felt that I could somehow
come close to this fire and close to these words'.[4]

Yet there was an awareness, even then, that out beyond the margins
of our Pentecostal community there were other voices with which I
would have to contend, voices which knew nothing of this fire and
which stood ready to offer a fiery challenge to the credibility of *my*
ever knowing it. I suppose I first learned to fear these other voices
from the same source that had first made me to desire holy fire, that is,
the faces of my elders.

I finally encountered these voices in their full force when, as a
young man, I left my father's house and took a journey into a far (different) country, where I spent all I had on a graduate program in Old
Testament studies. There I was directed once again to the first words
of the book of Deuteronomy, but now a mountain of scholarship

---

[4] The Hebrew name for the book of Deuteronomy is אלה הדברים (*ellah ha-debarim*),
'These are the words'.

stood before these words and yielded a very different reading, namely, 'these are *not* the words of Moses'. I learned that to believe otherwise was to be 'pre-critical'. And I knew, without it having to be explicitly stated, that to be seen as 'pre-critical' in this environment was a fate to be feared worse than death. Being relegated to the camp of the pre-critical was cursed; being admitted to the guild of the critical was blessed. I survived that time mostly by hiding in a wilderness between the curse that I feared and the blessing that I could not bring myself to embrace.

To be more specific, the treatment of Deuteronomy that I encountered in my 'critical training' placed this book at the very center of the canons of modern biblical scholarship (as D in the JEDP hypothesis) with its elaborate body of writings and prevailing theories on the late dating and complex redactional history of the Pentateuch.[5] This towering fortress of scholarship, with its formidable conclusions about the text and methods used to reach them, was a far cry from the ethos and impulses of my Pentecostal confession. This was the case not only with respect to the book of Deuteronomy but across the entire range of my 'critical training'. In a way that went against my deepest and mostly unconscious longings, I was being relentlessly conditioned to experience criticism and confession as mutually exclusive opposites.

Then came the day that I was offered a teaching position at my denomination's Pentecostal seminary. And as Providence would have it, for the very first semester and on a recurrent basis thereafter I was expected to teach a course on the book of Deuteronomy. My initial reaction was anxiety. There was no area of study where I felt any wider gap between the critical approach in which I had been schooled and the confessional interests for which I was now to be responsible. To my relief, I soon discovered the work of certain Evangelical scholars who had found ways to defend against the skeptical critical conclusions as far as the late, post-Mosaic dating of Deuteronomy and had done so by re-employing the very methods developed by the mainstream of historical critical scholarship, namely a form-critical argument that links the structure of Deuteronomy to an international treaty form found to be extant during the time of Moses but not in later centuries.[6] In this I found a new way to survive. I came out of hiding, but not much more than that. My new occupation essentially amounted to trying not to

---

[5] A representative survey of the historical critical scholarship on Deuteronomy can be found in R.E. Clements, *Deuteronomy,* Old Testament Guides (Sheffield: Sheffield Academic Press, 1989).

[6] M.G. Kline, *Treaty of the Great King: The Covenant Structure of Deuteronomy* (Grand Rapids, MI: Eerdmans, 1963) and K.A. Kitchen, *Ancient Orient and the Old Testament* (London: Tyndale Press, 1966), pp. 90-102.

offend a confession that still seemed threatened, while trying to defend against a criticism that continued to intimidate me.

As my journey in teaching Deuteronomy continued, the book that I had expected to be the last place for discovering an interface between Pentecostal confession and critical biblical scholarship started becoming for me the place of liveliest intersection and greatest potential. This took place under the impact of changes which were happening on several fronts: (1) in the field of biblical studies, (2) in Pentecostal scholarship, and (3) in my own relationship to both as a result of my return to a context of study within a Pentecostal community.

In critical biblical scholarship there was the growing impact of the paradigm shift from modernism to post-modernism, which is now the rage in Western culture. The undermining of modernity's foundation upon an epistemology claiming neutral objectivity eliminated any credible basis for keeping marginal perspectives, such as my Pentecostalism would represent, from being given a hearing in the academic arena. I encountered a new permission to look at the biblical text through Pentecostal eyes.

Furthermore this was reinforced by the related shift in academic scholarship away from the dominance of historiographical concerns and toward literary approaches and interest in narrative and story.[7] In Pentecostal scholarship this encouraged a conscious interest in the narrative orientation of Pentecostalism's own theological heritage. Story or testimony had been the prime vehicle and mode of discourse in Pentecostal faith from its beginnings, long before it had become fashionable in academic circles.[8] Still the turn toward narrative and literary concerns in critical scholarship was undoubtedly important in helping Pentecostal scholars like myself to get in touch with their native 'tongue'. I began teaching Deuteronomy at a time when Robert Polzin's work had made a significant case for the value of pursuing literary study of this book as well as biblical literature in general.[9]

Alongside of these important changes in academic biblical study and in Pentecostal scholarship, however, there was for me the even more decisive change of becoming part of a community of Pentecostals where I began daily to be challenged and helped toward bringing my own faith perspective into conscious, thoroughgoing dialogue with my

[7] The literature is voluminous, but the shift is well represented by G.W. Stroup, *The Promise of Narrative Theology* (Atlanta, GA: John Knox Press, 1981). See also the seminal article of S. Crites 'The Narrative Quality of Experience,' *JAAR* 39 (1971), pp. 291-311.

[8] See M. Dowd, 'Contours of a Narrative Pentecostal Theology and Practice' (paper presented to the 15th Annual Meeting of the Society for Pentecostal Studies, 1985), and J.-D. Plüss, *Therapeutic and Prophetic Narratives in Worship: A Hermeneutic Study of Testimony and Vision* (Bern: Peter Lang, 1988).

[9] *Moses and the Deuteronomist,* cited earlier.

biblical scholarship for the first time. It was not that my own life experiences had been without relation to my critical studies before this time. Part of the discovery was that they had been having a great deal of effect on my research, but in ways that were largely in the background and out of conscious view. I found out that although I had spent many years being trained to interpret texts, I had learned very little about interpreting my own story.[10]

I believe I can honestly say (or testify!) that this conscious move to begin bringing my own faith confession into interaction with my technical work on the text, instead of a compromise or contamination of my critical study (which is what I had been led to expect from such a move), was actually encountered as the most *critical* step I had ever taken in studying biblical texts. It is precisely what enabled me and forced me to realize that many of my earlier research choices and conclusions, which had passed for *critical* scholarship,[11] had actually been the product of largely *uncritical* impulses, such as social conformity and intellectual intimidation. I encountered a great deal of self-discovery, some of it unwelcomed and painful, which made biblical study more critical and yet at the same time more confessionally invigorating for me than it had ever been. As I continued teaching Deuteronomy in this vein and in this setting I became more and more convinced that it was opening me toward a fresh approach to the biblical text that could prove very significant and helpful to both Pentecostalism and biblical scholarship as a whole. I did not see some great new hermeneutical formula. What I saw instead were more and more instances in the particular text of the book of Deuteronomy where Pentecostalism's narrative orientation and instincts seemed capable of freshly informing and benefiting from a literary-theological approach to the book of Deuteronomy.

First, I was struck by the way that Deuteronomy went beyond merely utilizing narrative (a great deal of the literature of the biblical canon does this) to commending it as the prime means of expressing and keeping the faith. No urging of the book is more prominent than

---

[10] A book which focused this insight for me at the time was C.V. Gerkin, *The Living Human Document: Re-Visioning Pastoral Counseling in a Hermeneutical Mode* (Nashville, TN: Abingdon Press, 1984). Far more important than this book, however, was the person who recommended it to me, Robert D. Crick, an elder on my faculty who took a personal interest in me in those early years and 'read me like a book' with his brilliant pastoral counseling skills and fathering compassion. He was to me what Morrie Schwartz was to Mitch Albom in Albom's wonderful autobiographical account, *Tuesdays With Morrie* (New York: Doubleday, 1997). I will be forever grateful.

[11] I refer here mainly to papers written for courses in my graduate program at Vanderbilt University, 1976-1981.

the call to remembrance.[12] What's more, as the Hebrew canon's own paradigm for passing the faith to a new generation,[13] Deuteronomy succeeds through its own example in elevating narrative to a place of primacy and centrality for the whole canon. The work of Walter Brueggemann was especially important in helping me begin to see 'narrative as Israel's primal mode of knowing' and the significant implications which flow from this.[14] Yet I knew another means of access to such insights. I knew from my own background as a Pentecostal what it was like to be on the inside of a testifying, witnessing community where narrative was the central mode of theological expression. I began to sense that Pentecostals had significant insights to offer as well as receive in the study of this important aspect of Deuteronomy.

Specific elements in the narrative content of Deuteronomy began to appear especially relevant as I continued to pursue what seemed like a convergence of critical and Pentecostal perspectives on the text. Foremost here was the emphasis given in the book to the theophanic experience and revelatory testimony of Mount Horeb. The striking feature was not just that Deuteronomy repeatedly recalls this event (1.6; 4.10-15; 5.2-33; 18.16-20; 34.10) but also that it seems to strive to make it available and present to the new generation (see esp. 5.2-4). Once again I encountered something that seemed familiar in the light of my experience as a Pentecostal. I knew something first-hand about a community called to gather around a root experience of visionary and revelatory encounter with God in a way that expects the ushering of the present into that encounter.[15] It became apparent that the role of the Pentecost event (cf. Acts 2) in my own faith tradition suggested important parallels with the role of the Horeb event in the book of Deuteronomy, parallels of spiritual and experiential dynamics which went beyond the historical evidence which modern scholarship had turned up for linking the Feast of Pentecost to the commemoration of the giving of the Law at Horeb or Sinai.[16]

I do not think it is going too far to say that I sensed the affirmation of a *charismatic dimension* in Deuteronomy that scholarship was ill

---

[12] Especially prominent examples are seen in chs. 4 and 8. For a full survey see Edward P. Blair, 'An Appeal to Remembrance: The Memory Motif in Deuteronomy', *Int* 15 (1961), pp. 41-47.

[13] On this see esp. D.T. Olson, *Deuteronomy and the Death of Moses* (Minneapolis, MN: Fortress Press, 1994), pp. 7-14.

[14] See esp. his *The Creative Word: Canon as a Model for Biblical Education* (Philadelphia, PA: Fortress Press, 1982), pp. 15-27.

[15] For a recent attempt to develop this insight into a central thesis for Deuteronomy see J.G. McConville and J.G. Millar, *Time and Place in Deuteronomy* (Sheffield: Sheffield Academic Press, 1994).

[16] See R. Stronstad, *The Charismatic Theology of St. Luke* (Peabody, MA: Hendrickson, 1984), pp. 58-62.

equipped to probe. I found one OT scholar who had seen the category of charisma and the notion of a charismatic tradition as being decisive for understanding the book of Deuteronomy. Joseph Blenkinsopp, in his book *Prophecy and Canon*, argues that the book of Deuteronomy along with the three divisions of the Hebrew canon were formed in response to an ongoing conflict of authority claims between an institutional tradition of 'normative order' and a charismatic tradition of 'free prophecy'.[17] Blenkinsopp links these traditions and categories of analysis on the one hand to OT scholarship's longstanding debate on the relationship between law and prophecy and on the other hand to Max Weber's sociological typology of institution versus charisma.[18] The view of Deuteronomy that emerges in Blenkinsopp's treatment appreciates the strategic impact of a charismatic tradition on the book, but sees this tradition as a social threat which the book of Deuteronomy was fashioned to mitigate and control. Blenkinsopp sees a book 'deeply indebted to prophecy', but nevertheless shaped by an opposing clerical scribalism that sought to neutralize charismatic claims by assimilating their insights and impulses 'within its own institutional grid'.[19] Rather than 'ascribing cynical self-interest to these Torah scribes', Blenkinsopp wants to respect 'that they were persuaded of their own legitimacy and of the inability of prophecy to provide a sound basis for the life of the community'.[20]

I do not know whether Blenkinsopp's analysis was consciously affected by the charismatic renewal that peaked on his campus of the University of Notre Dame in the seventies, right before the time his book appeared.[21] However, I have come to realize, along with most of the scholars in this generation, I suppose, that where we stand pro-

---

[17] *Prophecy and Canon: A Contribution to the Study of Jewish Origins* (Notre Dame, IN: University of Notre Dame Press, 1977).

[18] Blenkinsopp, *Prophecy and Canon*, pp. 7-9, 39-46, 147-52. Blenkinsopp cites translations of several of Weber's major works, originally published just before and after the sociologist's death in 1920: *Ancient Judaism* (New York: The Free Press, 1952); *The Sociology of Religion* (London: Methuen, 1965); and *The Theory of Social and Economic Organization* (New York: The Free Press, 1964).

[19] *Prophecy and Canon*, p. 8.

[20] *Prophecy and Canon*, p. 8.

[21] For an account of the Catholic Charismatic Renewal and the early role of the Notre Dame University campus as a center of this movement, see F.A. Sullivan, 'Catholic Charismatic Renewal', in S.M. Burgess and G.B. McGee (eds.), *Dictionary of Pentecostal and Charismatic Movements* (Grand Rapids, MI: Zondervan, 1988), pp. 110-26. It is perhaps confirming of my own lack of truly critical engagement at this time to admit that, despite my knowledge of and interest as a Pentecostal in this well-publicized event, the question of any relationship between the clash of institution and charisma on the Notre Dame campus and the discussion of such a clash in ancient Israel by this Notre Dame professor never entered my mind when I first encountered Blenkinsopp's book during this time.

foundly affects our reading of the data. Scholars did not talk much about 'readings' back during the time when Blenkinsopp's volume appeared. However, things have changed dramatically since then. It is surely becoming much clearer to us all now that the historical critical methods of that day, though still very much in use, have themselves given decisive ground on their authority claims. In the end they too produce nothing other than 'readings'.[22]

Blenkinsopp offers *one reading* of a charismatic dimension in the book of Deuteronomy, one that is not neutral with respect to the sociological categories he utilizes. The modern Western academic tradition, which Blenkinsopp represents with his historical critical methodology and Weberian sociological analysis, is surely one that sides overwhelmingly with 'normative order' over against 'charisma'. Notwithstanding the relative value he might ascribe to the latter, it is clear that he comes from a perspective that is defining and viewing charisma from the outside. How would the charismatic dimension in the book of Deuteronomy read to someone coming from the other side? I have become convinced that this latter question is worth pursuing to the potential benefit of all. At the same time, I recognize that any attempt on my part to do so immediately encounters some serious problems. First, there is the question of whether my life-long participation in a North American 'classical' Pentecostal denomination, not to mention my graduate training at a secular university, qualifies me to attempt a reading from 'the other side'. Margaret Poloma's sociological study of the leading North American Pentecostal denomination, *The Assemblies of God at the Crossroads*, utilizes the same Weberian categories to show that we North American Pentecostals have gone a long way already down the road of institutionalization and loss of our 'charismatic' identity.[23] Then there is the problem that even with *this* insight we find ourselves appropriating definitions, methods, and approaches to interpretation that derive from 'outside' sources.

---

[22] I make this latter point not in order to dismiss but rather properly to appreciate Blenkinsopp's contribution. I believe his analysis is seminal and helpful in pointing to a decisive charismatic dimension and tradition in the book of Deuteronomy. His application of Weber's sociological categories of charisma and institution has allowed him to get at larger dynamics and concerns in the literature than what one usually finds in historical-critical work of this sort, and this is to the benefit not only of the study of Deuteronomy but also of its application to matters of contemporary concern. Blenkinsopp, in fact, uses his canonical study to suggest a more positive appreciation for charisma in the life of established religion than one usually finds in modern Western scholarship (*Prophecy and Canon*, pp. 151-52), and as a Pentecostal I welcome this as a positive and long overdue step.

[23] *Assemblies of God at the Crossroads: Charisma and Institutional Dilemmas* (Knoxville, TN: University of Tennessee, 1989), pp. 232-41.

Yet then does it not require precisely such sources 'outside' our-selves to make our interpretation something more than a self-serving projection of our own experience and ego, in other words, to make our interpretation *critical?* Is it the case, then, that any attempt to read the charismatic dimension of the biblical text from the inside, such as I am here proposing, will inevitably shut down the 'outside' perspective, or critical principle, which alone delivers us from self-serving subjec-tivity? Does a critical approach to interpretation invariably end where a confessional approach begins? It is at the heart of my purpose here to indicate how I have come to believe otherwise.

On the surface of things, it should not be surprising that modern thought has been so successful in training us to see criticism and con-fession as clear opposites. There is no doubt that the embrace of con-fession has too often served the avoidance of criticism, the stifling of voices different from or outside of our own. I say, 'no doubt', because I have seen this dynamic not just in others but also in myself. Biblical criticism helped me to get in touch with a lot of this. Yet I came to find another dimension of criticism that academic criticism, as I have experienced it, scarcely touches. It is a level of criticism that I find, if anything, *more critical* insofar as it unleashes a starker challenge to the self-securing tendencies of my own interpretive standpoint. It is the criticism which I found and experienced when I pushed more deeply *into* rather than *away from* my Pentecostal confession and experience.

I began to encounter a voice from the text of Deuteronomy that was more critically demanding of me than critical scholarship ever had been. This was the voice that brought me to the self-effacing realiza-tion that my academic training as an Old Testament scholar had been dominated largely by suppressed embarrassment and fear. These two things had driven me *everywhere* in my study, but I was too *uncritical* to notice. I was secretly embarrassed about the uncredentialed heritage and humble status of my uneducated Pentecostal elders. Notwithstand-ing the fiery 'mountain top' experiences to which my elders bore wit-ness, and perhaps more and more *because* of them, it was a past I wanted to forget and one which I was desperately trying to 'rise above'. As far as fear, I was afraid of scholars and smart people. I was constantly intimidated by them and in awe of them, never realizing at the time that this was the fear of which worship is made. I had a chance to recognize the power with which both of these passions were acting upon me one day when a friend and fellow graduate student, a Lutheran who had turned down an offer to study at Yale, asked me what church I attended. My face flushed with shame as he identified my denomination as Pentecostal and even asked me about speaking in tongues. I was so afraid of my friend's 'educated' opinion of me that I could do little more than stammer and grope for an awkward escape from the encounter. I shook off the potential self-revelation of this moment and went right back to my study carrel that day, suffering no loss of faith in my critical access to how the ancient authors came to compose the biblical writings, even though I was completely out of touch with the decisive factors at work behind *my* scholarly writing, right there in front of my nose.

When I finally made the turn toward a self-consciously Pentecostal approach to the text, Deuteronomy met my past-negating embarrass-ment with its sustained call for God's people to remember. Remember your background of homelessness in an extremely rural area where you depended on a welfare system of daily food allotments (e.g. 8.2-16); remember that your ancestors were known not for their education but for a lack of knowledge (8.3, 16); remember that your pedigree traces not from the upper class, middle class or even lower middle class but rather from slaves (5.15; 15.15); remember even that your background reveals a humiliating negation of national honor (9.7, 13, 25).

Deuteronomy met my fear of intellectual giants with its condemna-tion against fear of all the giants that faced God's people (1.28-35; 7.17-18). In fact the very context of Deuteronomy is determined by a lamentable episode of capitulation to this fear (ch. 1). The fear of an old generation postponed entry into the land, so that a new generation had now to be addressed with the same covenant choice. This kind of fear is found thriving here in the absence of the one fear that is promi-nently commended in the book of Deuteronomy and one that, I had to admit, was virtually non-existent in the context of my academic training – the fear of God (e.g. 4.10; 5.29). Deuteronomy helped me to see the underlying issue whenever fear was directed to anything other than God. The issue was idolatry. I had never realized before how much fear had to do with worship.

To put it succinctly, in the face of Deuteronomy's principal call to have no other gods before Yahweh, I found that another fear had claimed my allegiance. Before the call to remember the past and to honor my father and mother, I found myself given over to repression, embarrassment and dishonor. Interpreting Deuteronomy through the grid of my Pentecostal experience and vice versa brought me to a new interpretation of myself – a rigorously critical interpretation.

I realized at the same time that the book featured a rather rigorous criticism of the people of Israel and even Moses, who repeatedly is seen acknowledging his own weakness, failure, and consequent debarment from the promised land.[24] In fact, I cannot remember ever seeing this

---

[24] See J.G. McConville, *Grace in the End: A Study in Deuteronomic Theology* (Grand Rapids, MI: Zondervan, 1993), pp. 133-34, who is the only scholar I have found who acknowledges the remarkably critical thrust of this literature.

degree of self-critical rigor anywhere in the discourse of modern criticism. Was this critical perspective of Deuteronomy achieved through bracketing out the 'inside' confession while opening to the scrutiny of 'outside' sources? Reading Deuteronomy in intersection with my Pentecostal experience led me to another possibility and explanation. For I found on the inside, indeed at the very heart, of my Pentecostal experience and, I believe, the charismatic dimension of the book of Deuteronomy as well, an overwhelming encounter with the ultimate 'outside' source, so that the most radical criticism is disclosed precisely at the core of this confession. Against modernity's longstanding dichotomization of confession and criticism, there is found here a surprising fusion. It may, in fact, be the constitutive fusion in the radical inaugural moments of charismatic experience and tradition. I am proposing that in such moments utter confession and utter criticism implode. It is an utterly confessional moment, for everything yields to the claim of a theophanic experience. The claim is not decided but evoked, so that it is not so much a matter of *making a claim* as a matter of *being claimed*. Yet because this is the case, it is a moment of utter criticism. To be thus claimed is at the same time to be disclaimed, to be seized, taken captive and dispossessed of everything previously claimed. It is to know what it is to stand stripped down to the nakedness and weakness of one's confession. It is to know how vulnerable one's claims were all along and ever will be. It is an experience so radically confessional that we, like Isaiah, can say nothing less than, 'I saw God!' Yet it is so radically critical at the same time that we cannot help but exclaim, 'Woe is me!' Over against this kind of experience I find the tradition of Enlightenment criticism somewhat trivial and not nearly critical enough.[25]

Coming from this kind of critical-charismatic experience opens up a different reading of reality and a different reading of Deuteronomy. The way I read it (*and the way it has read me!*), Deuteronomy is itself

---

[25] At least one scholar within the critical guild has ventured to consider how that the witness to divine wonder in the biblical text represents a *critical* challenge to the sociology and epistemology of the Western academic establishment. See W. Brueggemann, *Abiding Astonishment: Psalms, Modernity, and the Making of History* (Louisville, KY: Westminster/John Knox Press, 1991). 'Abiding astonishment' is a phrase and a formulation which Brueggemann takes up from Martin Buber (M. Buber, *Moses* [Atlantic Highlands, NJ: Humanities Press International, 1946], pp. 75-77). He follows Buber in acknowledging that regardless of how one thinks about the possibility of *supernatural* phenomena, the experience of 'wonder must be accepted as a datum' that cannot be explained away. Indeed wonder happens precisely at the point where *'explanation'* has been overwhelmed and overridden. Brueggemann seems to think that a modern hermeneutic which has dismissed 'wonder' in the name of critical objectivity has done so at the cost of blinding itself from the most decisive aspect of the literature and the people it has sought to understand, but even more than that, it has blinded itself from its own ideological stake in the dismissal, evading the key clue to a truly critical understanding of itself (pp. 41-53).

coming from this kind of experience, and it is grounded and driven by the theophanic encounter with Yahweh at Horeb. This overwhelming revelatory moment, I would contend, is the prime issue and theme of the book. This is where Moses is coming from and where he is insisting that the new generation, and by extension *every* new generation, must come from if they are to live, keep the faith, and inherit the promises of God.

The Death of Moses and the Fire of God

The quickest and clearest way for me to present the outline of this literary-theological interpretation of Deuteronomy is to do so in contrast to an alternative one that has recently been offered by Dennis Olson of Princeton Theological Seminary. Olson's comprehensive treatment of Deuteronomy is the first thoroughgoing literary-theological approach to the book that has appeared in mainstream biblical criticism.[26] His grasp of the book's structure offers what I believe is a breakthrough insight. His convincing identification of the parts into which the canonical form of the book has been arranged sets the stage for identifying the theme that holds the parts together. Thus I follow Olson's literary insight into the book's structure in my own effort to identify the book's main theme. Yet our different theological perspectives, which surely have to do with different ways of perceiving and pursuing *critical* interpretation (and perhaps charismatic encounter as well), yield starkly contrasting understandings of Deuteronomy's primary theme. Olson argues that the book's governing theme is *the death of Moses*,[27] whereas I find it in the theophanic encounter with *the fire of God*. I will summarize Olson's interpretation before offering my own.

---

[26] Olson, *Deuteronomy and the Death of Moses*, pp. 4-5, presupposes some of the broad conclusions of historical critical scholarship as far as attributing the book to a Deuteronomistic school whose composition of Deuteronomy took place in multiple stages over a range of time that turned on two major events: (1) the fall of the northern kingdom, the place where the Deuteronomists were thought to have originated before being forced to migrate to the south when the fall of the north occurred; (2) the fall of the southern kingdom, a crisis that provided the Deuteronomic tradition with a chance to offer the nation a viable way forward in the face of the collapse of the 'establishment' traditions of Judah. Olson does not offer any argument for these conclusions nor does his central argument depend upon these conclusions in any significant way, since he is treating the book in its final form. Conversely, his central argument demonstrates such a thoroughgoing coherence, integrity and balance in the final shape of Deuteronomy that it would seem to have the unintended effect of posing a formidable challenge to the historical-critical claims for multi-staged, multi-layered composition. For a recent and *intentional* challenge to these long-held critical positions on the book of Deuteronomy see the historical-critical treatment of J.G. McConville, *Grace in the End*, pp. 45-64.

[27] Olson, *Deuteronomy and the Death of Moses*, pp. 6-22, in presenting his argument for the theme of Moses' death, calls it 'an important recurring theme' (p. 7) and 'a central metaphor' (p. 17), seemingly careful not to overstate. However, his claims for the theme's

Olson introduces his reading of Deuteronomy with the observation that a series of parallel superscriptions mark the respective beginnings of all the major sections of the book in its present form.[28] The book itself begins with the most inclusive such superscription: *'these are the words of Moses'* (1.1). This phrase stands before not only the whole book but also the initial narrative section, which reviews the events leading up to the present context of Moses' address to the new generation.

In 4.44 we encounter the second superscription, *'this is the torah'*. It introduces what Olson takes to be the most defining section of the book. This is so since *torah*, Olson argues, is the most adequate genre term for Deuteronomy as a whole, and this short section, which recounts the giving of the decalogue or ten commandments, presents what Olson sees to be a nutshell summary of the entire book.

The next section begins in 6.1 with 'This is the commandment, statutes and ordinances'. The singular noun 'commandment' refers, so Olson maintains, to none other than the great commandment of the *Shema*, which is presented right away in 6.4-5. This command, which only states in a positive way what the first commandment of the decalogue expresses negatively, is seen to be elaborated in the remainder of this longest section of the book. First there is commentary on the great commandment itself extending through ch. 11, argues Olson, and then comes the lengthy subsection of chs. 12–28, which begins by reiterating the second part of the earlier superscription, 'These are the statutes and the ordinances' (12.1). These detailed laws which, as others have recognized,[29] expand upon the commands of the decalogue, are ultimately to be seen as expansions of the single great commandment.[30]

Chapters 29–32 form the next section and are introduced with, 'These are the words of the covenant' (29.1) – not the one made with

---

integral relationship to the book's entire structure and theological movement (pp. 21-22) indicate nothing less than seeing the death of Moses as *the* leading theme.

[28] Olson, *Deuteronomy and the Death of Moses*, pp. 14-15. Olson points to other scholars who have noted the editorial structuring role of the superscriptions, as early as P. Kleinert, *Das Deuteronomium und der Deuteronomiker* (Leipzig: J.C. Hinrich, 1872), p. 167, but Olson breaks fresh ground in finding in these headings the key for grasping the overall literary shape of the book and the interrelationship of its parts. Here and in the following paragraphs I draw from Olson's own summary of Deuteronomy's structure, as presented on pp. 14-17.

[29] See esp. S. Kaufman, 'The Structure of the Deuteronomic Law', *Maarav*, 1.2 (1979, pp. 105-158, whose proposal for seeing the laws of Deut. 12–28 in terms of a series of legal expansions of the ten commandments in the same order of the decalogue has been widely accepted in recent scholarship.

[30] Olson, *Deuteronomy and the Death of Moses*, pp. 49-51, points to the long tradition of recognizing the inclusive role of the great commandment. He cites rabbinic comment as well as the words of Jesus (Mark 12.28-31).

Israel at Horeb, the verse quickly qualifies, but rather the present one 'in the land of Moab'. These chapters feature three new measures, Olson argues, that are meant to provide for Israel's future covenant life: (1) a liturgy of covenant renewal (chs. 29–30; cf. 31.10-13), (2) a transfer of leadership from Moses to Joshua along with the writing down of *torah* (ch. 31), and (3) the giving of the Song of Moses as a continuing witness (ch. 32).

The final superscription, 'This is the blessing', stands before the book's last two chapters. They present the last words of benediction that Moses pronounces over the children of Israel (ch. 33) and then the ensuing account of Moses' death, which includes a kind of eulogy of last words pronounced over Moses (ch. 34).

So the sections of Deuteronomy can thus be summarized:[31]

Chapters 1–4 'These are the words' (1.1)	Past Story
Chapter 5 'This is the torah' (4.44)	Torah in a Nutshell
Chapters 6–28 'This is the commandment, statutes and ordinances' (6.1)	Law for the Present
Chapters 29–32 'These are the words of the covenant' (29.1)	New Covenant for the Future
Chapters 33–34 'This is the blessing' (33.1)	Blessing for the Future

The theme of Moses' death, which obviously dominates Deuteronomy's final section, is found by Olson in all the previous sections as well. He finds that it is not only present in each part but also strategically placed in a way that unites all the parts together.[32]

The first section (chs. 1–4), which highlights the story of judgment upon the old generation (1.19–2.25), links this death outside the promised land with Moses' own death (1.37; 3.22-23). Furthermore, an additional reference to Moses' death seems to indicate that it somehow opens the way, pursued throughout the rest of the book, for the new generation to enter into life in the promised land (4.21-22).

---

[31] Olson, *Deuteronomy and the Death of Moses*, p. 16.

[32] Olson, *Deuteronomy and the Death of Moses*, pp. 17-22. Here Olson presents a preview summary of the theme's recurrence in each section. He elaborates this in the subsequent chapters of his study.

As regards the second section (ch. 5) Olson acknowledges that there is no direct mention of Moses' death.[33] However, he argues that the theme indirectly 'creeps again upon the stage' when the people request that Moses go near and listen to God in their stead, so that they will not have to risk being consumed by further exposure to the fire of God (4.24-27). In their words, 'Why should we die? For this great fire will consume us, if we hear the voice of God anymore' (4.25). The shadow of death, suggests Olson, is thus made to fall over the very essence of Moses' call and role as revelatory mediator.

In the following legal section, which elaborates 'the commandment, statutes and ordinances' (chs. 6–28), Olson again finds indirect references to the theme of Moses' death. He points to the golden calf story (9.8–10.11) where Moses recalls his intercession on behalf of the people before God. Moses' 40-day fast, in which he relinquishes the necessities of life, together with his prostration before Yahweh, wherein Olson sees 'a posture resembling death',[34] these suggest for Olson a *kind of* demise, a 'death' in quotation marks.[35] It is a mediatorial death, here again, by which the people of Israel are enabled to live.

Olson finds one more such reference to Moses' death in the law of 18.15-22, which anticipates God's future move 'to raise up a prophet' like Moses (18.15, 18). Not only does this passage point toward the time after Moses is gone, it also recalls once again how that the prophetic role of Moses was established at Horeb in the context of the people's reaction to the threat of death.

> You desired of Yahweh your God in Horeb on the day of the assembly, saying, 'Don't let me hear again the voice of Yahweh my God, neither let me see this great fire any more, so that I will not die' (18.16).

In addition to these references, Olson finds in many of the detailed 'statutes and ordinances' (chs. 12–28) something that 'resonates with the theme of Moses' death'.[36] He shows how that numerous laws, such as the laws of sacrifice, sabbath or of slave and debt release, 'have to do with giving something up, letting go, dying, or acknowledging the limits of human abilities, knowledge, and laws'.[37] These injunctions follow the trajectory of Moses' own fate, thinks Olson, in their underlying assumption that life somehow comes through death.

---

[33] Olson, *Deuteronomy and the Death of Moses*, p. 46.

[34] Olson, *Deuteronomy and the Death of Moses*, p. 19.

[35] Olson, *Deuteronomy and the Death of Moses*, p. 61. Olson here uses quotation marks repeatedly in making his point, 'Moses "dies"'.

[36] Olson, *Deuteronomy and the Death of Moses*, p. 20.

[37] Olson, *Deuteronomy and the Death of Moses*, p. 20.

The Moab covenant section of chs. 29–32 in its own way affirms this idea of life coming through death, argues Olson. This happens specifically in the way that the covenant mechanisms of the renewal liturgy of chs. 29–30 and the Song of Moses in ch. 32 provide for pre- servation of the community even beyond the anticipated curse of death and exile outside the promised land (29.16–30.7; 32.26-43). Olson sees these two communal provisions for 'life through death' framing a cen- tral subsection, chapter 31, which explicitly and repeatedly emphasizes the urgency of the occasion of Moses' impending death (31.2, 14, 16, 29). Here the transfer of Moses' leadership to Joshua and Moses' words to writing provide vital means for life to go on.

As Olson sees it, all the foregoing 'allusions to Moses' death finally flow into' the final section of Deuteronomy (chs. 33–34) and its ac- count of the actual death of Moses. Moses pronounces his last words of blessing upon the individual tribes, which is itself an act of final passage (ch. 33), just before the closing scene. The act of passing on final words to the children characterizes not only this concluding section but also the book as a whole. And it is an act that from the beginning has been occasioned and overshadowed, as Olson would emphasize, by the death of Moses.

There is no doubt that Olson has succeeded in demonstrating a greater place in Deuteronomy for the theme of the death of Moses than has heretofore been recognized. To see it as the leading or go- verning theme, however, is not justified according to my way of read- ing the book. Olson's view is most vulnerable in his discussion of ch. 5. Granting Olson's point that this is the book's most defining section, nothing less than a virtual blueprint summary of the whole book in line with its introductory superscription, 'This is the torah' (4.44), it should be quite telling that this key section offers no explicit reference to Moses' death. Olson finds no more than an *indirect* reference by way of the people's request for Moses to stand between them and the death that they fear before the fire of God. But is it not possible and even more likely that this reference to *encounter with divine fire* is not just an indirect allusion to the book's main theme but rather the main theme itself? It is surely the commanding theme of ch. 5, insofar as references to the fire of God and the people's response of fear frame the presenta- tion of the decalogue (5.4-5, 22-29) and come to an unparalleled cli- max of divine longing in v. 29, 'Oh that they had such a heart as this always to fear me and keep all my commandments'. If fear as well as obedience makes up the proper response to *torah,* then this living fire as well as the written commandments may be what this section has in view in announcing, 'This is the *torah*'.[38]

This crucial chapter replays Israel's fearful encounter with the fire of God at Horeb, and identifies it with what *torah* is all about and what God longs for 'always'. Even as it constitutes the sustained yearning of God, it can be seen as the sustained emphasis of Moses throughout the entire book in each of its major sections. Such emphasis belies the perpetual tendency of God's people to lose sight of the holy fire (cf. 5.24-27). I do not think that this is unrelated to modern scholarship's lack of recognition of the leading thematic role of the Horeb theophany in the book of Deuteronomy, which I now intend briefly to show.

Deuteronomy begins with reference to the revelatory event of Horeb (1.2-3).[39] The narrative immediately announces, 'Yahweh our God spoke to us at Horeb' (1.6). There unfolds from this announcement a story of how God's people then journey from this mountain, not just in a geographical way (cf. 2.3) but more importantly in a theological way. They soon journey away from the presence of Yahweh (1.29-33), who has promised, as Moses points out, 'to go before you' (1.30) even as he 'went in the way before you, as in the fire by night' (1.33). This, then, is a story about how the consuming fire of Horeb is illegitimately left behind, causing an unbelieving generation to be consumed (2.16). But this narrative that thus leads *away from* the Horeb theophany leads a new generation, and the reader of Deuteronomy, once again *back to* it. For the thrust and the heart of ch. 4 is a calling of Israel back to the overwhelming charismatic experience at the mountain of fire.

> Be careful and guard yourselves diligently lest you forget the things your eyes have seen and they depart from your heart, how that you stood before Yahweh your God at Horeb. . . You came near and stood before the mountain, and the mountain burned with fire unto the midst of heaven, with darkness, clouds, and thick smoke. Then Yahweh spoke to you from the midst of the fire. You heard the sound of the words but saw no form, only a voice (4.10-12).

The remainder of ch. 4 counters Israel's present and future tendencies to choose idolatrous forms over the living voice of Yahweh (cf. 4.15-16). This choice poses the burning issue of Deuteronomy: idol forms vs. the formless and form-annihilating fire. As this chapter declares, 'Yahweh your God is *a consuming fire*' (4.24).

---

[38] For an elaboration of this point see my discussion, 'Canon and Charisma in the Book of Deuteronomy', in the previous chapter.

[39] One sees not only the geographical reference in v. 2 but also the theological reference in v. 3, which redefines 'these words of Moses' in the superscription as those 'according to all that Yahweh had given him in commandment to them', pointing to Moses' mediatorial encounter at Horeb between 'Yahweh' and 'them'.

The opening section of Deuteronomy thus moves *from* Horeb and then *back to* Horeb in an effort to show God's people that the way to keep the word is to keep coming from the fire from which the word keeps coming.[40]

If the first section of Deuteronomy intends to *take Israel back* to the Horeb theophany, then the second section (ch. 5), which is entirely devoted, as we have seen, to this revelatory event, aims to *bring the Horeb encounter forward* to God's people. As the introductory words of Moses flatly assert,

> Yahweh our God made a covenant with us in Horeb. Yahweh did not make this covenant with our ancestors, but with us, even all of us who are alive here today. Yahweh spoke with you face to face at the mountain from the midst of the fire (5.2-4).

It is obvious from this key passage, especially in view of its appearance in this most important section of Deuteronomy, that perpetual, living response to the fire of God is of central concern for the whole book. This verse provides for the perpetuation of Horeb's fire just as the recruitment of Moses in 5.31 provides for the extension of the decalogue revelation that we see in the legal section which comes next (chs. 6–28).[41] The people may incline toward having statutes and ordinances without the fire, but Moses clearly strives here to bring the fire forward with the words.[42] This would, then, apply to the rest of his words in the book.

The legal section (chs. 6–28), however, is not without its own direct reference to the theme of the fiery theophany at Horeb. In fact the two most prominent *allusions to the death of Moses* in Olson's reading of this section appear as *explicit and direct references to the theophanic encounter* on the holy mountain. The second of these references (18.16-18) replays the scene at Horeb (cf. 5.24-31) when the people react in fear before the fire of God and ask for Moses to mediate. This time the scene stresses divine provision for continuing mediation even after Moses with Yahweh's promise 'to raise up a prophet' like Moses in the future (18.18). Thus the mediation of holy words *and holy fire*, it would

---

[40] This reading of Deut. 1–4 is more fully elaborated in my discussion, 'Canon and Charisma in the Book of Deuteronomy', in the previous chapter.

[41] The relation of ch. 5 to chs. 12–28 is made explicit in the way that 5.31 recalls how Moses is commissioned to relay the 'statutes and ordinances', which are the very terms we meet in the superscription of 12.1. See Olson, *Deuteronomy and the Death of Moses*, p. 46.

[42] The same point can be seen in 4.7-8, which indicates that Israel is to be distinct from the nations not only in having 'statutes and ordinances so righteous' (v. 8) but also in having 'a God so near as Yahweh our God' (v. 7).

seem, is not to be limited to the time of Moses nor to the book of Deuteronomy.[43]

The legal section's earlier reference to the Horeb encounter involves the golden calf narrative, featuring Moses' 40 days of prostration on the mountain before Yahweh (9.25), the longest narration of a single episode in the entire book (9.8-10.11). Whereas Olson seems to find the significance of this elaborate narrative in the way it subtly points forward to Moses' actual death, I find it much more likely that this life-and-death encounter on Horeb is *the main event,* to which Moses' final appointment with God on Nebo (ch. 34) becomes a mere echo (note 34.10). For where did Israel first and most deeply discover the truth that life comes through death – a truth that permeates the specific laws of chs. 12–28, as Olson has so convincingly shown?[44] Was it through the natural death of Moses and the natural succession of one generation giving way to the next, such as Moses' death depicts? I suppose that if this is the only kind of death that one takes seriously, then this is where the given truth must be sought. But another possibility emerges for those who would take seriously a theophanic encounter that could 'scare you to death' and yet amazingly leave you alive (cf. 5.26 and 9.19).[45] This is the kind of theophanic experience into which this testimony of Moses' intercession leads God's people even more deeply than before.

The next section, as we have seen, explicitly differentiates the past covenant encounter at Horeb with the present one in Moab (29.1 introducing chs. 29–32). Yet a significant connection to the Horeb theophany occurs in what Olson recognizes as the central portion of this section. Olson, however, gives virtually no attention to it.[46] Surely it should be regarded as a major moment in the book when God, whose past words have until this point only been relayed and quoted, now, for the first time in the book, speaks for himself (31.14). God calls Moses to come with Joshua into the 'tent of meeting', where he 'appears' in 'a pillar of cloud' and speaks to Moses and then Joshua (31.14-23). This reference to the Horeb-like manifestation of God's own presence may not signify much to those who, here again, do not take such experiences very seriously, but for those who do, there is every reason to see in this theophanic account at this point in Deuteronomy a major dimension of God's provision for Israel's future covenant life. Alongside the provisions which Olson notices – a covenant

---

[43] Note how Jeremiah, who is often viewed as the Hebrew canon's prime example of a 'prophet like Moses', sees his prophetic word as divine fire (Jer. 20.9; 23.29).

[44] Olson, *Deuteronomy and the Death of Moses,* pp. 62-125.

[45] This kind of death experience just might be decisive enough to put 'natural death' in quotation marks.

[46] Olson, *Deuteronomy and the Death of Moses,* pp. 134-35.

liturgy (chs. 29–30), a human successor and written canon (ch. 31), and a covenant song (ch. 32) – there is surely something to be said for the manifestation of divine presence itself, which is here both demonstrated presently at the 'tent of meeting' and given future significance in the divine threats ('I will hide my face' 31.17, 18) and promises ('I will be with you', 31.23) which are spoken within the 'tent of meeting'. And surely a 'tent of meeting' in and of itself presupposes a major place for continuing revelatory encounter, at least for those who have ears to hear and eyes to see.[47]

The final section of Deuteronomy (chs. 33–34), though it has no extended reference to the Horeb theophany as we have found in all the other sections, does have two brief references that could not be more strategically located. One comes at the very beginning, the other at the very end. Moses' blessing on the tribes begins, 'Yahweh came from Sinai' (33.2). Just like the message of Deuteronomy as a whole (cf. 1.6), which altogether represents Moses' last words to Israel, these last words of benediction are seen to flow ultimately from Yahweh's revelation at Horeb. In the final paragraph of the book, concluding attention is brought to how Yahweh had known Moses 'face to face' (34.10). The narrator's accompanying comment that 'there had not arisen a prophet like Moses (in this regard) since', combines with Deuteronomy's earlier reference that God has promised 'to raise up a prophet like Moses' (18.18), and together these words prompt God's people forward toward the future prospect of 'face to face' encounter with the consuming fire.[48]

Conclusion

In the light of the foregoing interpretation, I would now offer some summary reflections and mention a few larger implications.

Approaching Deuteronomy from the inside of my Pentecostal confession has led me to the conclusion that the fiery theophany of Horeb is the central theme of the book. There are those who would criticize me for having read my own confessional experience into Deuteronomy. Yet would not the pronounced lack of attention to the Horeb theophany in Deuteronomy scholarship render the latter at least equal-

---

[47] It may be indicative of the negative national prospects which are emphasized in this chapter (31.16-18, 21, 29) that this people, who had earlier opted for their own tents rather than the burning mountain (5.30), now find themselves on the outside of the 'tent of meeting' looking on. Modern scholars, such as Olson, who scarcely acknowledge the theophanic significance of this meeting, seem to be looking on at an even greater distance. The 'classroom' can be a long way from the 'tent meeting'.

[48] On this eschatological effect at the book's conclusion see the perceptive comments of P.D. Miller, '"Moses My Servant": The Deuteronomic Portrait of Moses', *Int* 41 (1987), pp. 245-55 (p. 249).

ly open to the criticism of having read the book through its own experience or lack thereof. It all becomes a matter of what experiences and
indeed what criticism we are willing to take seriously.

My reading has pointed up a number of literary relationships and
connections, which can be judged on their own merits. Yet I am
forthrightly acknowledging that the coherence that I have discerned
and uplifted in this reading involves more than literary observations. It
has much to do with pursuing how things appear from the inside of
such a confession as opens Deuteronomy, 'Our God spoke to us'.
From the outside, such a confession is easily regarded as some primitive
notion belonging to a pre-critical world-view where such notions are
commonplace, and if commonplace, then not expected to be particularly noteworthy, much less central, in such literature as we have before us. However, from the inside, such a confession would easily
point to the singular claim which evokes the given worldview, which
divides time, and which commands and centers the deepest commit-
ments of the heart. It would thus not appear surprising to find this
claim occupying the thematic center of this writing, for it would point
to the heart of the hermeneutic which is generating the writing. And if
the heart of the hermeneutic, then not a mere buttress for some more
fundamental claim or a means to reinforce a standpoint already occupied. We are dealing rather with the point where standing and understanding have their beginning, because this is where they have been
completely lost and found anew. We are dealing, in other words, with
the point where confession becomes profoundly critical.

The voice that comes to claim central position on the inside of this
confession comes from the outside, from the wilderness, from 'other-
ness' itself. It comes from the margin and then marginalizes all who
claim it, who are claimed by it. It will ever put marginal voices in a
totally and radically new light – the voices of widows, orphans and
aliens. Without the experience of the voice that comes from the midst
of the fire, as it did on the day of Pentecost and as it did at Azusa
Street, we may never become critical enough to affirm as we should
the other voices from the margins.

4

The Prophetic Calling: An Old Testament Profile and Its Relevance for Today*

The place of the prophet in the body of Christ is a burning issue today in many quarters of the Pentecostal and Charismatic movements. This is the obvious context in which, and in response to which, I have taken up this topic. It surely stands behind the specific occasion that instigated the writing of this article, namely the gracious invitation to deliver the keynote address to the 2003 EPTA Conference, which convened under the theme, 'Prophecy Then and Now.'[1]

As an Old Testament professor, I assumed that my contribution to this theme would be expected to fall on the 'Prophecy *Then*' side of things. Accordingly, I sought to lay out a picture of the Old Testament prophetic calling[2] – one that is concerned not so much with the cutting edge of scholarship as with the center and heart of the OT prophets as I have come to see them over the course of twenty years of teaching. Yet I want to be 'up front' that what I sketch here about 'prophecy then' undoubtedly reflects my conceptions, convictions, and concerns about 'prophecy now'. In one sense, this could not be otherwise, for, as we all know, any view of 'then' is inevitably colored by the 'now' of the viewer. Yet in a more deliberate sense, as now indicated in my chapter title above, I have deliberately taken up the study of the OT prophets from the vantage point of being concerned about how 'prophecy now' could be and should be impinged upon by 'prophecy then'. I suppose my Pentecostal faith especially conditions

* First published in *Journal of the European Theological Association* 24 (2004), pp. 16-29.

[1] The original draft of this study was presented as the keynote address of the EPTA Conference at the International Apostolic Bible College in Kolding, Denmark on April 24, 2003 under the title, 'A Profile of the Prophetic Calling in Old Testament Perspective.' A later version of the study was presented at the 33rd Annual Meeting of the Society for Pentecostal Studies at Marquette University in Milwaukee, WI, USA on March 12, 2004 under the title, 'The Prophetic Vocation: An Old Testament Profile and Contemporary Points of Relevance.'

[2] For a recent and similar effort that I found after completing the present study – one with which my own effort has many points of resonance – see John Goldingay, 'Old Testament Prophecy Today,' *Spirit & Church* 3.1 (May 2001), pp. 27-46.

me to look for how this 'now' relates to that 'then', for how 'this' relates to 'that' goes as deep for me, and for most Pentecostals I suspect,
as Peter's words in Acts 2, *'This is that* which was spoken by the
prophet Joel, "In the last days," God says, "I will pour out my Spirit
upon all flesh, and your sons and daughters will prophesy"' (Acts 2.16-
17; cf. Joel 2.28).

I also want to admit up front that my sense of 'prophecy now' is
very much a North American Pentecostal 'now'. How relevant this
can be for contemporary contexts other than my own I must leave to
others to help me see.

My starting point, quite naturally, is the Hebrew word for prophet,
נביא (*navî*). As the noun is rooted in the verb 'to call', scholars have
debated whether the active or passive sense of the verb was determinative in the coining of the term, that is, whether *navi* originally pointed
to 'one who calls' (i.e. 'speaks forth a message') or to 'one who has
been called' (i.e. 'summoned or commissioned'). The primary verbal
activity of prophets in the OT could support the former possibility –
indeed prophets were speakers[3] – yet the prominence of the so-called
'call narrative' in the OT presentation of the prophets (Isa. 6; Jer. 1;
Ezek. 1–3) would just as strongly support the latter. I am thus inclined
to suggest seeing a 'both/and' rather than an 'either/or': the OT *navi*
was indeed 'one who had been called out by God to call out'.

This simple definition, drawn from the Hebrew term for prophet,
directly points to what I find to be the most prominent facet of the
profile of the OT prophet. *The prophet above all is a messenger.* This
identity is in play every time one hears what is surely the most common phrase in OT prophetic literature, 'Thus says the LORD', for, as
OT form critics have long noted, the phrase, 'Thus says X', is none
other than the 'messenger formula' used widely in ancient Near Eastern statecraft and diplomacy when a message was introduced by a royal
messenger.[4] Moreover, the book of Isaiah, which begins the Latter
Prophets, presents the call of Isaiah in a way (no doubt paradigmatic
for all the prophets) that clearly depicts the commissioning of a court
messenger. The scene in Isaiah 6 is plainly one of a royal court complete with regal entourage and sovereign deliberations about the sending of a messenger: 'Whom shall I send? And who will go for us?'
Then after the answer, 'Here I am; send me', comes the commissioning proper: 'Go and speak to this people' (Isa. 6.8-9). This is a depiction of the divine council on the model of the throne rooms of ancient

---

[3] Note how Ex. 7.1-2, the second occurrence of the term נביא (*navi*) in Scripture,
seems intent to define the word in terms of speaking on behalf of another.

[4] This is attested in many non-biblical as well as biblical texts, e.g. Isa. 36.4, 14; 37.3,
5, 21.

Near Eastern monarchies. And the prophet is clearly cast in the role of the ancient Near Eastern political messenger. This model, prominently and programmatically displayed in Isaiah 6, is widely represented and referenced throughout the rest of the OT prophets as well – e.g. in Jer. 23 (see v. 18); Ezek. 3; Hab. 2; Hag. 1; Mal. 3; 1 Kgs 22 (the Micaiah story).

If the prophet is a messenger, what then constitutes the message? The primary answer, in OT terminology, would be: 'the word of the LORD', that is, the 'דבר (*davar*) of YHWH'. As Jer. 18.18 reveals, *davar* was as quintessentially the subject matter for the prophet as תורה (*torah*) was for the priest and 'counsel' was for the sage. Accordingly, the second most common phrase in OT prophetic literature is, 'the *davar* of YHWH came to so and so'. More exactly the Hebrew phrase uses the verb 'to be' (היה, *hyh*), so it could more precisely be rendered, 'the *davar* of YHWH *was* to so and so' or '*occurred* to so and so'.

Since the expression, 'the *davar* of YHWH occurred to so and so', is so prominent, it is crucial to recognize its import. This is a common phrase that points to an uncommon experience. It is no mere transmission of information, insofar as God's word, his *davar,* is no mere *datum* of information. It is more like a *quantum of transformation,* an event[5] that *happens,* indeed *occurs* (היה, *hyh*) to the prophet. Thus, the term *davar* here entails a range of meaning that goes beyond our term 'word'. A *davar* can be more than a word that is spoken, heard, written, or read. It can be an *event* that is encountered, experienced, or seen.

The book of Hosea provides a particularly vivid demonstration of this point. After the first verse of Hosea announces that 'the *davar* of YHWH *occurred* to Hosea', the rest of this chapter proceeds to describe the life-engulfing experience that this entailed. It is an experience that stretched over a considerable span of time, enough time to marry and have and name three children (Hos. 1.2-8). The second verse of the book even draws attention to how God's word *through* the prophet begins with these events that God prescribes *to* the prophet. Specifically, Hos. 1.2 reads, 'when YHWH began to speak *through* Hosea, YHWH said *to* Hosea'. Obviously, the occurrence of the *davar* of YHWH to Hosea is much more than a momentary relay of communication. It is a lengthy, lived-out ordeal.

---

[5] The term *davar* has a range of meaning that is not fully represented by its usual English translation, 'word'. See W.H. Schmidt, 'The Word of God', in G.J. Botterweck and H. Ringgren, eds., *Theological Dictionary of the Old Testament,* vol. III. (trans. J.T. Willis, G.W. Bromiley and D.E. Green; Grand Rapids, MI: Eerdmans, 1978), pp. 111-25, esp. p. 113. See also my discussion in 'Canon and Charisma in the Book of Deuteronomy', in Chapter 2 of this volume.

This helps to explain why *davar* in prophetic literature can be presented as something that is seen, as well as heard or spoken. Thus, Amos 1.1 introduces 'the words (plural of *davar*) of Amos ... which he saw (חזה, *khazah*)'.[6] With the verb חזה (*khazah*: 'to see') we come to the related noun חזון (*khazon*: 'vision'), which is another important term alongside *davar* in OT prophetic vocabulary. The prophets were not only messengers of words but also messengers of visions, in other words, visionaries or seers (cf. 1 Sam. 9.9; Hos. 12.10; Isa. 29.10) who bore witness to things they were shown (e.g, Jer. 1; Amos 7–8; Hab. 2).[7]

The vision or *khazon* of the OT prophet, in line with the common use of the term 'vision', can refer to a momentary appearance or visualization of something by supernatural means, like having a dream while being awake.[8] Yet if we limit prophetic vision only to this, we have not said enough about the OT conception of vision. The book of Isaiah uses the term vision (*khazon*) in its first verse as a singular, inclusive term that encompasses all the prophetic words and experiences that constitute the entire book. This suggests that all of the discrete revelations that came to the prophet, in the form of both verbal or visionary experiences, come together to generate, to comprise, and to reflect an overarching perspective, a kind of God-induced view of reality or worldview, along the lines of what Walter Brueggemann has called 'an alternative consciousness'.[9] The visionary element of OT prophecy was, thus, about more than receiving any number of distinct revelations from God. It entailed being radically changed, in the light of such revelation, to see all things differently.

This heavier, more substantial definition of prophetic word (*davar*) and vision (*khazon*) correlates with one additional term that is prominently used to refer to the message of the OT prophet – the term משא (*massa*). Normally translated either 'burden' or 'oracle', the Hebrew term *massa* fuses together both of these conceptions. Thus, *massa* denotes a heaviness that is carried before (and sometimes after) it becomes a message that is delivered. The ordeal of pregnancy, labor, and deli-

---

[6] In similar fashion, Israel's first prophet, Moses, identifies the revelations of YHWH as 'words (again, plural of *davar*) that your eyes have seen' (Deut. 4.9).

[7] Habakkuk 2.1-2 brings prophetic vision together with the activity of a 'watchman', a vision-related role, which is another prominent and oft-emphasized dimension of the OT prophetic calling (see e.g. Jer. 6.17; Ezek. 3; Hos. 9.8), and consequently, it could very well be developed as another facet of the OT prophetic profile.

[8] See e.g. Joel 2.28, where the term 'visions' is paired with the term 'dreams'.

[9] See Brueggemann, *The Prophetic Imagination* (Philadelphia, PA: Fortress Press), ch. 1, esp. p. 13, where the programmatic definition of this term is given: '*a consciousness and perception alternative to the consciousness and perception of the dominant culture around us*' (Brueggemann's italics). A similar view on what the prophets *see* is explicated by Christopher Dube, 'From Ecstasy to *Ecstasis*: A Reflection on Prophetic and Pentecostal Ecstasy in the Light of John the Baptizer', *JPT* 11.1 (2002), pp. 41-52 (esp. pp. 42-43).

very makes a particularly fitting metaphor,[10] and it is one that the prophets themselves can be found appropriating repeatedly. For example, Isa. 21.1-3 introduces a *massa* of the prophet that is explicitly elaborated in terms of the experience of the pangs of a mother in childbirth. In Isa. 42.14 the experience of a mother's travail that punctuates Isaiah's message is ascribed to God himself. Jeremiah who foresees (or fore*hears*) the travail of his people in 4.31, feels the birth pains himself in 6.24.

Thus I maintain that in the full scope of this ordeal of prophetic revelation, one can see God doing more than just communicating his message; God is inculcating his passions. Surely this is the obvious import of the ordeal of the prophet in Hosea 1–3.[11] Accordingly, the prophet represents more than the mouth of God; the prophet mediates the heart of God. The divine words come forth, but in conjunction with the divine passions that are evoked and formed in the prophet through the entire experience of the *davar* of God.[12]

The acknowledgment that the Hebrew prophets were about experiencing and expressing the passions of God brings me to the point of identifying a second major facet of the profile of the OT prophet. *The prophet was a poet or minstrel.*[13] My assertion here points to the fact that poetry was the primary medium of prophetic communication in the OT.[14] This is where the OT prophet departed from the conventions of

---

[10] For discussion of another important metaphor that registers the heaviness of the prophetic experience, see J.J.M. Roberts, 'The Hand of Yahweh,' *VT* 21 (1971), pp. 244-51 and see also the following biblical references: 1 Kgs 18.46; Isa. 8.11; Jer. 15.17; Ezek. 1.3; 3.14, 22; 8.1; 33.22; 37.1; 40.1.

[11] For an exposition that elaborates this very point, see Scott A. Ellington, 'When God Gets Too Close for Comfort: Hosea's Prophetic Ministry of Sharing God's Suffering,' *Spirit & Church* 3.1 (May 2001), pp. 5-26.

[12] Perhaps Jonah is the exception that proves the rule. He carries the word of God (ch. 3), but then he is found to lack the passion of God (ch. 4), so it becomes easier to see why God revokes the word. See my, 'And Also Much Cattle?!: Prophetic Passions and the End of Jonah', Chapter 7 of this volume. No one has discerned and discussed this crucial role of passion in the ancient Hebrew prophets better than Abraham Heschel, *The Prophets* (New York: Harper & Row, 1962). See also Brueggemann, *Prophetic Imagination*, ch. 3.

[13] I choose the term 'minstrel' for its alliterative, mnemonic effect alongside 'messenger' and the other facets I develop hereafter in my prophetic profile. My utilization of 'minstrel' here follows an early usage that denotes a synonym of 'poet', not one that necessarily involves the term's more popular associations with music. Yet the latter associations are not entirely alien to the practice of Old Testament prophecy, as can be seen from such prophetic texts as 2 Kgs 3.15-16; Isa. 5.1-7; Ezek. 33.30-33.

[14] Brueggemann, *Prophetic Imagination,* pp. 44-61, has offered the most informative discussion on this point, and my own discussion here reflects, at a number of points, what I have learned from Brueggemann in this important book and in his other writings on the prophets; see e.g. his *The Creative Word: Canon as a Model for Biblical Education* (Philadelphia, PA: Fortress Press, 1982), pp. 51-54.

the messenger role. The ancient Near Eastern messenger appears typically to have spoken in the precise and pragmatic prose of politics, but
the Hebrew prophet's characteristic idiom was the emotive and highly
symbolic language of poetry, the language of the heart.

The artistic rhetoric and, on occasion, theatrical actions of the OT
prophets moved at a level deeper than rational discourse. It was generated from and directed toward more than merely the goal of instruct-
ing or informing the mind. It was more about the moving, the
provoking, and the transforming of the imagination. Like the parables
of Jesus, the poetics of the Hebrew prophets functioned to challenge
and upend settled fields of perception and frames of reference. The
force of God breaking in and shattering the prophets' own frames of
reference no doubt drove them to find in poetic language their only
available means even to hope to make reference to something so inde-
scribable. Poetic symbolism and figurative language are well suited, if
not humanly necessary, when it comes to giving utterance to a reality
beyond the confines of the presently experienced and explained world.
And the prophets, here again, were extensively and intensely occupied
with envisioning a reality that moved outside the boundaries of conventional perception or what Brueggemann calls the 'royal consciousness',[15] so called because it is a view of the way things are that is
perpetrated, programmed, promoted, protected, and presided over by
those in charge, because it regularly serves the interests of those in
charge.

Against the power of the royal clamp on present perception, the Old
Testament prophets unleash poetry that both rekindles revolutionary
memories of a long-buried past and sparks never-before-conceived
glimpses of a breathtaking future[16] – like when Isaiah or Hosea re-
appropriates the radical memory of the Exodus (Isa. 43; Hos. 11) or
when Joel, Micah or Ezekiel catches a fresh vision of God's international aims for Zion (Joel 2; Mic. 4; Ezek. 47). In all of this the prophets expose and challenge the underlying presumption that the royal
'now' is the only arrangement of life that is thinkable, that ever was or
that ever could be. Kings are inclined to think 'no news is good news',
because significant change is scarcely welcomed by those on top.
However, the prophets know better. They recall that once upon a
time the world was otherwise, and they come to the stunning and
seizing conviction that it will be otherwise again. The recalling of the
old reality and the heralding of a new world coming can be seen to cut
both ways. They spell judgment for those invested in the status quo

---

[15] Brueggemann, *Prophetic Imagination,* chs. 2–3.
[16] Brueggemann, *Prophetic Imagination,* chs. 3–4.

but hope for those who are already aching for an altered quo.[17] Yet, either way there is real news, and it is ultimately *good* news, because it is *God's* news, indeed late-breaking news of the truly *final* edition. This is regime change of the ultimate kind.

So, while the poetry of the prophets is markedly distinct from political discourse, it nonetheless has the capacity to produce powerful political effects.[18] Poets often do, which is why totalitarian regimes so soon see the need to get rid of them,[19] especially when the poetry is not confined to some quaint and sequestered literary circle or fine arts guild but rather is set loose in the public square, as is characteristically the case for the OT prophets.

Yet the prophets' poetry, true to the very nature of poetry, typically does not pursue a pragmatic strategy that takes on power in direct ways. Instead it is subtle, prodding, puzzling, and probing. What, after all, can mere words do? Not much, it seems, at least in the immediate, in the face of 'real' political power. Yet, on the other hand, poetic images, rhetorical flourishes, and symbolic actions can be hard for conventional forces to combat. They can slip beneath the radar of public resistance and sow seeds of alternative thinking deep in the psyche of a person or a people. They might take a long time to germinate, longer even than a prophet's life, but poetic visions spoken with conviction have been known to outlive and finally overtake many a regime.

Still, we should make no mistake about it. In the context of public power the prophet as minstrel occupies a position of weakness. With poetic craft as their primary tool, the prophets at best seem to be at the mercy of the facileness and fickleness of public opinion that is usually disinclined to take them seriously. The prophet Ezekiel explicitly testifies to how he was made aware of this very situation by God himself:

> As for you, son of man, your people ... come to you as people come, and they sit before you as my people, and they hear what you say ... but, lo, you are to them like one who sings love songs with a beautiful voice and plays well on an instrument, for they hear what you say, but they will not do it (Ezek. 33.30-32, RSV).

[17] Brueggemann, *Prophetic Imagination,* chs. 3–4. Brueggemann's terms for these two dimensions are 'prophetic criticizing' (ch. 3) and 'prophetic energizing' (ch. 4), respectively.

[18] Thus, the *davar* of YHWH can be seen constituting an 'event' both as it comes to and is experienced by the prophet, as discussed earlier, and also as it goes forth from and evokes effects beyond the prophet. Classic examples of prophetic texts that voice this perception include Isa. 55.10-11; Jer. 1.9-10; 23.29. See the suggestive analysis of Gerald T. Sheppard, 'Prophecy: From Ancient Israel to Pentecostals at the End of the Modern Age,' *Spirit & Church* 3.1 (May 2001), pp. 47-70, who focuses on prophecy in terms of its power to effect communal survival and societal change, from its ancient Israelite to its modern Pentecostal expressions.

[19] Brueggemann, Prophetic Imagination, p. 45.

This striking testimony of the prophet as minstrel can help us see the point that the poetic medium, by its very nature, possesses an elusiveness that easily results in its meaning, logic, and practical applicability being lost on the listener and at times even on the prophet's own consciousness. While poetry does a good job of offering a glimpse, a hint, a clue, a lure, enough to provoke a question, it is usually not enough to produce the full grasp of an answer. This keeps prophets speaking in a language not altogether known – indeed *an unknown tongue* that can render the prophet an alien even in the prophet's own culture.[20] As Isaiah was told,

> Go and say to this people,
> 'Hear and hear, but do not understand;
>   see and see, but do not perceive.'
> Make the heart of this people fat,
>   and their ears heavy,
>   and shut their eyes;
> lest they see with their eyes,
>   and hear with their ears,
> and understand with their hearts,
>   and turn and be healed (Isa. 6.9-10, RSV).

This last point brings me to a third facet of my OT prophetic profile. *The prophet is a madman.*[21] One prophetic text states this quite flatly. In Hos. 9.7 we find the assertion, 'the prophet is a fool; the man of the spirit (רוח, *ruach*) is mad (מְשֻׁגָּע, *meshuga*, from the verb שָׁגַע, *shaga*: 'to be mad')'. In this text Hosea seems to be representing not his own view but rather the very negative consensus view of the prophets held by the Israelite public during his day and time. Yet a survey of OT prophetic literature reveals that this association between the prophets and madness runs throughout the history of OT prophecy.[22] For ex-

---

[20] This theme of the prophet's alienness is tied, quite naturally, to one of the most prominent focal points of OT prophecy: to announce the coming Exile of the Hebrew people. The marginalizing and rejecting of this message and the prophetic messengers who carried it, meant that these prophets entered the experience of exile beforehand. They were forerunners of the exiled, insofar as they suffered an alienation from their own people that prefigured the alienation their people would meet at the hands of the Assyrians and Babylonians. As I tell my students, the prophets were the first to enter the judgment they prophesied.

[21] I use the male reference 'mad*man*' here, being conscious of its shortcomings in relation to gender inclusiveness – a problem that attends the use of the term 'prophet' as well, insofar as there are widely distributed (even if numerically few) references in the OT to women who are called 'prophetess' (*naviah*): Ex. 15.20; Judg. 4.4; 2 Kgs 22.14; Neh. 6.14. Thus, I would acknowledge the female inclusiveness of my entire profile, despite the shortcomings of my terms.

[22] See Heschel's extended and discerning discussion on this point in *Prophets*, vol. II, pp. 171-89. He even goes so far as to note one etymological theory that proposes a root connection between the term נביא (*navi*) and madness (p. 175).

ample, when Jeremiah writes a letter from Jerusalem to the exiles in Babylon, the Jewish officials there write back with directives to the Jerusalem priest to arrest 'every madman (*meshuga*) who prophesies (Jer. 29.26). When Elisha sends one of the sons of the prophets to anoint Jehu to be king of Israel, Jehu's military colleagues refer to this prophetic figure pejoratively and dismissively as a 'madman' (*meshuga*) in what appears to be, here again, a popular class slur of the time (2 Kgs 9.11). Similarly there is a popular saying that arises about King Saul and his association with the prophets that would not appear to be unrelated to his mental instability, which crops up more than once in the Samuel narratives.[23] It takes the form of the sarcastic question, 'Is Saul also among the prophets?' (1 Sam. 10.11, 12; 19.23).

In these Samuel texts as well as the text of Hos. 9.7 the presence of *ruach*, the Spirit from Yahweh, plays a prominent role in the associations with madness. Perhaps it is easy to see why, since *ruach* is wind, the untamed and untamable energy and dynamic controlled only by God – indeed, 'the wind blows where it wills' (Jn 3.8). It is a force that can come upon persons, seize them, and cause them to get beside themselves in prophetic ecstasy, like we see in the case of Saul and his men who come upon a company of prophets in 1 Sam. 19.20-24. Such turbulence of spirit can seem rather wild, unnatural, abnormal, and even crazy to civilized society – something to be kept out of bounds.

There is even a tradition of modern OT scholarship, led by Scandinavian scholar, Sigmund Mowinckel, that has tried to see ecstatic prophecy or *ruach* prophecy as something to be marginalized in the OT as an early, primitive, foreign-based phase of prophecy (a 'prophecy of the spirit') that was displaced by the distinctly Israelite tradition of 'prophecy of the word'.[24] Yet this evolutionary denigration of spirit as giving way to word seems to reflect more of what is to be found in modern interpretation than in the biblical text, for there are references widely distributed throughout the OT prophets of all time periods that, when not arbitrarily dismissed as editorial glosses or otherwise explained away, show that the Hebrew prophets were not at all averse to association with the untamed *ruach* of YHWH (e.g. Mic. 3.9 [cf. 1.8-9]; Isa. 32.15) as modern scholars like Mowinckel appear to be.[25]

---

[23] See e.g. 1 Sam 16.14-23; 18.10; 19.9. Note particularly how Saul's prophesying and madness come together in 1 Sam. 18.10.

[24] Mowinckel, 'The Spirit' and the 'Word' in the Pre-exilic Reforming Prophets,' *JBL* 53 (1934), pp. 199-227.

[25] Micah, in an effort to contrast himself with popular prophets who please the people with a message of false peace (Mic. 3.5), says, 'But truly I am full of power by the Spirit (*ruach*) of the LORD, and of justice and might to declare to Jacob his transgression and to Israel his sin' (Mic. 3.9). Micah shows already in an earlier verse how intensely he is affected by this experience of God's revelation, when he says, 'I will wail and howl. I will go stripped and naked; I will make a wailing like the jackals and a mourning like the

Clearly the OT prophets were prophets of Spirit as well as word, and the argument for a distinction between a rational type of prophecy (associated with word) and a more non-rational or irrational type (associated with spirit) evidences a distorting, artificial imposition of modern biases, categories, and methods on the evidence.

Jeremiah, granted, does not use the term *ruach*, but he still can testify to his encounter with YHWH's word in terms of an experience of raw force, in line with our earlier consideration of דבר (*davar*): 'like a burning fire shut up in my bones (that) I could not hold back' (Jer. 20.9; cf. also 23.29). Not only is Jeremiah thought by others to exhibit an extreme and altered state of mind (Jer. 20.10; 29.26), he forthrightly confesses to it himself, saying in 23.9, 'My mind within me is shattered; all my bones shake. I am like a drunken man, like a man overcome by wine, because of YHWH, and because of his holy words'. As we Pentecostals well know, this is not the last time that an experience of prophetic revelation would provoke a comparison with drunkenness (cf. Acts 2.13-15).

This last quote from Jeremiah helps to establish the point that the prophets at times experienced a kind of madness that was not merely ascribed from without by others but also experienced from within by encounter with God's word (*davar*) and Spirit (*ruach*). The prophets were not mad or drunk as some would suppose, rather they were staggered by the radical effects of being lifted up, as I like to put it, into the sanity of God – a sanity that all of a sudden made them realize how crazy the 'normal' world had actually become, like Isaiah when he cried, 'Woe is me, for I am undone! I am a man of unclean lips, and I dwell in the midst of a people of unclean lips; for my eyes have seen the King, the LORD of hosts' (6.5; cf. also Hab. 3.16).

This is a jolting reversal where normal is revealed to be woefully abnormal and where sane now appears crazy. The reversal is so stark that even to begin to represent it will inevitably mean to appear crazy in the eyes of most people (indeed seeing, they will 'not see' – Isa. 6.9). Yet even more, the reversal can at times be so overwhelming and arresting to the prophets that they know themselves to be going, in some

---

ostriches, for her wounds are incurable' (Mic. 1.8-9). We see Isaiah speaking hopefully in the first half of the book of a time when 'the Spirit is poured upon us from on high' (Isa. 32.15), and in the last part of the book we hear his words, 'the Spirit of the Lord God is upon me, because the LORD has anointed me to preach good tidings to the poor' (Isa. 61.1). Then, in addition to the classic references of Zechariah, 'by my Spirit says the LORD of hosts' (Zech. 4.6), and Joel, 'I will pour out my Spirit upon all flesh' (Joel 2.28), there are Ezekiel's many references to being encountered by God's *ruach*. It would not appear incidental that Ezekiel, whose association with God's Spirit is more prominent than that of any other OT prophet, is also the prophet most known for erratic and bizarre behaviors.

sense, out of their own minds, carried away by the zeal of the LORD. Indeed, YHWH's zeal (קָנָא, *qana*) is another term that comes to be associated with this theme of prophetic madness. Zeal, even the zeal of the LORD, is an extreme and volatile passion that is not without its potential dangers, as the stories of Elijah's suicidal self-inflation (1 Kgs 19.9-18) and later Jehu's bloodthirsty zealotry (2 Kgs 9–10) help to show. Yet the zeal of the Lord, fully experienced, is a passion that sets the prophet not only over *against* people but ultimately *for* people, for this and nothing less than this is the end of God's passions. Short of this, prophetic zeal can become either suicide or terrorism, but carried to its proper and divine end, the zeal of the LORD consumes the prophet (cf. Jn 2.16-22) and such madness is fulfilled in martyrdom.

This brings me to a final (at least for this paper) facet of the profile of the OT prophet (and what could be more final?): *the prophet is a martyr*. Although it is not a Hebrew word, *martyr* seems to me a particularly apt term for drawing together and identifying the summarizing trajectory and convergence of the other facets of the OT prophetic vocation as previously delineated. Given the shattering weight of the prophetic message, the passion-provoking poetic form it took, and the 'alien' mentality it effected in its bearers, prophets characteristically lost their lives. So it is quite fitting to connect the OT prophets to this term drawn from the Greek, for martyrdom can be seen as the bottom line of their job description (cf. 1 Kgs 19.10; Neh. 9.26), as several New Testament summations on the Old Testament prophets would bear out (Mt. 5.12; 23.29-37; Lk. 11.47-49; 13.33-34; Acts 7.52). Moreover, true to the more juridical New Testament sense of μάρτυς (*mártus*), they were indeed witnesses unto death; they died because of their witness (μαρτυρία, *marturia*) for God. Yet I would want to stress that even more fundamentally, they died because *they witnessed God*. One is reminded of the persistent Old Testament conviction that to see God meant death (Gen. 32.30; Ex. 33.20; Deut. 4.33; 5.23-26; Judg. 6.22-23; 13.22). And the OT prophets regularly testified to experiences of seeing God that entailed the recognition that their lives were over – 'over' not merely in the sense of being destined for some future persecution and physical execution, but rather 'over' already, in every sense that mattered, in the primal, defining moment when they first saw God. Thus, we read Isaiah's words, 'Woe is me, for I am undone (doomed, wasted)! ... for my eyes have seen the King, the LORD of hosts!' (Isa. 6.5). What Isaiah saw had already sawn him asunder. We can read similar testimonies from other OT prophets (Ezek. 1-4; Mic. 1.3-8; Hab. 3, esp. v. 16). Martyrdom was not merely the culminating climax of the OT prophetic vocation but its initiating crisis. The prophets' readiness to face death in the literal sense finds its generative source, I would suggest, in the radical theophanic encounter that had, in the deepest sense, already claimed their lives.

My conclusion, given the confines of the present study, will be brief. I have sketched a profile of the OT prophet in terms of four facets: messenger, minstrel, madman, and martyr. I have done so with a sense that these facets and the composite profile they yield are relevant for informing prophetic vocation in the body of Christ today and within Pentecostal and Charismatic circles in particular. There is much teaching about prophecy circulating in these circles of late and much controversy stirring, and I do not claim to be 'on top' of this entire burgeoning arena of discussion and publication.[26] Neither do I pretend to have it all figured out as far as the full scope and shape of the prophetic vocation for our current context. Yet, from what I have seen, not just from those who are skeptically resisting the push for a more expanded role for the contemporary prophet but also from those who are enthusiastically pushing for it, there is frequent appeal, in either case, to some proposed normative pattern for the prophetic vocation in the contemporary church that appears superficial – superficial, I believe, because it has been cut off, in varying degrees, from its biblical roots and its biblical end.

Of course, this disconnection with prophecy's OT roots, such as I have explicated them above, is usually supported and justified with the doctrine that Old Testament prophecy has now been displaced by 'New Testament prophecy' (so called) as a pattern for the church.[27] Yet in response to this dispensational demarcation and displacement, I am always prompted to ask, what about the book of Revelation? Can we not see in John's Apocalypse a manifestation of prophecy that has more in common with the radically concentrated, spiritually overwhelming, poetically mind-boggling, and culture-confronting form reflected in the Old Testament profile sketched above than in the prophecy of the dispensationally delimited and downsized variety that is now so commonly circumscribed and prescribed under the name 'New Testament prophecy' (which is itself not a NT term, as far as I can tell)?[28]

---

[26] See the recent survey of Charismatic ministries that have been most influential in the practice and teaching on the prophetic by Michael R. Cooper, 'Inspiration and Institutions: A Place for Prophets,' D.Min. thesis, Regent University, 2004.

[27] Perhaps the most influential effort to draw such a sharp line of discontinuity between prophecy in the OT and 'New Testament prophecy' is Wayne Grudem, *The Gift of Prophecy: In the New Testament and Today* (revised ed., Wheaton, IL: Crossway Books, 2000), who limits his definition of NT prophecy to 'speaking merely human words to report something God brings to mind' (p. 51).

[28] Grudem, of course, relegates and restricts any elements associated with OT prophecy that he finds in the book of Revelation (or elsewhere in the NT, for that matter) either to an apostolic age and agency he dogmatically presumes to have ceased (*Gift of Prophecy*, pp. 43-45) or, in the case of the prophets in Rev. 11, to 'special . . . figures' of

My essential point in this chapter is that the biblical roots of the prophetic vocation intrinsically come together with its biblical end – I mean 'biblical end' here both in the sense of prophecy's *theological and experiential consummation* in martyrdom, as traced above, and also in the sense of its *canonical culmination* in the (New Testament!) book of Revelation, where the Holy Spirit, faithful prophetic witness, and martyrdom come together in the most explicit and decisive way of all,[29] all the way to the final summation of Rev. 19.10: 'For the witness (the μαρτυρίαν, *marturian*, the martyrdom) of Jesus, is the Spirit of prophecy'.[30] Has not the time come in our contemporary church for a teaching and mentoring of the prophetic vocation that, like Jesus' teaching of the disciples,[31] envisions, prepares for, and leads God's people unto this end?[32]

the 'end-time', who cannot, therefore (according to Grudem's dispensational presuppositions), be relevant as examples of prophecy for *our* time (p. 364 n. 5). Throughout his study Grudem narrowly delimits 'New Testament prophecy' in order to protect Scripture's sole authority to speak directly for God in our day, and he does this, ironically, by following a dispensational paradigm (indeed, a church tradition) of interpretation that is not explicitly to be found in Scripture. For a more historically disciplined study of prophecy in the NT that acknowledges its many aspects of continuity with prophecy in the OT, particularly in the prophecy represented in the book of Revelation, see David Hill, *New Testament Prophecy* (Atlanta, GA: John Knox Press, 1979), esp. pp. 70-93.

[29] While I am out of my depth when it comes to critical New Testament scholarship, I would appeal here to the recent study of my colleague, Robert Christopher Waddell, *The Spirit of the Book of Revelation* (JPTSup 30; Blandford Forum: Deo Publishing, 2006), whose primary conclusion is that the 'role of the Spirit in the Apocalypse is best defined as the Spirit of Prophecy' (p. 191).

[30] I wish to acknowledge Peter Prothero's extremely helpful elaboration of this verse in his presentation on prophecy in the church that similarly argues for the consummating convergence of prophecy and martyrdom, 'The Testimony of Jesus is the Spirit of Prophecy', delivered at the EPTA Conference in Kolding, Denmark on April 24, 2003. In translating πνεῦμα (*pneuma*) in Rev. 19.10 as a reference to the (Holy) Spirit and not just (human) spirit, I follow Waddell, *Spirit of the Book of Revelation*, pp. 190-91, who gives grounding for this reading in the literary and thematic continuities of the entire Apocalypse.

[31] See esp. Lk. 11.45–12.12.

[32] I wish to express my gratitude to the officers and members of EPTA, whose kind invitation to the 2003 EPTA Conference provided the initial impetus for this study. I also thank them for their engaging and stimulating dialogue there that was responsible for further development of the paper, though not at all responsible for its remaining shortcomings. I am also grateful for those who listened and responded to a later version of the paper at the Society for Pentecostal Studies meeting in March 2004 at Marquette University.

5

The Prophet as Mentor: A Crucial Facet of the Biblical Presentations of Moses, Elijah, and Isaiah*

This study forms a sequel to the study presented in the previous chapter where I sketch a profile of the Old Testament prophet in terms of the following facets: the prophet as (1) messenger, (2) minstrel, (3) madman, and (4) martyr. Here I extend the profile to a fifth facet: the prophet as mentor.[1]

In highlighting the mentoring role in OT prophecy, as I am proposing to do in this paper, I am coming against a long-standing stereotype of the OT prophet as a 'lone ranger' figure, who stands completely outside of and over against the rest of society as an independent, starkly isolated individual. This stereotype was once an attractive, romanticized notion in modern Western biblical criticism, in a time, no doubt, when rugged individualism, the myth of the solitary hero, and, yes, even TV Westerns like the 'Lone Ranger' were more popular.[2] Robert Wilson's book, *Prophecy and Society in Ancient Israel*, published in 1980, deserves no small part of the credit for uprooting this stereotype in the field of OT studies, for he compiled abundant evidence from Hebrew Scripture for the pervasive and variegated relationships and interdepen-

---

* First published in *Journal of Pentecostal Theology* 15.2 (April 2007), pp. 155-73.

[1] I credit Janet Everts Powers for the suggestion of extending my study to include an additional section on 'the prophet as mentor'. My work was already moving in this direction when she proposed the term 'mentor' as an appropriately alliterative parallel to the other facets I had developed. The Greek roots of the term notwithstanding (cf. Mentor, the friend and advisor of Odysseus in Homer's *Odyssey*), 'mentor' is an apt term in contemporary discourse for the role that I am addressing in this chapter. I do not use the term here according to some precise definition but rather according to general popular usage as an umbrella term associated with person-to-person eldering, discipling, training, teaching, modeling and such.

[2] A helpful summary of modern biblical scholarship (up to the 1970s) on the OT prophets that points to this romantic Western view of their stark individuality and originality can be found in Ronald E. Clements, *One Hundred Years of Old Testament Interpretation* (Philadelphia, PA: Westminster Press, 1976), ch. 4.

dencies between Hebrew prophecy and the social structures of ancient Israel.[3]

Yet the stereotype still persists in many quarters in the church today, especially in discussions where Old Testament prophecy is contrasted to New Testament prophecy.[4] Here one sees the dispensational contrast that is overdrawn between the solitary prophet of OT times and a much more corporately interrelated and communally integrated form of prophecy for the church of the NT and for today. This line of thinking is firmly positioned to miss all the ways, such as Wilson has shown, that OT prophecy supports and is supported by ancient Israel's community life and social relationships. The result of this line is a view of the OT prophet that is both misinformed and incapable of informing, as a more accurate picture could, the communal relationships and dimensions of prophecy that are relevant to Christian prophecy even for the church today.

Wilson presented a broad view of the social connectedness of the Hebrew prophets. I propose to add to the discussion by focusing more narrowly on the OT prophet's role in mentoring. And whereas Wilson undertook a sociological analysis of the OT data, I pursue a literary-canonical approach to the prophetic literature. The concern for mentoring is not only present in the literature but prominent to the point of making it arguably one of the constitutive facets of the OT prophetic vocation. Its prominence is manifest by its being featured in the canonical presentations of the three leading prophetic figures in the OT: (1) Moses, the foundational prophetic figure in the canon's foundational section – the Torah, (2) Elijah, the leading prophet of the Former Prophets, and (3) Isaiah, the preeminent prophet of the Latter Prophets. This study will now proceed to look at the mentoring theme as it appears in relation to each of these prophets in turn.

Moses as Mentor
We begin, as the Hebrew canon would naturally prompt us, with the Torah's presentation of Moses. While Moses fills a broad spectrum of

---

[3] Robert R. Wilson, *Prophecy and Society in Ancient Israel* (Philadelphia, PA: Fortress Press, 1980). Wilson's introductory review of scholarship on OT prophecy's relation to ancient Israelite society (pp. 1-19) notes the important antecedents for his own contribution in the form-criticism of H. Gunkel, S. Mowinckel, and others who first began to raise the issue of social context (*Sitz im Leben*) and in the tradition criticism that first began to appreciate the role of distinct social groups that transmitted the prophetic traditions. See also the more recent and concise summary of the matter by Walter Brueggemann, *Theology of the Old Testament: Testimony, Dispute, Advocacy* (Minneapolis, MN: Fortress Press, 1997), pp. 622-625, who sees the tradition criticism of Gerhard von Rad as particularly influential in leading up to Wilson's sociological work.

[4] E.g. Mike Bickle, *Growing in the Prophetic* (Orlando, FL: Creation House), pp. 93-95.

leadership roles in Israel's formational phase,[5] the Torah's most explicit projection of his identity is as the prophet *par excellence*,[6] the exemplar for all Hebrew prophets to come. 'The LORD your God will raise up for you a prophet like me from your midst' (Deut. 18.15), says Moses to Israel as he recalls what God had said to him on Horeb: 'I will raise up for them a prophet like you from among their kindred, and will put my words in his mouth, and he shall speak to them all that I command him' (Deut. 18.18).[7] While this programmatic text registers respect for the notion that the source of the OT prophet's vocation rests ultimately and singularly in divine choice and initiative, beyond the jurisdiction of family inheritance, human appointment, or social instigation, it also at the same time shows respect for the idea of Moses' function as human model, even if this does not yet involve a direct mentoring role.

Something a step closer to the latter can be seen in the other classic Torah text on the succession of prophets after Moses, found in Numbers 11. Here we have Moses' famous wish that takes on the force of solemn prophetic prediction, 'Would that all the LORD's people were prophets and that the LORD would put his Spirit upon them! (Num. 11.29). Again we can note the emphasis on divine agency; it is the LORD who would put *his* Spirit upon them. Yet the narrative leading up to this pronouncement begins with God initiating this line of action in a way that brings his involvement into close association with that of Moses. He tells Moses,

> Gather seventy elders ... and bring them to the tabernacle of meeting, so that they may stand there with you. Then I will come down and talk with you there, and I will take of the spirit that is upon you and will put it upon them. Then they shall bear the burden of the people with you, so that you might not bear it yourself alone (Num. 11.16-17).

This statement seems to go out of its way to emphasize to Moses that these elders would experience this call to prophetic activity *'with you'*, repeating this otherwise superfluous phrase two times. It is not only that their prophesying would originate with the spirit that is taken from that which is upon Moses, but also that their prophesying would continue in close proximity and connection to the attending presence of Moses. Conversely, one might see this latter emphasis offset by the subsequent turn in the story when two of the 70 elders are exonerated

---

[5] See George W. Coats, *Moses: Heroic Man, Man of God* (JSOTSup 57; Sheffield: JSOT Press, 1988), esp. his summary in ch. 12.

[6] For a clear statement on this see Dewey M. Beegle, *Moses, the Servant of Yahweh* (Grand Rapids, MI: Eerdmans, 1972), ch. 4, esp. pp. 76-78.

[7] Translations from Hebrew Scripture in this chapter are my own, unless otherwise noted.

by Moses after they continue prophesying in the camp outside the presence of Moses (Num. 11.25-29). Yet this only serves to set up the story's culminating and forward-looking declaration by Moses that acknowledges that the prophetic vocation is something that is not always to be tied immediately to Moses' physical presence and historical time.

The element in this story in Numbers 11 that is most pertinent to the proposal at hand is that the prophetic role is here presented in direct association with eldering. The prophetic call is directed specifically to a group of 'elders', who in exercising this call will be assisting Moses explicitly in the task of 'bear(ing) the burden of the people' – an expression that, in light of Torah usage elsewhere,[8] quintessentially represents the parental, eldering role. Thus, we see elders being raised up to prophesy as a means of extending their function as elders.

Thus this passage weighs significantly for my thesis in the way it presents (1) a clear OT precedent for prophetic community in terms of a corporate experiencing of the prophetic vocation, (2) the first indications of prophetic mentoring, (3) and a culminating declaration that has the effect of projecting the expectation of such phenomena into the future of God's people.

The implicit connections between the prophetic vocation and mentoring that appear in Numbers 11 are greatly enhanced in the light of the explicit concern, which runs through the entire Moses macronarrative, for the teaching and raising up of the next generation.[9] This can be seen in a passage no less pivotal than the Passover story, recorded in Exodus 12. This crucial event turns on the institution of a solemn observance that is framed as an exercise in parental instruction to the children.

> And you shall observe this word as an ordinance for you and your children forever ... And when your children say to you, 'What do you mean by this service?', you shall say, 'It is the sacrifice of the Passover of the LORD, who passed over the houses of the children of Israel in Egypt when he struck the Egyptians and delivered our households.' So the people bowed the head and worshipped. Then the children of Israel went away and did as the LORD commanded Moses and Aaron' (Ex. 12.24, 26-28).

---

[8] Note how the same verb, 'bear' (נשא, *nasa*), is used earlier in the same passage (Num. 11.12 – Moses says, 'Did I conceive this whole people? Did I birth them that you should say to me, "*Bear* (*nasa*) them in your bosom, as a nursing parent carries the suckling child"?') as definitional for the parental responsibility that is taken to characterize the eldering role. See such a usage also in Deut. 1.31.

[9] For the importance of this theme in the canonical shaping of the entire Torah, see Walter Brueggemann, *The Creative Word: Canon as a Model for Biblical Education* (Philadelphia, PA: Fortress Press, 1982), pp. 14-38; esp. 14-15.

Yet an even more significant display of this theme of parental faith instruction of the children comes in the last book of Moses, Deuteronomy, where it is the dominant concern from start to finish. Following the book of Numbers, which is itself structured to highlight the shift of focus from the old generation that perished in the wilderness to the new generation that would enter the promised land,[10] Deuteronomy is presented as a grand, culminating, divinely inspired effort by Moses to disciple the new generation toward the promised future of God's covenant (1:5; 5:31; 31:19).[11] Moses is an elder who, in the end (as I like to tell my students), becomes a youth minister. He is a father who functions as mentor to the children of Israel. And he does so in a paradigmatic way, for in exercising the mentoring role he also models it and mandates it, explicitly and repeatedly, as the future responsibility and expectation of both this new generation and all subsequent generations of the children of Israel (Deut. 6.7-9; 20-25; 11.19-21; 29.9-15).

While the instructional character of Moses' activity in Deuteronomy is not contested, there would be those who would not see this as especially linked to his prophetic vocation but rather see Moses in Deuteronomy more in the role of teacher or priestly figure responsible for Torah instruction (cf. Deut. 31.9-13).[12] Yet, even though Moses is featured throughout Deuteronomy as the subject of many verbs having to do with teaching,[13] when it comes to the specific nouns used to identify him in the book, it is his role as prophet that is expressly highlighted (Deut. 18.15-18; 34.10).[14] And this goes right to the point: Moses' crowning role in Torah is presented precisely and paradigmatically as that of the prophet as mentor.

This is not to say that mentoring in Deuteronomy is restricted to the prophetic vocation, for Moses clearly expects the priests, elders, and parents of Israel to be actively engaged in this crucial effort. Yet Moses here takes up this task in special relationship to his prophetic call and commission, for the whole message of Moses in Deuteronomy is in-

---

[10] On this and its implications for the entire Pentateuch, see the authoritative work of Dennis T. Olson, *The Death of the Old and the Birth of the New: The Framework of the Book of Numbers and the Pentateuch* (Chico, CA: Scholars Press, 1985).

[11] It is not my purpose here to establish this point, seeing it is already a well-established consensus of Deuteronomy scholarship (see e.g. Dennis T. Olson, *Deuteronomy and the Death of Moses: A Theological Reading* [Minneapolis, MN: Augsburg Fortress, 1994]), who can even insist on seeing the genre of the book as 'catechesis'). My only purpose here is to relate this consensus to the thesis at hand.

[12] See Olson, *Deuteronomy and the Death of Moses,* pp. 11-14, and G. von Rad, *Deuteronomy* (OTL; trans. D. Barton; Philadelphia, PA: Westminster Press, 1966), pp. 23-30.

[13] See Olson, *Deuteronomy and the Death of Moses,* p. 11 and esp. n. 10.

[14] Cf. also Deut. 33.1, where Moses is called, 'man of God', a term that substitutes for 'prophet' elsewhere in the OT (e.g. 1 Kgs 13), and Deut. 34.5, where Moses is called 'servant of the LORD', but in a text that explicitly highlights his status as a prophet.

troduced as something both *pedagogical* ('Moses began to explain this Torah', so 1.5) and *prophetic* ('Moses spoke ... according to all the LORD commanded him', so 1.3). We can see prophecy here in the service of pedagogy, just as we could see prophecy in Numbers 11 in the service of eldering.

Perhaps one last connection between Moses and mentoring should be noted. In Deuteronomy 31 Moses presents Joshua as his successor (vv. 1-3), exhorting Joshua before the people (vv. 7-8), and summoning him, at God's command, to go with him to the 'tent of meeting' where the transaction is completed and sanctioned through an encounter with the presence of God (vv. 14-23). This passage by itself may yield no more than a slight indication of a mentoring relationship. Yet it gains more weight by the way it arcs back to Moses' summoning of the elders in Numbers 11 to the same 'tent of meeting', while also pointing forward to the only other comparable story of leadership succession in Hebrew Scriptures, that of Elijah and Elisha, with its long-noted Moses–Joshua parallels[15] that can be found alongside numerous indications of the mentoring relationship. And to this we now turn.

Elijah as Mentor

Elijah's presentation in Scripture may yield the strongest example in the Old Testament of the prophet as mentor. In addition to his relationship with Elisha, the protégé with whom Elijah's ministry is inseparably linked in Israel's memory, there is the culminating canonical reference that associates Elijah for all time with the divine aim 'to turn the hearts of the elders to their children and the hearts of the children to their elders' (Mal. 4.6; cf. Lk. 1.17).

It is somewhat ironic that Elijah's legacy would arrive at this end in view of how his story begins. He bursts on the scene of Israel's history in 1 Kings 17 without antecedent or genealogical introduction. We simply and abruptly hear, 'Now Elijah the Tishbite, of the inhabitants of Gilead, spoke to Ahab' (17.1). It appears to me to be without precedent in the OT for a character of such magnitude to be introduced without reference to his father.[16] Could it be that Elijah had no

---

[15] See R.P. Carroll, 'The Elijah–Elisha Sagas: Some Remarks on Prophetic Succession', *VT* 19 (1969), pp. 400-15, and A.W. Jenks, *The Elohist and North Israelite Traditions* (SBLMS, 22; Missoula, MT: Scholars Press, 1977), p. 95. Among a number of parallel motifs noted is the particularly striking one that presents the successor miraculously crossing the Jordan and then journeying to Jericho. Reinforcing these parallels would be that the successor's name in each case is formed by a divine appellation joined to the root (ישע, *yasha*), 'to save' (Joshua – 'Yahweh saves' and Elisha – 'God saves'; see my *God Saves: Lessons from the Elisha Stories* (JSOTSup 95; Sheffield: JSOT Press, 1990).

[16] One could perhaps find a later example of this magnitude in Daniel. His lack of genealogical identification in the book of Daniel might serve to register the force of the

father worth referencing? Such a thought is reinforced when we hear Elijah saying to God in his moment of despair, 'Take now my life, O LORD, for I am no better than my fathers' (1 Kgs 19.4). This at least points to a fathering deficit in Israel – one that Elijah is at once divinely called out of his despair to address in the form of anointing leaders for the next generation, including 'Elisha, son of Shaphat of Abelmeholah, to be prophet in your place' (1 Kgs 19.16). So whether the fathering problem in Israel extended to the personal level for Elijah or not, this canonically 'fatherless' one proceeds to become Scripture's primary paragon for restoring fatherhood among God's people.

At their final parting, Elisha calls Elijah 'my father, my father' (2 Kgs 2.12), a title that obviously corresponds to 'the *sons* of the prophets' who appear in the background of this event and in the subsequent ministry of Elisha, clearly pointing to the relationship of a prophetic leader among a small group of disciples (2 Kgs 2.3, 5, 7, 15; 4.1, 38; 5.22; 6.1; 9.1; cf. 13.14). Identified elsewhere as the one 'who poured water on Elijah's hands' (2 Kgs 3.11 – a metaphorical expression that obviously connotes in this context an apprentice relationship), Elisha inherits from Elijah the role of 'father' to the 'sons of the prophets', and the entire narrative of 2 Kings 2 is plainly designed to highlight this.

What makes 2 Kings 2 even more significant in its bearing on my thesis is the central placement this story of prophetic succession is given in the literary structure of 1 and 2 Kings. It forms the midpoint not only of the Elijah and Elisha materials (1 Kgs 17 – 2 Kgs 13) but also of the entire Kings corpus, as the literary analysis of George Savran has convincingly shown.[17] Prophetic mentoring is thus not merely a peripheral motif but a central concern of the books of Kings and the Elijah–Elisha materials in particular. Centered in a long and largely sad saga of royal succession that finally ends in failure, 2 Kings 2 presents a divinely graced instance of prophetic succession that offers the best model and hope for all Israel finally to succeed – indeed, to experience the ultimate success of succession, which is all about transmitting the sacred inheritance to the next generation.

---

break in familial connection and native identity that the Babylonian captivity was deliberately aiming to carry out, as the story of Daniel 1 seems intent to show.

[17] George Savran, '1 and 2 Kings', in *The Literary Guide to the Bible* (R. Alter & F. Kermode, eds., Cambridge, MA: Harvard University Press, 1987), pp. 148-49. Savran sees 2 Kings 2 standing at the midpoint of the Elijah and Elisha stories, which form the Kings corpus' middle section (1 Kgs 17–2 Kgs. 12), which is itself flanked by an inner frame featuring alternating coverage of the Northern and Southern kingdoms (1 Kgs 12–16 and 2 Kgs 13–17) and then the outer frame covering the unified kingdom of Solomon on one side (1 Kgs 1–11) and the single remaining kingdom of Judah on the other (2 Kgs 18–25).

Elisha poses the very issue of the transference of the covenant inheritance in 2 Kings 2 when he asks Elijah, 'Please let a double portion of your spirit be upon me' (v. 9). The 'double portion', of course, refers to the eldest son's share of the patriarchal inheritance, according to the standards of patrimonial lineage as represented in Israel's covenant law (Deut. 21.17). Granted, 'spirit' is not the normal 'stuff' of the patrimonial inheritance. 'Spirit' obviously does not lend itself to being measured and apportioned like property and land. So we have here a figurative application of the 'double portion' that specifically pertains to the endowment of the prophetic vocation – a point that could be reinforced by the Numbers 11 passage, viewed earlier, where God took of 'the spirit that was upon (Moses) and placed it on (the 70 elders)' (v. 17), whereupon they were empowered to prophesy (v. 25).

Conversely, we should perhaps not be so quick to restrict the idea of the transference of 'spirit' exclusively to the prophetic role. In Israel's covenant, a father's bestowal of inheritance upon his son was never simply reduced to what was material. There was an obvious element of spiritual transfer involved in the transaction, where the father laid hands upon the son and uttered solemn, prophetic pronouncements of favor and blessing over the son's future and destiny (Gen. 48.8-22). That these words were seen to bestow a spiritual force that would effect their fulfillment was not doubted (Gen. 27.18-40). So if Elisha in 2 Kings 2 is speaking of the 'double portion' in a fresh, figurative way in reference to a bestowal of spiritual power, it is not entirely beyond the bounds of what had always been expected to be passed on from Israel's elders to those being raised up after them. And here again, the prophet Elijah, like the prophet Moses before him, is modeling a role of spiritual eldering that is not the exclusive domain of the prophet but belongs finally to all the people of God (again, cf. Mal. 4.5-6).

Beyond 2 Kings 2 uplifting the crucial *fact* of mentoring, this chapter also highlights, I would suggest, some key clues to its characterizing *features*. I detect one of these in Elijah's initial reply to Elisha's request for 'a double portion of your spirit' (v.9). Elijah says, 'you have asked a difficult thing' (v. 10). One finds in this response a forthright recognition that the completion of the nexus between mentor and mentoree is something that moves a bit beyond one's capacity to master.[18] It takes us into untamed territory beyond our ken and control – territory that

---

[18] One might have already gotten the impression that Elijah had thoughts along this line from the beginning when he first throws his mantle upon Elisha in 1 Kgs 19.19-21. When Elisha follows after Elijah on this occasion, the older prophet seems awkward and at a loss as to what to do, saying to Elisha, 'Go back again; for what have I done to you?' (v. 20). Elijah here seems anything but a 'master', the preferred title, apparently, that the 'sons of the prophets' come to ascribe to him (2 Kgs 2.3, 5).

is effectively symbolized in this very story by the region beyond the Jordan, which Elijah's miracle of parting the water has just allowed the two prophets to enter before they have this exchange. [19]

The goal of mentoring, then, is 'a difficult thing', not reducible to a formula, program or technique. Indeed, it involves an element of the spirit that cannot be packaged, manipulated or controlled, for, as the Lord knows, 'the wind blows where it wills' (Jn 3.8) – a notion clearly signified in the story's moment of truth when a divinely sent 'whirlwind' at once both separates Elijah and Elisha and binds them together for good, as the mantle of the elder falls down to the successor (vv. 11-13).

This succession is predicated upon only one condition that must be fulfilled – one that, in the light of this story's paradigmatic centrality, may point to the most defining characteristic of the mentoring relationship. After telling Elisha that he has 'asked a difficult thing', Elijah continues, 'nevertheless, if you see me when I am taken from you, it will occur for you, but if not, it will not occur' (2 Kgs 2.10). [20] Thus, the one thing necessary is that Elisha be tenacious in staying with Elijah to the end. This could seem rather random if it were not for the fact that the first half of the story features a repetitive series of instances where Elijah urges Elisha to stay behind while he keeps proceeding to the next phase of his final journey, whereupon Elisha repeatedly vows, 'As the LORD lives and you yourself live, I will not leave you' (vv. 2, 4, 6). Thus, Elisha has already proven his determination to be tenacious in sticking with Elijah to the end, even before it explicitly becomes his mentor's final pre-condition for succession. It is as if Elisha has all along been passing the test that qualifies him to receive Elijah's mantle. The success, indeed, the succession of this mentoring relationship is shown to turn not so much on the *doing* of mentoring[21] but rather on simply *being* a mentor and *being with* a mentor.

[19] See the incisive comment of W. Brueggemann, *1 & 2 Kings* (Macon, GA: Smyth & Helwys, 2000), pp. 294-95: 'The two of them now cross the Jordan, departing the settled land governed by the king into the wilderness, the inscrutable land of mystery. In this territory Elijah began his own dangerous ministry that refused any royal authority (1 Kgs 17:1-6). That the two of them go into the untamed land parallels the entry of Moses into the wilderness where reliance upon the raw power of Yahweh is a necessity' (Exod. 15:22). One thinks here also of John the Baptist and Jesus.

[20] Note how the elusiveness of this transaction is registered by the phrasing, 'It will occur (היה, *hayah*)', rather than something like, 'I will do it'. There is a sense of something being imparted by Elijah that is essentially 'out of his hands'.

[21] One can recall here when Elijah first puts his mantle upon Elisha and then says, 'Go back again; what have I *done* to you?' (1 Kgs 19.19-21). From beginning to end, it would seem, being a mentor does not depend upon knowing how it is done.

Isaiah as Mentor

My final OT case for the prophet as mentor is Isaiah.[22] Raising up the next generation is one of the most crucial and comprehensive themes in the book of Isaiah, but this has not been recognized in previous Isaiah scholarship. In this brief study I attempt only to sketch the evidence, which merits a fuller exposition in the future.

In the first chapter of Isaiah the first issue raised comes in God's words, 'I have reared and raised up children, but they have rebelled against me' (1.2). The thrust of chs. 1–5 is to elaborate this point. Chapter 6 presents Isaiah's dramatic call from God to address the point by delineating the entire course of his subsequent ministry – (1) delivering a message that will be disregarded and refused by those of his own generation, bringing about their devastation down to (2) a remnant, which will then itself be destroyed until only a stump remains, whereupon (3) a 'holy seed' (זרע, *zara*) at last will appear (6.8-13). At the beginning of the book we see God's desire for holy offspring (1.2) and its fulfillment is now foreseen in the end. Indeed, the last word of the book features a reverse match of the first word of the book:

Hear, O heavens,	For as the new heavens
And give ear, O earth,	and the new earth, which I make shall
	remain before me
For the LORD has spoken.	Says the LORD
I have reared and raised up children,	Your seed (*zera*) and your name
But they have rebelled against me (1.2)	shall so remain (66.22)

Within this frame, after elaborating the problem (chs. 1–5) and previewing both the consequences and the course toward the solution (ch. 6), the rest of the book of Isaiah (chs. 7–66) elaborates the course of Isaiah's commission in terms of his prophetic ministry to each of three successive generations (linked to the three parts in 6.8-13 noted above), whereby his ministry successively moves toward the end goal of raising up 'holy seed'. The shifts in Isaiah's ministry from the first generation to the second and then from the second to the third, turn respectively on the two historical narratives that distinguish and domi-

---

[22] The scope of this study limits me to this one final example. By no means do I regard this as the only remaining place in the Old Testament to find evidence for the prophet as mentor. For example, evidence can be gleaned from the Samuel narratives, specifically where Samuel is raised up from childhood as a prophet (1 Sam. 3) at a time when righteous fathering had fallen down (1 Sam. 2.22-36). Supplementing this, we also find in the Samuel narratives further appearances of the 'sons of the prophets' (1 Sam. 10.5-6; 19.20). Then there is the prophecy of Joel that begins with a prophecy to elders about how nothing remains for them to leave to their children (1.2-4) but afterward opens up to a word that reverses this curse with a promise for an outpouring of Spirit with prophetic manifestations upon both elders and their children (2.28-29) and culminates finally in a promise of covenant blessing that will continue 'from generation to generation' (3.20).

nate the internal structure of the book.[23] The first narrative recounts a national crisis under king Ahaz in ch. 7; the second recounts a manifold national crisis under his son, king Hezekiah, in chs. 36–39. In both cases Isaiah plays a pivotal role that culminates in a judgment on these kings and the generations they represent for their failure to attend to God's will, with particular respect to their children – a failure that sets up a call for Isaiah to turn his attention, in each case, to these very children who constitute the generation that will follow. Laying out the parallels between these two historical narratives will begin to clarify this structural and thematic matrix for the book.

The Ahaz narrative and the Hezekiah narrative are both initially set in the same geographical spot: 'at the end of the conduit of the upper pool in the highway of the fuller's field' (7.3; 36.2). In both cases this clearly represents a trusted resource at a time of military threat (Ahaz, from an Aramean-Israelite coalition, 7.1; and Hezekiah, from the empire of Assyria, 36.1-4). Both kings are confronted by a messenger (Ahaz, by Isaiah saying, 'Thus says the LORD', 7.7; and Hezekiah, by an Assyrian officer saying, 'Thus says the great king, the king of Assyria', 36.4) bearing a message in each case about the focus of their belief or trust (7.9; 36.5-7). Alongside both messages stands a reference to children who represent 'a remnant' that signifies the gravity of the crisis (for Ahaz, the presence of Isaiah's child, named 'Remant-shall-return', 7.3; and for Hezekiah, his own word to Isaiah, 'This is a day of distress, rebuke, and scorn; for children have come to the point of birth and there is no strength to deliver ... so lift up a prayer for the remnant that is left', 37.3).

Amid these many parallels there is one stark contrast: Ahaz immediately turns away from the word of the LORD (7.10-13), whereas Hezekiah promptly turns toward the word of the LORD (37.1-2). Significantly, both kings, after being given divine words, are then given prophetic signs with pregnant references about children, but whereas Ahaz's sign (one featuring an expected child to be named 'Immanuel') is unclear, confusing and disquieting (7.14-25),[24] Hezekiah's sign (one

---

[23] The first scholar to draw attention to the pivotal role of the Ahaz and Hezekiah narratives in the structure of the entire book of Isaiah was E.W. Conrad, 'The Royal Narratives and the Structure of the Book of Isaiah', *JSOT* 41 (June 1988), pp. 67-81. See also his *Reading Isaiah* (Minneapolis, MN: Augsburg Fortress Press, 1991), esp. ch. 2, and C.R. Seitz, *Zion's Final Destiny: The Development of the Book of Isaiah; A Reassessment of Isaiah 36-39* (Minneapolis, MN: Augsburg Fortress Press, 1991, who takes up and develops this same view.

[24] For example, the 'curds and honey' that the child will eat in 7.15 seem to constitute the delicacies of prosperity, but in 7.22 'curds and honey' seem to be all that is left in a land where cultivation has been destroyed. Clarity as to the sign's sense of weal or woe is thoroughly lacking, especially since the child and land are not plainly identified, as the enormous diversity of scholarly opinion on the passage can stand as proof. But the confu-

featuring a 'remnant who ... will again take root downward and bear fruit upward') is clear, concise and reassuring (37.30-32).

Yet Hezekiah's crisis does not end here or even with the complete withdrawal of the Assyrian army the next day (37.36-38), for ch. 38 promptly begins,

> In those days Hezekiah was sick unto death ... and Isaiah the prophet ... said to him, 'Thus says the LORD, "Set your house in order, for you shall die"' (38.1).

Again Hezekiah responds by turning to the word of the LORD, which again brings a reprieve – this time a divine promise of fifteen years added 'to your days' (38.2-5). This prompts Hezekiah to write a psalm of praise for God's granting him health (שׁלוֹם, *shalom*, 38.17) that significantly culminates in a vow concerning his children:

> The living, the living one shall praise you,
> As I do this day.
> The father shall make known your trustworthiness (אמת, *emeth*) to the children (38.19).

Yet what happens next brings Hezekiah to the breakpoint of his crisis, which has everything to do with failing his children, about whom he has just made a vow. After Babylonian officials pay a state visit to toast his recovery and he shows to them all the treasures 'in his house and in all his kingdom' (39.1-2), Isaiah confronts him with a word from the LORD that indicts him for showing off the covenant inheritance that 'your fathers have preserved until this day' (39.5-6). This evokes the announcement of divine judgment:

> Behold, the days are coming when everything in your house and what your fathers have preserved until this day shall be carried to Babylon, nothing shall remain, says the LORD. Furthermore, they shall carry away some of your sons who come forth from you and whom you bear – they shall become eunuchs in the house of the king of Babylon (39.6-7).

Hezekiah's response, which comes in the following and final verse of the entire Hezekiah narrative, is stunning and absolutely pivotal in its relation to the governing theme of raising up children, as we have traced it through the hinge points of the book:

---

sion of the sign, I believe, is precisely the point, so that 'hearing they do not hear and seeing they do not see', as Isaiah had already been told would be the case in the previous chapter (6.9). The ambiguous form the word takes is the judgment for refusing it in the first place.

Then Hezekiah said to Isaiah, 'The word of the LORD that you have spoken is good.' For he said, 'There will be health (שָׁלוֹם, *shalom*) and trustworthiness (אֱמֶת, *emeth*) in my days' (39.8).

Whereas he had sought God to change the decree of death upon his own days, there is a telling absence here of any intercession for the sake of welfare and trustworthiness in the days of his children, countering the thrust of his own earlier vow (38.19). In the end Hezekiah, no less than his father Ahaz, abandons the children of the next generation to a rather dim prospect. Yet Isaiah had been told from the beginning that hope did not lie in the remnant itself but in something deeper – deep in the stump after the cutting off of the remnant (6.13).

Having traced out the parallel's between the Ahaz and Hezekiah narratives, we can now proceed to see the subsequent shifts that take place in the prophetic vocation of Isaiah, particularly with respect to the children who are left in the lurch by these two kings and the generations they represented.

Directly after the Ahaz episode, which ends with God's giving the king a sign, God speaks to Isaiah a word, which begins with a sign (8.1-4). While both signs have to do with a child to be born, Ahaz's Immanuel sign was confusing, whereas Isaiah's sign is clear. He is to notarize a name, 'Spoil-speeds-plunder-hastens', then give it to the child that his wife soon bears, and then know that before the child is able to say 'Mommy' or 'Daddy'[25] Assyria will spoil and plunder the Aramean-Israelite coalition, thus eliminating the immediate national threat. However, the sign is then further extended to clarify as well what had remained obscure in Ahaz's sign: Assyria will continue its sweep like a flood 'through Judah' and 'rise up to the neck ... and fill the breadth of your land, O Immanuel' (8.5-8). God here makes privy to Isaiah what Ahaz and his generation could not see in the Immanuel sign, *viz.* that 'God with us' means threat. Indeed 'seeing, they do not see' (6.9). The pivotal issue here comes down to seeing or not seeing the sign, the signification, indeed the significance in the identity of the children.

Isaiah is given eyes to see, and so now he is ready to receive a further divine directive about his own calling:

'Bind up the testimony,
seal the teaching (תּוֹרָה, *torah*) among my disciples'
I will wait on the LORD,

---

[25] In addition to the clear identity of the mother, the child's first utterance of 'Mommy' and 'Daddy' provides a clear time marker that contrasts with the more vague time marker in Ahaz's sign: 'before the child shall know to refuse evil and choose good' (7.16). Indeed most parents can mark the very moment that the former occurs, but the time of knowing right from wrong is ever hard to pin down.

> Who hides his face from the house of Jacob,
> And I will hope in him.
> Here am I and the children,
> whom the LORD has given me –
> signs and wonders in Israel
> from the LORD of hosts (8.16-18).

The 'Here am I' of ch. 6 is now sharpened to a focus on the new generation: 'Here am I and the children, whom the LORD has given me'. Isaiah, like Moses after the failure of the older generation in the wilderness, is called to be a minister to the youth. Isaiah knows the children are signs, he knows they are significant, and he knows his prophetic call is to be their mentor in the light of this revelation.

Thus, chs. 8–35, I would suggest, unfold as the *torah* of Isaiah (8.16), which, like the *torah* of Moses in Deuteronomy, is given to the children of a new generation in the shadow of the older generation's failure to prepare them for the threatened future that lies ahead. With Isaiah this future comes to meet the children, we have seen, in the crisis of Hezekiah, who is raised up to represent the remnant constituted by these children of the new generation (Isa. 36–39; see esp. 37.4). We have noted how that, at first, Hezekiah represents them well by turning toward the word of the LORD, but in the end he fails by turning away from his own children, resigning them to the dim fate of Babylonian exile that he and his generation had bequeathed them (39.5-8).

However, right after we see Hezekiah writing off the generation of his children (39.8), we turn to the next page and chapter and see Isaiah writing *to* them (chs. 40–66).[26]

This lengthy section of the book of Isaiah has long been recognized as being addressed to the future generation of the Babylonian captivity and has for this reason long been thought to have come from hands much later than Isaiah's. Yet this widely followed conclusion has failed to recognize the parallel between (1) Isaiah's call in ch. 8 to the new generation left in the lurch by the Ahaz crisis and (2) the prophet's call in ch. 40 to the new generation left in the lurch by the Hezekiah crisis. The historical-critical focus on how ch. 40's sudden shift ahead to another generation does not conform to Isaiah's time has completely missed how thoroughly this shift conforms to Isaiah's call and the theme on which the structure of the book has been shown to turn. It is the call to mentor the children of the next generation to the end of raising up holy seed.

Significantly, the prophetic call of ch. 40 is first issued ('Speak comfort', v. 1), then taken up ('a voice of one calls out', v. 3), and then

---

[26] For helping me to arrive at this way of putting it, I credit a conversation with one of my former students, Jonathan Stone.

transferred to another ('a voice says, 'Call out', v. 6).[27] Like with Moses in Deuteronomy passing on the mentoring call, Isaiah's call to the children of this future generation is urgently commended to being taken up by them – a most appropriate urging in view of the time gap beyond Isaiah's days, which now must be bridged.[28] So throughout this part of the book, Isaiah's call to this future generation points beyond itself to the raising up of others to take up the call. Many points could be noted here, but most crucial to Isaiah's purpose, as well as ours, is what can be found in the call of the servant of Yahweh, presented throughout the so-called 'servant songs' of Isaiah 42–53,[29] but particularly in the climax of Isaiah 53. I note the following points.

(1) For Isaiah, the call of the servant in ch. 53 points to the depths from which the holy seed springs forth. Accordingly the servant is identified in 53.2 as a 'root out of dry ground' – one who, like the stump of 6.13, is 'cut off from the land of the living' (53.8).

(2) Accepting the servant's call requires faith – 'Who will believe our report?' (53.1). This is the same issue (and Hebrew term, אמן, *amen*) of belief posed to Ahaz (7.9), whose own response to the call failed here.

(3) Fulfilling the servant's call entails enduring affliction from the LORD for the sake of the promise of one's offspring and finding fulfillment therein for one's own life – 'it pleased the LORD ... , to afflict him (or 'make him sick' [כלה, *khalah*], the same term used of Hezekiah's sickness in 38.1) ... for he shall see his seed (זרע, *zera*); he shall prolong his days' (53.10). Hezekiah's response to the call failed here, for after prevailing upon God to take away his sickness and to prolong his days (ch. 38) Hezekiah was content in the gain of his own added days to accept, without objection, the loss of his children's (ch. 39).

(4) The servant's call entails sacrificing one's life for the life of one's children[30] – 'He shall see the travail of his soul and be satisfied; by his knowledge my righteous servant shall make many righteous ... for he poured out his soul unto death' (53.11-12). The travail of Isaiah 53 opens up to the birth announcement of Isaiah 54 – the promise of

---

[27] Cf. v. 9 where Zion is addressed as the 'bringer of good tidings'. For the scholarly suggestion that Isaiah 40 features a kind of second 'call that parallels Isaiah 6', see W. Brueggemann, *Isaiah 40-66*. Westminster Bible Companion (Louisville, KY: Westminster John Knox Press, 1998), pp. 17-19.

[28] Scholars estimate the end of Isaiah's ministry to be some time soon after 700 BCE and mark 586 BCE as the beginning of the Babylonian exile.

[29] These 'servant songs' (42.1-4; 49.1-6; 50.4-9; 52.13–53.12) were first demarcated and designated as a discrete grouping by B. Duhm, *Das Buch Jesaia*. HKAT III, 1 (4th ed.; Göttingen: Vandenhoeck & Ruprecht, 1922 [first published in 1892]).

[30] Thus, the call of the prophet as mentor and as martyr converge in the end (cf. my discussion of the prophet as martyr in the previous chapter of this volume, 'The Prophetic Calling').

many children (54.1), 'your *seed* [זרע, *zera*]' (54.3), 'taught of Yahweh' (54.13), 'established in righteousness' (54.14), and surely representing the 'holy seed' envisioned in Isaiah's call in 6.13. The final verse of Isaiah 54 declares, significantly, that 'this is the heritage of the *servants* [plural!] of Yahweh' (54.17).

(5) Thus, the call of the servant in Isaiah 53 is commended to all who would be servants of Yahweh.[31] While this call points us ahead as Christians to Jesus, the ultimate example of the prophet as mentor, it also points us back to the prophet Isaiah, whose faithfulness as a servant of Yahweh,[32] according to the call of Isaiah 53, can be traced in clearly drawn contrast to Ahaz and Hezekiah, as we have seen, through the course of the entire book. And so we are led by the prophetic example of Isaiah to respond as servants of Yahweh, 'Here am I' (6.8), indeed, 'Here am I and the children the LORD has given me' (8.18).

In conclusion, I offer a few brief reflections on how the foregoing evidence for the OT prophet as mentor could be relevant for the church today. I merely mention a few leads that might be further pursued.

First, this study of the three leading prophets of the OT shows the extensive biblical grounding for the role of the prophetic vocation in addressing and calling all of God's people to the responsibility of mentoring the next generation, 'turning the hearts of the elders to their children and the hearts of the children to their elders'. It is a role that becomes especially critical, as we saw, in contexts of blatant dereliction of the eldering generation, such as can be seen today in almost any direction one looks.

Secondly, this study points up the importance of prophetic insight in recovering and reclaiming a divine revelation of the intrinsic significance of children. There is a profound spiritual dimension to raising up and blessing a new generation that includes but goes beyond a systema-

---

[31] For a study that points up the prominence of the theme of the 'servants of Yahweh' in the latter part of Isaiah, albeit in a way that is somewhat different than what I am suggesting here, see W.A.M. Beuken, 'The Main Theme of Trito-Isaiah, "The Servants of YHWH"', *JSOT* 47 (June 1990), 67-87. For an example of how Christians in the NT understood themselves to be recipients of the call of the 'servant of Yahweh' in Isaiah, see Acts 13.46-49.

[32] The call of the servant of Yahweh could also point back to Moses, as well, for he is called 'servant of Yahweh' (Deut. 34.5) in the very passage that reviews his legacy as a prophet (Deut. 34.5-12). See G. von Rad, *Old Testament Theology, Volume II: The Theology of Israel's Prophetic Traditions* (trans. D.M.G. Stalker; New York: Harper & Row, 1965), pp. 250-62, esp. 261-62, for the view that the figure of Moses as suffering prophetic intercessor is the prime biblical tradition behind the 'servant of Yahweh' in Isaiah 53. See also D. Olson, *Deuteronomy and the Death of Moses*, pp. 35-39, 45-48, 57-58, and 150, for a sustained argument on the presentation of Moses in Deuteronomy as one who suffered vicariously for God's people.

tized catechism or curricular program of discipleship. It is more about *being* and *being with* someone than knowing what to *do*.

Consequently and thirdly, spiritual succession, as the prophet Elijah recognized and can still help us to see, is 'a difficult thing' that in the end will call elders to go to places beyond themselves where only a vision of God can overcome the *di*vision between generations.

Finally, this study shows that the call of the prophet as mentor is ultimately the call addressing us all to follow, even to *be*, the suffering servant of the LORD, giving up our lives for our children, indeed seeing the holy seed from the travail of our souls and being satisfied.[33]

---

[33] My special thanks go to Walter Brueggemann, who was kind enough to respond to this study when it was first published by offering his own affirming reflections, 'A Response to Rickie Moore's "The Prophet as Mentor",' *JPT* 15.2 (April 2007), pp. 175-77.

6

Jeremiah against the Prophets: Discerning the Truth in the Light of the End

Who, for God's sake, is telling the truth? This is a question as contemporary as today's newspaper, yet the question is entirely fitting to introduce a study on the ancient Israelite prophet, Jeremiah. There is no part of Scripture that engages this question more intensely than the book of Jeremiah, and there is no place where the stakes for answering it are higher.

Jeremiah learned at the beginning of his life what we learn at the beginning of his book. He was to deliver to his generation a message that would be vigorously countered from every quarter of society, as 1.18 says, 'the whole land (אֶרֶץ, *eretz*) – the kings of Judah, its princes, its priests, and the people of the land.' Why? It is because Jeremiah would announce nothing less than the coming of complete destruction 'upon the whole land (*eretz*)' (4.27; cf. 1.14). God's death notice for Judah was as unwelcome and as unthinkable as the end of the world. Indeed this is surely the appropriate comparison for grasping the magnitude and the import of Jeremiah's message for Judah,[1] as Jeremiah's own poetry bears out:

> I looked on the earth (*eretz*) and lo, it was waste and void;
> and to the heavens, and they had no light.
> I looked on the mountains, and lo, they were quaking,
> and all the hills moved to and fro.
> I looked, and lo, there was no one at all.
> and all the birds of the air had fled.
> I looked, and lo, the fruitful land was a desert,
> and all its cities were laid in ruins
> before the LORD, before his fierce anger
>
> (4.23-26, NRSV; cf. 25.15-31)

---

[1] Walter Brueggemann has written helpfully and eloquently on this point. See his 'Cosmic Hurt/Personal Possibility: Jer. 4.23-28; Isa. 45.18-22; Luke 6.21-31', ch. 14 in his *Interpretation and Obedience: From Faithful Reading to Faithful Living* (Minneapolis, MN: Fortress Press, 1991), pp. 313-21; and also his *To Pluck Up, To Tear Down: A Commentary on the Book of Jeremiah 1-25* (Grand Rapids, MI: Eerdmans, 1998).

The world against which Jeremiah hurled such words naturally had strong motivations for refuting them and also had, throughout most of Jeremiah's ministry, some formidable resources for doing so. Specifically, there were significant political, social and theological factors that weighed heavily against Jeremiah's case. Politically, when Jeremiah first began to warn of the coming 'foe from the North' (cf. 1.14)[2] the viable military threat of the superpowers of that time had clearly diminished in Judah. Thus, the practical likelihood of national devastation seemed remote. Also the covenantal reform of Josiah (2 Kgs 22-23) in the time of Jeremiah's early ministry,[3] with its dramatic turn back toward the religious foundations and the traditional values of the nation, had surely engendered a strong sense of social and religious improvement and well-being. Thus the perceived level of national guilt did not seem to warrant such extreme judgment. Not unrelated to this factor and perhaps most importantly of all, Judah's most hallowed theological tradition, which centered on Yahweh's enduring promises concerning the throne of David, the city of Jerusalem and the temple of Zion (2 Sam. 7.1-17; 1 Kgs 9.1-5), was widely and solemnly believed at this time to place Judah beyond the possibility of ruination (cf. Jer. 7). God's *gospel through David* was appropriated in a way that saw God's *law through Moses* as something finally indecisive and inconsequential for the nation's destiny.

Thus, while seeing Jeremiah as a 'man of contention,' and indeed that was his own self-description (אִישׁ רִיב, *ish riv*),[4] it is important to see that the contention was a two-way affair. The *words of Jeremiah* pressed an explicit case against Judah,[5] but the *world of Judah* pressed back constantly, if not always explicitly, with its own antithetical claims.[6]

[2] The critical issues connected with this so-called, 'foe from the North' are covered extensively in *A Prophet to the Nations: Essays in Jeremiah Studies*, ed. Leo G. Perdue and Brian W. Kovacs (Winona Lake, IN: Eisenbrauns, 1984), pp. 129-73 (articles by Henri Cazelles, Brevard S. Childs and C.F. Whitley).

[3] For a thorough discussion of Jeremiah's relationship to the reform, again, see *Prophet to the Nations*, pp. 89-127 (articles by Henri Cazelles and J. Philip Hyatt).

[4] See Jer. 15.10.

[5] For the importance of the legal lawsuit or covenant lawsuit form in Jeremiah and classical prophecy generally, see B. Gemser, 'The RIB or Controversy Pattern in Hebrew Mentality', VTSup 3 (1995), pp. 120-37; H. Huffmon, 'The Covenant Lawsuit in the Prophets', *JBL* 78 (1959), pp. 285-95; and J. Harvey, 'Le *rib*-Pattern, requisitoire prophetique sur la rupture de l'alliance', *Bib* 43 (1962), pp. 172-96. For a recent critique of this view, which sees a more limited appropriation of actual lawsuit procedure, see Michael De Roche, 'Yahweh's *rib* against Israel: A Reassessment of the So-Called "Prophetic Lawsuit" in the Pre-exilic Prophets', *JBL* 102 (1983), pp. 563-74.

[6] Having discerned this fact better than most, Brueggemann discusses it throughout his commentary (*To Pluck Up*) under the terms 'royal temple ideology' and 'the Jerusalem establishment' (see esp. pp. 5-7).

This paper will focus upon one aspect of Jeremiah's contention, perhaps the one most explicit and intense of all: Jeremiah's contention with other prophets of his time. I have arrived at this focus as the result of the convergence of two major interests. First of all, as a Pentecostal I am interested in exploring Old Testament prophecy as an essential background for understanding the revelatory work of the Spirit in the New Testament. More specifically, I am concerned with the ongoing relationship in the Old Testament between inscripturated word and inspired utterance. I have argued that an urgent theological concern of the book of Deuteronomy (esp. Deut. 4 and 5) is the continuing complementary role of inspired utterance alongside God's written word.[7] I see the book of Jeremiah as a natural place to continue pursuing this issue, in light of the prominent way that new prophetic revelation comes together in this book and in Jeremiah's time with earlier written revelation, indeed with the canonical tradition of Deuteronomy itself.[8] Yet my focus in this paper upon Jeremiah's conflict with other prophets forces attention to a threat that seems to stand opposite to the one addressed so prominently in Deuteronomy. There the prime threat to God's revelation was that the fire of prophetic utterance would be quenched in favor of static idolatrous forms (cf. Deut. 4.12-24).[9] Yet in Jeremiah's conflict with the prophets, we confront a proliferation of prophetic utterance, which seems to rage wildly out of control (cf. Jer. 23.21-40). Thus God's truth can be missed through overplaying and not just underplaying the place of prophetic utterance, and Jeremiah's contention with the prophets offers an important paradigm for addressing this side of the issue.

Another aspect of my interest as a Pentecostal in Jeremiah's confrontation with other prophets is its relation to a context of eschatological expectancy.[10] The last ten years in Judah before the fall of Jerusalem was a time of intense preoccupations about the end. Spanning the years between Babylon's first and final deportations of the citizenry of Judah, this decade, not surprisingly, featured vigorous eschatological reflection and discourse, as Jeremiah's own recorded prophetic experiences and encounters with other prophets so clearly show.[11] As the apocalyptic

---

[7] See Chapter 2 above.

[8] The relationship of Jeremiah and Deuteronomy has been a central concern of Jeremiah studies. Again see the articles by Cazelles and Hyatt in *Prophet to the Nations*, pp. 89-127.

[9] Again, see my discussion in Chapter 2.

[10] On the importance of eschatology to Pentecostal tradition, see Steven J. Land, *Pentecostal Spirituality: A Passion for the Kingdom* (JPTSup 1; Sheffield: Sheffield Academic Press, 1993).

[11] It is likely that there was a heightening of prophetic activity generally and prophetic conflict involving Jeremiah specifically in the decade before Jerusalem's fall. While it is

currents intensify in our own terror-ridden world, I believe that the texts that take up Jeremiah's struggle with the prophets can offer some crucial canonical clues on how God's truth is discerned in eschatologically intense times.

Examining Jeremiah's clash with opposing prophets as a way to gain leverage on the issue of true vs. false revelation is a well-worn path. A number of scholars have taken up this issue.[12] My treatment here does not presume to offer any comprehensive analysis designed to surpass the previous scholarly discussion. Rather my reason for pursuing this study has to do with my sense that approaching the given topic and biblical material from the vantage of Pentecostal experience[13] may open up some fresh angles on what the Bible is saying through Jeremiah's battle with the prophets. I am suggesting, in other words, that the distinctive eschatological and revelatory claims, for which Pentecostals have stood and withstood,[14] open up an existential identity with Jeremiah which could reveal things in the biblical text which others might not notice.

I propose to look first at Jeremiah 28, the passage considered to be the *locus classicus* on true vs. false prophecy in the Old Testament.[15] Then I will offer some brief comment on Jer. 23.9-44, a collection of diverse materials that the biblical text introduces with the words, 'concerning the prophets.'

In approaching ch. 28, it is crucial to see its close linkage to ch. 27.[16] This is seen from the very first verse, which points back to the time reference of 27.1, 'in that same year, at the beginning of the reign of

true that Jeremiah denounces certain prophets and prophetic activity in oracles considered to be early (e.g. 2.8, 26; 4.9), all of the specific confrontations between Jeremiah and other prophets, which have been recorded in the biographical accounts, take place in this final ten-year period (see 28; 29.29). It stands to reason that the puncturing of belief in Jerusalem's impregnability, which Babylon's first deportation surely must have caused, would have encouraged looking for oracular reinforcement for the old static structures and religious symbols, which in earlier times would probably have appeared not to have needed such help. I am suggesting that Jeremiah's clash with the world of Judah took more of a *charisma vs. institution* shape before 597 BCE (cf. the Temple Sermon, as recorded in Jer. 7 and 26) and more of a *charisma vs. charisma* character afterward. One undated text that clearly suggests an intensification of the latter kind of conflict at some point in Jeremiah's ministry is the oracle prohibiting oracles in 23.33-40.

[12] For a treatment of the issue, which takes note of the major treatments of the past and offers some original proposals, see Gerald T. Sheppard, 'True and False Prophecy within Scripture', in *Canon, Theology, and Old Testament Interpretation: Essays in Honor of Brevard Childs*, ed. Gene M. Tucker, *et al.* (Philadelphia, PA: Fortress, 1988) pp. 262-82.

[13] See Roger Stronstad, 'Pentecostal Experience and Hermeneutics', *Paraclete* 26 (1992), pp. 14-30.

[14] Again, see Land, *Pentecostal Spirituality*.

[15] See Sheppard, 'True and False Prophecy', p. 268.

[16] Cf. B. Childs, *Old Testament Theology in a Canonical Context* (Philadelphia, PA: Fortress, 1985), pp. 133-44.

Zedekiah' (28.1). As the beginning of Judah's last decade, this year has obvious eschatological import, especially so since, as ch. 27 has also made clear, this is the year when Jeremiah had first heard God tell him to don the ox yoke that would symbolize Babylon's impending conquest (vv. 2-7). Chapter 27 goes on to relate the oracular message of the ox yoke. In first-person testimony, Jeremiah recounts his experience of delivering this message, first to the envoys coming to Jerusalem from surrounding nations (vv. 3-11), then to king Zedekiah (vv. 12-15), and finally to 'the priests and all the people' (vv. 16-22). While each delivery of this message is unique to its respective audience, the same essential points are made in all three cases: (1) the nations must serve Nebuchadnezzar (vv. 5-8, 12, 17); (2) failure to submit totally to Babylon will result in total removal from the land; and (3) the prophets who are saying otherwise are lying and must not be heeded (vv. 9-10, 14, 16).[17]

When Brevard Childs finds these same essential points in Jeremiah's oracle to Hananiah in ch. 28 (vv. 14, 16, and 15 respectively) he uses this to argue that ch. 28 is only a 'concrete illustration of the one message against false prophets,' with the implication that the canonical presentation is not at all interested in depicting an existential crisis about the problem of discerning the truth.[18] It is as if the reiteration of a comprehensive theocentric message in ch. 27 undercuts any existential tension in ch. 28. Gerald Sheppard has recently restated Childs's point this way:

> Rather than inviting interpreters of scripture to 'relive' the moment and to speculate regarding the criteria of discernment, the canonical context now casts the issue of true and false prophecy in thoroughly 'theocentric' terms.[19]

As Childs proceeds with his interpretation of Jeremiah's encounter with Hananiah, he at first seems willing to allow that the original episode, before its present canonical positioning, intended to represent a crisis of discernment.[20] However, he goes on to minimize this possibility by arguing that,

> Even without an appeal to the effect of the later canonical framework, vv. 5-9 cannot be read in terms of Jeremiah's self-understanding. To interpret the text as reflecting Jeremiah's personal uncertainty as to his

---

[17] Childs, *Old Testament Theology*, pp. 137-38.

[18] Childs, *Old Testament Theology*, p. 138. Cf. Childs's earlier statement, 'For years I thought that I understood the passage (Jer. 28). Now I am prepared to disagree with a widespread interpretation, shared by Zimmerli and von Rad, which I would probably classify as existential (cf. also Buber).'

[19] Sheppard, 'True and False Prophecy', p. 263.

[20] Childs, *Old Testament Theology*, p. 138; cf. also p. 141.

own previous message, and to see no continuity between the past and the present, is to psychologize the text. The issue of ch. 28 is not about Jeremiah's psyche. Rather, the exegetical issue turns on God's will for the nations under the rule of Nebuchadnezzar. The theological focus is fully theocentric.[21]

But after saying this, Childs has to admit that vv. 5-9 do in fact register a theological restraint in Jeremiah's immediate response to Hananiah that indicates an openness or uncertainty as to the possibility that God had changed his plan.[22] Despite Childs' insistence at this point that the issue here is theocentric ('What is God's purpose?') rather than psychological ('How does Jeremiah know whether or not he is right?'), as if these questions could ever be separable (!), I do not see how, even from this perspective, that one can deny the text's initial aim here to pose the existential crisis of discernment.[23] This is especially the case when the question of discernment is considered not just in relation to Jeremiah, as Childs limits the issue, but also in relation to the people, who are repeatedly mentioned as witnesses in Hananiah's encounter with Jeremiah (28.1, 5, 7, 11). I would even propose that the subsequent canonical framing that the narrative of ch. 28 has received from ch. 27, far from lessening or eliminating this existential dimension, as Childs has argued, rather enhances it.

The stage for Jeremiah's encounter with Hananiah is set and the initial pole of dramatic tension is established by the thrice-repeated delivery of Jeremiah's ox-yoke message in ch. 27. This repetition has the

---

[21] Childs, *Old Testament Theology*, p. 139.

[22] Childs, *Old Testament Theology*, p. 139.

[23] I believe Childs is denying the narrative its dynamic function of reactualizing the existential experience of revelatory process not because of what's in the text, but because Childs is committed to a view of canon (and perhaps even a view of reality) that sees canon as a *product* which terminates the revelatory *process* (cf. Sheppard's 'canonical' argument for the 'end of prophecy' in the article previously cited, pp. 273-80). Thus Childs says, "The initial assumption of seeing a simple analogy between the prophet's function and ours subverts the essential role of the canon which established theological continuity between the generations by means of the authority of sacred scripture. We are not prophets nor apostles, nor is our task directly analogous" (p. 137). The end result of this kind of view, I suppose, is that a biblical narrative has nothing left to do than be a 'concrete illustration,' to use Childs' term (p. 138), of a settled theological position. Yet it is amazing how differently biblical narratives will appear (1) when the possibility of continuing prophetic process is taken seriously (cf. Thomas Overholt's view of the continuing possibility of prophecy from the perspective of sociological phenomenology: 'The End of Prophecy: No Players without a Program', *JSOT* 42 [1988], pp. 103-15); or (2) when the canon is viewed in the light of the experience and the urgency of social *transformation* and not just community *formation*, in other words, when the canon is related not just to the establishment of what is but also to the possibility of the end of what is (see Henri Mottu, 'Jeremiah vs. Hananiah: Ideology and Truth in Old Testament Prophecy', in *The Bible and Liberation: Political and Social Hermeneutics*, ed. Norman K. Gottwald [Maryknoll, NY: Orbis, 1983], pp. 235-51).

literary effect of accentuating the extent to which Jeremiah, if you would pardon a pun, has stuck his neck out. For Jeremiah the three groups addressed move increasingly closer to home, from the international envoys, to king Zedekiah, to 'the priests and all the people'. This last-mentioned audience is important in that it is specifically mentioned, with duplicate wording, at the beginning of ch. 28. Hananiah addresses Jeremiah in the presence of 'the priests and all the people' (v. 1), thus the earlier sequence of oracles can be seen to lead directly into this encounter.

The Hananiah narrative is not to be seen, as Childs indicates, as a particular example of something typified in the previous chapter. Chapter 27 relates a sequence of unique events in first-person narration, and chapter 28 only extends this sequence to present another new and this time very different encounter. Thus Jeremiah recounts that 'in that same year', that is, the year in which he had spoken the three oracles just reviewed, 'Hananiah ... spoke to me' (v. 1). The roles of the previous chapter are abruptly reshuffled. We last saw Jeremiah as the speaker, the priests and all the people as the addressee, and the salvation-proclaiming prophets as a central topic of the message. However, now we see one of those very prophets assuming the role of speaker, Jeremiah is the addressee, and the priests and all the people are looking on.

Of course, in the first verse, we do not yet know what kind of prophet Hananiah is. As has often been noted, the Hebrew text, unlike the Septuagint, does not employ the qualification, *false* prophet, but instead uses the same term for Hananiah (נביא, *navi*) that is used of Jeremiah several verses later (v.5). It is only with Hananiah's words that follow in vv. 2-4 that he can be associated with the prophets about whom Jeremiah spoke in ch. 27. And yet Jeremiah, who at this point is still continuing the first-person narration begun in 27.2, quotes Hananiah without any editorial comment that would presently discredit his oracle – an oracle that, at least in style, has a remarkably orthodox ring to it. We see the typical messenger formula, 'thus says the LORD,' an appropriately reverential and traditional reference to God as 'LORD of hosts, the God of Israel,' and a salvation pronouncement that, though in direct opposition to Jeremiah's unretracted message to submit to Babylon, could find precedent in the salvation oracles of the sacred traditions that even Jeremiah would undoubtedly have embraced. All of these things are routinely noticed by commentators, but it is worth underscoring that these are precisely the things that would have been noticed by 'the priests and all the people,' in whose presence (literally, 'before whose face'), as Jeremiah's narration seems careful to mention, Hananiah spoke his message to Jeremiah.

What is *not* adequately noticed is that after the quotation of Hananiah's opening message to Jeremiah, Jeremiah's first-person narration abruptly gives way to third-person narration (v. 5).[24] The literary effect of this unexpected transition is to distance the reader from Jeremiah's own perspective right at the moment of truth. The reader is forced to relinquish his or her privileged perspective alongside Jeremiah and is made to take a seat in the gallery, as it were, alongside 'the priests and all the people', whose mention again at this very point in the narrative (v. 5) surely functions to accentuate this effect. We no longer will see Hananiah through Jeremiah's eyes, but we will see Jeremiah and Hananiah from the same point of vantage, standing side by side on the same footing.

If the shift in point of view establishes this leveling juxtaposition, then the parallel wording of v. 5 gives explicit reinforcement: 'Then *the prophet* Jeremiah spoke to Hananiah *the prophet* in the presence of the priests and all the people who were standing in the house of the LORD.' Assigning the same identification, 'the prophet,' to the names of both men here as they are shown standing before the crowd, points not so much to Jeremiah's dilemma of discrimination but to the crowd's, and now the readers' who are positioned to look on from the crowd's perspective. And we should realize that it has not been usual up to this point in the book to see references to Jeremiah followed with this epithet. Before this occurrence in 28.5, the words 'Jeremiah the prophet' occur only three times (1.5; 20.2; 25.2). Yet this chapter proceeds to use this phrase no less than six more times (vv. 6, 10, 11, 12a, 12b, 15), over against the four additional occurrences of 'Hananiah the prophet' (vv. 1, 10, 12, 15). Such use of this epithet in this chapter seems to stress the seriousness of Hananiah's prophetic image, while making Jeremiah's prophetic identity appear as if it were on the defensive.

The speech of Jeremiah, which now follows (vv. 6-11), further reveals Jeremiah's struggle to show himself a match to Hananiah. He first says, 'Amen!', expressing his wish, perhaps with sarcasm, that Hananiah's words would come true (v. 6). Unlike Hananiah, however, Jeremiah has no 'thus says the LORD' to offer on this occasion. Jeremiah speaks here with explicit appeal to no authority beyond his own, and he seems to be trying hard to make the most of this by introducing his

---

[24] There is no textual basis for the suggestion of John Bright, *Jeremiah* (AncB 21; Garden City, NY: Doubleday, 1965), p. 197, that the first-person reference in 28.1, 'to me' (אֵלַי, *elay*), should be understood as an abbreviation of 'to Je[remiah]' (אֶל־יִ[רְמִיָה], *el-ye[remya]*), thus bringing v. 1 into conformity with the third-person style of the rest of the chapter. Cf. also BHS footnote. The literary continuity with ch. 27, noted earlier, is stronger weight for retaining the first-person reference in 28.1 in the absence of any textual support or any other kind of support for such a dubious proposal for abbreviation.

words with solemn formality: 'Hear now this word which I speak in your hearing and in the hearing of all the people' (v. 7). Without the authority of divine revelation, Jeremiah presses to persuade through argument. His argument entails appeal to normative traditions, but such appeal seems less than decisive, because it is clearly selective. The likes of Isaiah's message of salvation for Jerusalem during the siege of Sennacherib in 701 BCE is conveniently ignored when Jeremiah says in v. 8, 'the prophets who preceded you and me from ancient times prophesied war, famine, and pestilence against many countries and great kingdoms.' Similarly, in v. 8, when Jeremiah appeals to the Deuteronomy fulfillment principle for identifying a bogus prophet (Deut. 18.22), he selectively shifts attention away from Deuteronomy's emphasis on false predictions of disaster to his present concern with false predictions of peace.[25] 'As for the prophet who prophesies peace,' he says, 'when the word of that prophet comes to pass, then it will be known that the LORD has truly sent the prophet' (v. 9). Yet the weakness of this test, as has often been noted, is that Jeremiah's assurance that '*then* it will be known' is offered to those who are being asked to 'hear *now*' (v. 7). How can a future proof commend a present word?

The climax of this prophetic stand-off comes when Hananiah answers Jeremiah's weak words with a bold action. His taking the yoke-bars from Jeremiah's neck and smashing them is forceful in spectacle as well as symbolism (v. 10). The grandstand opportunity and impact of this act is not lost on Hananiah, who immediately follows his spectacular gesture with an oracle explaining it: 'Thus says the LORD: Even so will I break the yoke of Nebuchadnezzar king of Babylon from the neck of all the nations within two years' (v. 11). Nor is the grandstand effect lost on the narrator, who for the third time mentions that the given words were spoken 'in the presence of all the people' (v. 11). Although the narrative remains completely silent on the nature of the people's response, the repeated reference to 'the presence of the people' tenaciously rivets attention upon the question of their perspective and their reading of this event.

But the question is abruptly suspended, as is the episode itself, when Hananiah's oracle is immediately followed with the unexpectedly terse phrase, 'But Jeremiah the prophet went his way' (v. 11). Here he is identified once again as 'Jeremiah *the prophet*.' At this point in the narrative are we in need of reassurance that he still is a prophet?! Could this be how it looked from the perspective of 'all the people'? The narrative does not give any answer. The narrative's silence matches Jeremiah's silence, and this is what forces the question. We have a narrator to reassure us that the man leaving, the man who had no oracle to

---

[25] This is noted by Childs, *Old Testament Theology*, p. 133.

give, is nevertheless a prophet. Yet what about the people? I would suggest that this silence is the loudest point of the story.

For Jeremiah the silence is broken in the very next verse. 'Sometime after,' we are told, 'the word of the LORD came to Jeremiah' (v. 12). He is told, 'Go, tell Hananiah (note that God does not call him "the prophet"), "Thus says the LORD (at last the prophet Jeremiah will speak a prophetic word): You have broken the wooden bars, but I will make in their place bars of iron"' (v. 13). For this previously silent prophet, a second 'Thus says the LORD' quickly follows, spelling out the fulfillment of this symbolism in terms of Babylon's iron grip (v. 14). And then yet a third and final 'Thus says the LORD' is given – this time an oracle directed to Hananiah personally. 'Behold, I will remove you from the face of the earth. This very year you shall die, because you have uttered rebellion against the LORD' (v. 16). There remains only the final verse that validates the word of *the prophet* Jeremiah. 'In that same year, in the seventh month, the prophet Hananiah died' (v. 17).

What is noteworthy about Jeremiah's words from the LORD, however, is that they are presented to Hananiah with no mention of 'all of the people'. The earlier public encounter contrasts this private exchange. While in the presence of all the people, Hananiah had the first and the last word, and Jeremiah's words seemed weak by comparison. Yet at the end, Jeremiah has all the say, while Hananiah is the only audience in sight. Earlier Jeremiah, with all the force he could muster, had been conscious to speak out his human word not only in Hananiah's hearing, but also 'in the hearing of all the people' (v. 7). Yet now his divine word claims no surrounding audience. The true word is set apart from the presence of the people, and all by the little phrase, 'sometime later' (v. 12). How much later? That doesn't seem to matter. All that seems to matter is that the word *comes* only after Jeremiah *departs*, after he is no longer in the presence of all the people.

As readers, we also leave the presence of the people. We follow Jeremiah by way of the narrator, not through Jeremiah's own first-person narration as before. Jeremiah, as it were, led us into the presence of the people, and the narrator in the end leads us out. From this point we are even allowed to look forward to Hananiah's death to see a demonstration of the very fulfillment principle that Jeremiah had so earnestly projected 'in the hearing of all the people' (v. 7). In a sense we did not have to wait for this demonstration, for we came to the whole book in the light of the fulfillment of Jeremiah's word concerning the exile (cf. Jer. 1.3). We knew Jeremiah was right; Hananiah was wrong. This was available to us all along. Yet the power of this narrative, it seems to me, is the way it leads us back through and makes us reconsider what was available 'in the presence of the people' and 'in the hearing of all the people' in the last days of Judah.

We see Hananiah's role in making 'this people trust in a lie' (v. 15). We also see Jeremiah's attempt to persuade the people with his best theological arguments (vv. 8-9). Yet even more significantly, I think, we see God withholding his own decisive and determinative word until 'sometime later' when all of the people are no longer in view. While this insight might hold implications for what it was like to *be* a true prophet (and this question is certainly pursued in Jeremiah's confessions), I believe that the primary thrust of this narrative is rather toward what it was like to *see* a true prophet, particularly in the time of the end. My suggestion is that Jeremiah 28 points toward God's active agency in the eschatological crisis of discernment. We see God making his own prophetic word more distant and unavailable at the very time the public seems ready for prophetic answers. I see God making his prophetic word more distant in this narrative not only by his withholding his decisive oracle until 'sometime later' out of the public view, but also by leaving Jeremiah to appear weak, outstripped, and finally silent in his unforgettable encounter with Hananiah.

As I have argued previously,[26] Deuteronomy, which explicitly sets forth Israel's theology of revelation, introduces the distinctive role of the prophet and prophetic revelation in relation to the manifestation of divine nearness. Essentially because of the continuing voice of God through prophetic utterance, Israel could testify, 'What great nation is there that has *a god so near* to it as the LORD our God is to us, whenever we call on him?' (Deut. 4.7; cf. 5.27; 18.15-16). Yet what appears in Jeremiah, as we have seen, is a manifestation of prophecy that registers and accentuates divine distance rather than divine nearness.

The significance of this theme of divine distance with respect to Jeremiah's clash with false prophecy is made clearer when we turn to ch. 23. This theme, which Jeremiah 28 presents dramatically and narratively, is addressed explicitly and didactically in Jeremiah's oracles 'concerning the prophets'. After a series of oracular poems in which Jeremiah harshly condemns his counterparts for speaking false prophecies and sternly warns the people against listening to them (23.10-22), we come to the stark question, 'Am I a God nearby,' says the LORD, 'and not a God far off?' (v. 23; NRSV).[27] The thrust of this rhetorical

---

[26] See Chapter 2 of this volume.

[27] For an insightful study of this verse in relation to its immediate and wider biblical contexts, see Warner E. Lemke, 'The Near and the Distant God: A Study of Jer 23.23-24 in its Biblical Theological Context', *JBL* 100/4 (1981), pp. 541-55. Lemke considers the variant LXX reading of the verse as a statement instead of a question and appreciates ways that it could be seen to fit with Jeremiah's surrounding message. However, he finds an

question is obviously that, counter to what the lying prophets are representing, God is not merely immanent and at hand but he is distant and beyond human grasp. Here again, I would point to Deuteronomy, which, as I have shown,[28] grounds the origin of the prophetic office in relation to the manifestation of divine nearness. This text, however, offers a striking contrast, which seems to have more than coincidental connection. Whereas in Deuteronomy, God's distant and unapproachable essence was brought near through prophecy, here in Jeremiah, God's distance and unapproachableness are prophetically reasserted in the face of prophetic activities that have misrepresented and presumed upon the nearness of God.

This linkage with Deuteronomy seems to be reinforced in v. 29 with the use of the image of fire in reference to God and his word. Here as in Deuteronomy 4 (see vv. 9-24) the fundamental essence of God's mediation of his word is addressed in terms of fire. Complementing the question, 'Am I a God nearby, and not a God far off?,' v. 29 asks, 'Is not my word like fire?' Whereas in Deuteronomy Israel experienced God's word *coming out* of the fire (see 4.11-12), this verse of Jeremiah shows God's word, as it were, *turning back into* fire.

In this central section of Jeremiah ch. 23 (vv. 23-29), then, God and his prophetic word are represented in terms of distance. God's word stands over against these prophets, and as a result their judgment is declared both before (vv. 12, 15) and immediately after (vv. 29-32) this section. Yet, as in the case of the Hananiah narrative, ch. 23 is also interested in the people who listen in on the conflicting prophetic voices. In fact vv. 16-22 explicitly address these people. The section begins,

> Thus says the LORD of hosts: 'Do not listen to the words of the prophets who prophesy to you filling you with vain hopes; they speak visions of their own minds (לֵב, *lev*), not from the mouth of the LORD. They say continually to those who despise the word of the LORD, "It shall be well with you," and to every one who stubbornly follows his own *mind* (לֵב, *lev*), they say, "No evil shall come upon you"' (vv. 16-17).

This oracle is reminiscent of Jeremiah's own word to all the people in his encounter with Hananiah. It is followed, moreover, by what appears to be a word from Jeremiah (rather than God), which ends on a point strikingly similar to the point Jeremiah ends on in his speech before Hananiah and the people, where he says, 'when the word of the prophet comes to pass, *then it will be known* that the LORD has truly sent the prophet.' He says,

even stronger relationship between the MT reading and Jeremiah's surrounding polemic against the prophets, which moves in the same general direction as my own analysis.

[28] See my discussion in Chapter 2.

The anger of the LORD will not turn back until he has executed and accomplished the intents of his mind (לֵב, *lev*). In the latter days you will understand it clearly (v. 20).

What is so striking here is the implication that the clarity of understanding for which the mind now searches seems to be viewed as unavailable until the end. Is God's revelation in the time of the end being kept at a distance from the human mind? Note the three uses of the word 'mind' (*lev*) in this section in ch. 23 from which we have just read. At the end (v. 20) we see God accomplishing the 'intents of his *mind*'. In v. 16, the prophets are said to 'speak visions of their own *minds*'. They speak, says v. 17, to 'those who despise the word of the LORD', that is, to every one who 'follows his own *mind*'. Note how despising the word of the LORD is identified with following one's own mind. The word of God is thus placed over against not only the mind of the false prophets but the mind of the people as well. Indeed I believe that chapter 23 pushes this very point one step further. Note how the whole collection of material begins with Jeremiah's own words,

> My heart (or 'mind', לֵב, *lev*) is broken within me,
>   all my bones shake;
> I am like a drunken man,
>   like a man overcome by wine,
> because of the LORD
>   and because of his holy words (v. 9)

The prophetic word of God is placed over against not only the mind of the false prophets and the mind of the people, but the mind of the true prophet, as well.

Some time ago, the renowned British OT scholar, Robert P. Carroll wrote an article entitled, 'A Non-Cogent Argument in Jeremiah's Oracles against the Prophets'.[29] His study focuses on 23.22 where Jeremiah says of the lying prophets,

> If they had stood in my council,
> then they would have proclaimed my words to the people,
> and they would have turned them from their evil way,
> and from the evil of their doings.

Carroll reasons that, since the book portrays Jeremiah himself as failing to turn the people from their evil ways through his own oracles, then Jeremiah is either forced to see himself as a false prophet by his own logic or, more *reasonably* in Carroll's view, Jeremiah has simply stumbled into an illogical argument. I mention this article not to refute Carroll's point on this verse, though I have my thoughts on that.

---

[29] Robert P. Carroll, 'A Non-Cogent Argument in Jeremiah's Oracles against the Prophets', *Studia Theologica* 30 (1976), pp. 43-51.

Rather I am interested in the generalities that Carroll draws from this interpretation. He writes of Jeremiah,

> In a time of crumbling loyalties and disintegrating society he spoke out in passion and confusion against everyone and against everything. His evaluations of the prophets stem from his moral passion and rage. Such prophetic passion can so easily lapse into pathological forms of speech that it ceases to be rational, coherent thought. The prophetic tendency to 'rant and rave' can be seen in its most virulent form in Jeremiah's polemical oracles against the prophets.[30]

I do not believe Carroll's argument is at all a new one. I believe it is the same one with which Jeremiah had to contend. Carroll judges Jeremiah's prophetic ministry harshly. Jeremiah was likewise judged harshly within his own lifetime and likewise by those who presupposed a rationality that presumed to sit in judgment above all things, never realizing at the time that their rationality itself could be the object of judgment.

One might ask, if such a radical negation of human rationality is really to be this relevant to prophetic truth in the time of the end, then what is left to be said about discernment? I would suggest two clues that stand at the beginning and end of Jeremiah's oracles concerning the prophets. At the beginning there is Jeremiah's testimony of a broken heart (*lev*, 23.9), of which the confessions give us a running record. What clue might we draw from this? Perhaps discerning the truth in the end will end up breaking our hearts. At the end of ch. 23 there is a more explicit directive, wherein all claims for having an oracle or burden from the LORD are prohibited, but asking after the word of the LORD is permitted.

> As for the prophet, priest or one of the people who says, 'The burden of the LORD,' I will punish that man and his household. Thus shall you say every one to his neighbor and every one to his brother, 'What has the LORD answered?' or 'What has the LORD spoken?' But 'the burden of the LORD' you shall mention no more, for the burden is every man's own word, and you pervert the words of the living God, the LORD of hosts, our God. Thus you shall say to the prophet, 'What has the LORD answered you?' or 'What has the LORD spoken?' (vv. 34-37).

What clue might we draw from this? Perhaps discerning the truth in the end might end up turning not on determining the answer, but rather on persisting in the question, being able not to know, suffering the silence. Jeremiah might teach us that the world's truth in these times can often throttle God's truth. It did when Hananiah broke

---

[30] Carroll, 'A Non-Cogent Argument', p. 44.

Jeremiah's yoke. It did when Jesus stood in a Roman yoke before Pilate. Pilate asked, 'What is truth?' And like Jeremiah before Hananiah, Jesus didn't have a thing to say. Who could have known that this was the answer that we all were waiting for?

7

'And Also Much Cattle'?!:
Prophetic Passions and the End of Jonah

Introduction

This study proposes to take a look at the end of Jonah in order to pursue a much larger end. Contrary to the rhetorical strategy that I find in the book of Jonah, which ends with an unanswered question, I want to be 'up front' about this more ultimate aim. To put it pointedly, my intent is to point out passions that I take to be crucial right now to the process of Bible study in the Pentecostal tradition. My aim emerges from the attempt to conceive and to encourage others to conceive with me the need, the merit, and the possibilities for what I once heard William Faupel refer to as 'a Pentecostal reading of the Bible'.[1] While initial steps in this direction have previously been taken,[2] I believe that we Pentecostals have yet to envision the full and far-reaching prospects for a comprehensive exposition of the biblical text in accord with the heart of our distinctive ethos and experience.

I use the word 'heart' here rather deliberately and emphatically, for while the prevailing modern Western academic approach to the Bible, whether liberal or conservative, has been essentially a head trip, a distinctively Pentecostal approach promises to be much more a matter of the heart. Steven Land's ground-breaking work, *Pentecostal Spirituality:*

---

[1] Faupel, who is Director of the Library and Professor of the History of Christianity at Wesley Theological Seminary in Washington DC and past president of the Society for Pentecostal Studies, shared this with me several years ago in personal conversation,.

[2] See the numerous studies on Pentecostal hermeneutics that have appeared in recent years, as noted in the recent article by John Christopher Thomas, 'Women, Pentecostals and the Bible: An Experiment in Pentecostal Hermeneutics', *JPT* 5 (1994), pp. 41-56 (p. 43 n. 4). See also the survey article by French L. Arrington, 'Hermeneutics', in S.M. Burgess and G.B. McGee (eds.), *Dictionary of Pentecostal and Charismatic Movements* (Grand Rapids, MI: Zondervan, 1988), pp. 376-89, and *Pneuma* 15.2 (Fall 1993), an issue devoted entirely to articles on Pentecostal hermeneutics. I would also mention Jackie David Johns and Cheryl Bridges Johns, 'Yielding to the Spirit: A Pentecostal Approach to Group Bible Study', *JPT* 1 (1992), pp. 109-34.

A Passion for the Kingdom,[3] has shown that the heart of Pentecostal theology, spirituality, and hermeneutics *is all about the heart,* specifically a
heart that is shaped by a distinctive gestalt of apocalyptic passions
which lead from and back to the life of the Spirit. The experience of
the Holy Spirit not only changes the mind (*orthodoxy*) and the deeds
(*orthopraxy*), but also the affections (*orthopathy*) are radically transformed
to become the transforming and integrating fulcrum of everything
else.[4] As Land explicates this constellation of Pentecostal passions, it
becomes clear how they point the way to a radical new reading of
reality and, more particularly, the biblical text.[5]

While Jackie Johns, in his article, 'Pentecostalism and the Postmodern Worldview',[6] has taken up Land's lead on Pentecostalism's distinctive reading of reality, Larry McQueen, in his monograph, *Joel and
the Spirit: The Cry of a Prophetic Hermeneutic,*[7] and Robert Baker in his
article, 'Pentecostal Bible Reading: Toward a Model of Reading for
the Formation of Christian Affections',[8] have taken the next steps on
the matter of a distinctive Pentecostal approach to the biblical text.[9]
McQueen's study, the first fully developed Pentecostal reading of an
entire biblical book, freshly identifies and integrates the passionate
theological movements of the book of Joel in the light of their trajec-
tories through the New Testament and into contemporary Pentecostal
experience – experience in which McQueen's first-hand participation
is acknowledged as having vitally informed his insights. Baker's brief
but provocative article shows how that reading the Gospel of John in a
way that is similarly attuned to the affective dynamics of his Pentecostal
faith, leads him to notice striking indications of this Gospel's own concern for affective impact.

These studies by McQueen and Baker are highly suggestive not only
in showing the compelling place of passion in the process of Scripture
study, but also in pointing up the prominent presence of passion in the

---

[3] Steven J. Land, *Pentecostal Spirituality: A Passion for the Kingdom* (JPTSup 1; Sheffield:
Sheffield Academic Press, 1993).

[4] Land, *Pentecostal Spirituality*, pp. 32-57.

[5] Land, *Pentecostal Spirituality*, pp. 71-81.

[6] Jackie Johns, in his article, 'Pentecostalism and the Postmodern Worldview', *JPT* 7
(1995), pp. 73-96.

[7] Larry R. McQueen, *Joel and the Spirit: The Cry of a Prophetic Hermeneutic* (JPTSup 8;
Sheffield: Sheffield Academic Press, 1995).

[8] Robert O. Baker, 'Pentecostal Bible Reading: Toward a Model of Reading for the
Formation of Christian Affections', *JPT* 7 (1995), pp. 34-48.

[9] Following now in this same vein of distinctively Pentecostal readings of entire bibli-
cal books are the still more recent studies of Robert Christopher Waddell, *The Spirit of the
Book of Revelation* (JPTS 30; Blandford Forum: Deo Publishing, 2006), and Lee Roy
Martin, *The Unheard Voice of God: A Pentecostal Hearing of the Book of Judges* (JPTSup 32 ;
Blandford Forum: Deo, 2008).

biblical writings themselves, a presence which has been long over-looked or dismissed by the *dispassionate* modes of scholarship that have until recently monopolized modern biblical study.

I am convinced that pursuing such a reading of the Bible is extreme-ly relevant right now for the Pentecostal movement. We are in need of Scripture exposition that represents and addresses the deep passions that have characterized our faith and propelled our movement. However, I do not believe that such a pursuit is relevant only to Pentecostalism, as a kind of in-house conversation among ourselves and for ourselves. As the studies by McQueen and Baker help to illustrate, reading the Bible through the lens of our Pentecostal passions can open up dimensions and dynamics *at the heart* of the biblical text in a way that is extremely relevant to a contemporary scholarly discussion grown weary in its distance from the text. Deep calls to deep. Apocalyptic times call to apocalyptic passions – passions that connect the heart of the Pentecostal movement with the heart of Scripture and with the troubled heart of a post-modern world.

We Pentecostals, then, are not the only souls who are ready to ad-mit passions into the workings of our biblical hermeneutics. I can point to several recent studies that have made this clear to me. There is W. Dow Edgerton's book, entitled *The Passion of Interpretation*,[10] in which this University of Chicago professor presents the daring proposal that passion underlies *all* interpretation. He pursues this thesis by relating the crisis of interpretation in our current post-modern situation to classic texts, both biblical and non-biblical, which narrate the crisis origins of our western Judeo-Christian hermeneutical traditions.

Then there is Walter Brueggemann's small but important book, *Ab-iding Astonishment: Psalms, Modernity, and the Making of History*.[11] Here Brueggemann challenges the historical-critical establishment to take seriously the alternative modes of reading reality that are represented in the Bible's testimony to pivotal divine interventions. Brueggemann contends that the modern rationalistic dismissal of this testimony ob-scures the fact that the latter reflects not just naive notions that con-form to some primitive worldview, but rather the enduring wonder of a people who have had their worldview shattered through such expe-riences – a prospect that rationalistic modernity, Brueggemann suggests, has an ideological stake in not seeing in the interest of its *own*

---

[10] W. Dow Edgerton, *The Passion of Interpretation* (Louisville, KY: Westminster John Knox, 1992).

[11] Walter Brueggemann, *Abiding Astonishment: Psalms, Modernity, and the Making of History* (Louisville, KY: Westminster John Knox, 1991).

worldview – a worldview where reason *overules* such passions as surely as moderns *rule over* such primitives.[12]

I would also mention the recent book by Jeffrey L. Staley, *Reading with a Passion: Rhetoric, Autobiography, and the American West in the Gospel of John*.[13] Taking a critical step beyond reader-response criticism, this New Testament scholar and son of a Plymouth Brethren missionary, proposes and demonstrates the merits of an autobiographical dimension in Scripture study. Here again we see a case made for the integration of biblical interpretation and the personal passions of faith experience.

There is much here in these recent studies that should speak to Pentecostal Bible scholars and show us that we indeed have much to speak! It is time for us to look more deeply into and then from our Pentecostal passions and into the passions of the biblical text. In the remainder of this paper I want to offer another modest attempt to do just that in terms of the ending of the book of Jonah. Before moving to this, however, I would want to give brief mention to one other work of biblical scholarship that I find significantly relevant to this whole effort that I have been discussing.

Almost a generation ago now, the great Jewish scholar Abraham Heschel published his two-volume work, *The Prophets*.[14] In it he attempted to convince the scholarly world that *pathos* was the most important key for understanding the Hebrew prophets and the biblical materials that stem from them. Although Heschel's work was respectfully acknowledged in the critical biblical scholarship of that time, there was not much response in the way of following up or building upon Heschel's leads, and that remains largely the case, it seems to me, even to this day. Perhaps it took a Jewish scholar, living and writing in the shadow of Auschwitz,[15] to inject the issue of *pathos* into the discourse of modern biblical study. Perhaps it will be the task and the privilege of Pentecostal biblical scholars, living in the light of the end, to see where this *pathos* will lead.[16]

[12] Relevant here is the recent rise and explosive growth of post-colonial hermeneutics.

[13] Jeffrey L. Staley, *Reading with a Passion: Rhetoric, Autobiography, and the American West in the Gospel of John* (Lexington, KY: Continuum, 1995).

[14] Abraham Heschel, *The Prophets* (New York: Harper & Row, 1962).

[15] The dedicatory statement that Heschel placed at the beginning of *The Prophets* is telling in this regard: 'To the martyrs of 1939-1945'.

[16] Heschel's work on pathos should be relevant to Pentecostal scholars working in other areas besides biblical studies. One such Pentecostal scholar in the area of theology whose efforts are informed by Heschel is Samuel Solivan, *Spirit, Pathos and Liberation: Toward an Hispanic Pentecostal Theology* (JPTSup 14; London: Continuum, 1999).

The End of Jonah

Biblical scholars and translators have long struggled with the oddness of the phrase found at the very end of the book of Jonah, וּבְהֵמָה רַבָּה (*webehemah rabbah*), 'and many cattle.' The King James Version represents this oddness well, as it follows closely the Hebrew word order. It renders the entire verse, which is God's concluding question to the prophet Jonah, with these words:

> And should not I spare Nineveh, that great city, wherein are more than sixscore thousand persons that cannot discern between their right hand and their left hand; and *also* much cattle? (4.11).

It is as if the entire story leads up to the final punch of this divine question, only to have the force of the punch undone by the appended reference to the Ninevites' livestock. The New International Version, avoids this by rendering a completely different grammatical structure and word order:

> But Nineveh has more than a hundred and twenty thousand people who cannot tell their right hand from their left, and many cattle as well. Should I not be concerned about that great city? (NIV).

Numerous commentators have tried their hand at explaining how the book of Jonah has come to end with such a curious bovine reference. Most follow the line that it merely points up Yahweh's concern as extending even to animals.[17] A contrast is seen in relation to Jonah's gourd. Although not on the level of humans, beasts are vastly more significant to God than the plant for which Jonah is concerned. A few other scholars have argued that the reference is intended as a concluding humorous twist, which links with other humorous elements in the book, such as the fish ordeal, the worm scene, and especially where the Ninevites cover even their cattle with sackcloth (3.8).[18] These explanations, though common, are not obvious and still fall short of any compelling reason for the concluding mention of Nineveh's many cattle.[19] I want to suggest that where *reason* is lacking, on the surface at least,

---

[17] See e.g. John Calvin, *Commentaries on the Twelve Minor Prophets,* vol. III (trans. John Owen; Grand Rapids, MI: Eerdmans, 1950), p. 144; Hans Walter Wolff, *Obadiah and Jonah* (Minneapolis, MN: Augsburg, 1986), p. 175; Leslie C. Allen, *The Books of Joel, Obadiah, Jonah and Micah* (NICOT; Grand Rapids, MN: Eerdmans, 1976), p. 234; James Limburg, *Hosea-Micah* (Interpretation Series; Atlanta, GA: John Knox, 1988), p. 157; Douglas Stuart, *Hosea-Jonah* (Word Biblical Commentary; Waco, TX: Word, 1987), p. 508; Terrence E. Fretheim, *The Message of Jonah* (Minneapolis, MN: Augsburg, 1977), p. 129.

[18] See Jack M. Sasson, *Jonah* (AncB; New York: Doubleday, 1990), p. 319, who mentions several others who offer various versions of this view.

[19] See Sasson, *Jonah,* p. 319, who admits that the reference is 'a seemingly incongruous afterthought'.

there might just be some *passion* beneath the surface that can account for Jonah's unusual ending.

In making my case, I would first of all point out how important passions are to the book of Jonah. This can be seen first in the depiction of the sailors. The words that introduce them to the story are, 'all the sailors were afraid and each cried out to his god' (1.5). It is understandable that these men would respond emotionally with their lives being threatened by the sea storm, but their passion seems to be highlighted, as they are contrasted in the very next verse to the sleeping Jonah's lack of urgent response. The captain asks him, 'How can you sleep? Get up and call upon your god!'

We see the passions of the sailors again in 1.10. This is right after we see Jonah being singled out as culprit by the casting of lots and then complying when the sailors ask him to identify himself. At this we are told, 'and the men were gripped with great fear, and they said, "What have you done?!"' This seems a bit over-reactive to Jonah's preceding answer, 'I am a Hebrew and I worship Yahweh, the God of heaven who made the sea and the land' (1.9). Indeed it is only *after* we are told that the sailors were terrified that we are filled in on what else they had heard from Jonah that had disturbed them so. As if to explain the terror reported at the beginning of v. 10, the rest of the verse informs us, 'the men knew he was running away from Yahweh, because he had told them'. By giving the reader this information only *after* the fact, the sailors' passion is highlighted. We see their passion even before we see the reason for it.

Feelings surge again for the sailors in 1.14 when the sea grows wilder and they are driven to the decision of accepting Jonah's proposal to be thrown overboard.

> Then they called unto Yahweh and said, 'O Yahweh, please do not let us be destroyed because of the life of this man. Don't put innocent blood upon us, for you, Yahweh, have done as you pleased' (1.14).

We reach the final scene with the sailors when the sea calms, but even here their emotions are stirred. Parallel to the first reference in 1.5, the final reference to the seamen tells us, '*the men were greatly afraid of Yahweh, and they offered sacrifices to Yahweh and made vows*' (1.16, emphasis mine).

It is striking, in view of this graphic portrayal of the sailors' terror at several points during this turbulent ship ride, that there is no reference at all here to any such emotion in Jonah. This, together with the mention of Jonah's needing to be roused from sleep in the middle of the storm, seems almost to make a statement about Jonah's lack of noticeable passion. At least the narrative at this stage is not noticing. When Jonah is thrown overboard, the narration's point-of-view does not immediately take us over the side of the ship with Jonah, but rather we are left on deck with the mariners to see their reaction to the calming of the waves (1.15-16). Then, when we move ahead in the next verse to see Jonah's outcome, we see none of the dramatic characterization for Jonah (in this most climactic moment of all!) that we saw for the sailors in the previous verses. Instead the narrative quells all such drama by the matter-of-fact assertion, 'and Yahweh appointed a great fish to swallow Jonah; and Jonah was in the belly of the fish three days and three nights' (1.17, Hebrew 2.1). We now know what is inside the fish, but we still do not know what is inside of Jonah!

Chapter 2, of course, finally draws a focus upon Jonah's reaction. We are told, 'then Jonah prayed to Yahweh, his God, from the belly of the fish' (2.1, Hebrew 2.2). There is no prefacing reference to Jonah's emotional state here, such as we were given for the sailors when their acts of prayer were reported in 1.5 and 1.16. Yet what is even more striking in this regard, I would suggest, is the form that Jonah's prayer takes in the verses that follow (2.2-9, Hebrew 2.3-11). A far cry from the spontaneous outbursts depicted for the seamen, Jonah's prayer is a highly formal and stylized expression, as scholarship has long noted.[20] It fails to reveal much of what Jonah himself is feeling, especially considering the kind of psalm that it is. For it is not so much a direct, much less urgent, address to God, as it is a second-level reflection upon an earlier act of prayer.[21]

> I called in my distress to Yahweh, and he answered me (2.2, Hebrew 2.3).

Such an opening does less to take us into the raw interior life of Jonah than it does to distance us from it. It is as if the distress is now over and composed reflection has taken its place. Accordingly we proceed to hear only what Jonah did, said, and experienced *in the past tense* (2.2-7, Hebrew 2.3-8), even what he will say to Yahweh *in the future* (2.9, Hebrew 2.10), without ever once hearing how Jonah *feels presently* about his immediate plight, even though he is still far from being out of the woods, so to speak.

Jonah's prayer in the midst of the fish (ch. 2) stands narratively in between the sailors' prayers that precede (in ch. 1) and the Ninevites' prayers that follow (in ch. 3). And just as the fomality of Jonah's psalm contrasts with the fervency of the sailors on the one side, it contrasts with the urgency of the Ninevites on the other.

---

[20] See this discussed in the review of Jonah scholarship by Brevard S. Childs, *Introduction to the Old Testament as Scripture* (Philadelphia, PA: Fortress Press, 1979), pp. 419-26.

[21] See Childs, *Introduction*, p. 423, where we find Childs's observation, 'the Hebrew text is unequivocal in its use of verbs of completed action in striking contrast to the Septuagint's attempt to remove this problem'.

The response of the Ninevites is shown to be swift, sweeping, and intense. Straightway upon hearing Jonah's succinctly reported message of judgment (3.4), we are told that 'the people of Nineveh believed God, proclaimed a fast, and put on sackcloth, from the greatest of them to the least' (3.5). In the next verse the *'greatest of them'* himself, the king of Nineveh, hears the message and immediately responds *in the same way*, donning sackcloth and proclaiming a fast (3.6-8). Ironically, and in a way that only accentuates the intensity of response, the royal call to fast is redundant by the time it is issued, for a call to fast has already gone forth from the people (3.5)![22] Thus we do not sense the following of a form but the transformation of a following. We see not the prayer of established liturgy (as Jonah's in ch. 2) but rather the cry of intense emergency[23] (as the sailors' in ch. 1). It is a cry, so we promptly learn, that moves God (3.10).[24]

The artistically crafted contrast we have traced up to this point between the *expression of passion,* in the case of the Gentiles, and the *suppression of passion,* in the case of Jonah, prepares us precisely for the focus of the final chapter. For here the book comes to a culminating and penetrating gaze upon what Jonah is feeling.

On the heels of God's reversal of his edict to destroy Nineveh, ch. 4 begins, 'But it displeased Jonah greatly, and he was angry' (4.1). What wind, storm, and gastric expulsion had failed to surface in the story, is at last evoked by God's act of clemency for the Ninevites. We finally see the passion of Jonah. Now Jonah prays again, but it is no longer stylized psalmody and second order reflection on petitions of the past, as in ch. 2. Now Jonah is shown praying in a way reminicent of the sailors and the Ninevites. His words erupt out of the particularity, immediacy, and passion of the moment. 'O Yahweh! Is not this what I said when I was still in my country?' (4.2a). This latter statement confirms the suspicions that the previous narrative depiction of Jonah has planted. Jonah's deep feelings have been kept from view. He now proceeds to reveal them.

---

[22] See the keen observations on the king's actions by Phyllis Trible, *Rhetorical Criticism: Context, Method, and the Book of Jonah* (Minneapolis, MN: Fortress Press, 1994), p. 185, 'authorization replaces spontaneity. . . the monarch who emulates his subjects decrees that they emulate him'.

[23] Note the reference in 3.8 to the cry which the king is calling for: 'Let them cry mightily' or 'with violence (בהזקה, *bekhazqa*)'.

[24] God moves after Jonah's prayer, as well, but it is perhaps not insignificant that there he does not directly respond to Jonah, but rather he 'speaks' (אמר, *amar*) to the fish (2.10)! Here in 3.10 he responds more directly to the praying Ninevites, observing (ראה, *ra'ah*) 'what they did'.

> For this reason I made haste to flee to Tarshish, because I knew that you are a gracious God, merciful, slow to anger, abundant in covenant love, and relenting when it comes to calamity (4.2b).

Jonah points behind his own passion to the passion of God. This familiar quote from Exodus (Ex. 34.6) is surely an important underlying theme for the whole book. While this classic faith statement acknowledges divine anger, which God's word of judgment against Nineveh had clearly conveyed,[25] it gives overriding emphasis to divine mercy, and this is what the story of Jonah so exceptionally illustrates, from the sparing of the endangered sailors to the rescue of Jonah and, especially, to the extraordinary pardon of a notoriously evil city.

Yet even though God's passion is the book's underlying theme, Jonah's passion, in the end, is the primary focus. The text zeroes in on this with Jonah's death wish in 4.3. 'So now, Yahweh, take my life from me, for it is better (טוב, *tov*) for me to die than to live'. This extreme point of prayer provides God the occasion to probe further into the feelings of this prophet. Playing off Jonah's own word, God asks him, 'Is it good (יטב, *yatav*) for you to be angry?' (4.4). The question clearly carries the connotation, 'Is there good reason for you to be angry?'[26]

No answer is given. The narrator earlier acknowledged Jonah's anger (4.1), but the prophet has not yet owned up to this emotion. Echoing the story's beginning, Jonah just leaves. Yet his divine interrogator, having now pressed in upon the deeper issue, follows his probe with pursuit. Jonah goes outside the city and covers himself with a shelter (4.5), and God moves in upon him and covers him with a plant (4.6). However, we quickly learn that it is only a set-up for the purpose of *uncovering – uncovering Jonah,* not just physically but emotionally. This becomes obvious through the way that the plant's rise and fall brings Jonah right back to the pathos of his prior statement to God ('It is better for me to die than to live', 4.8b) and thus right back to God's same emotion-probing question to him: 'Is there good reason for you to be angry, specifically over the plant?' (4.9a). 'Good enough to be angry, angry unto death!' (4.9b), comes Jonah's reply.

While Jonah's statement certainly brings us to an extreme expression and admission of his passion, God's final words to the prophet indicate that we have not yet gotten to the bottom of the reason *or the passion* of Jonah's anger. God pushes deeper, I would suggest, by coming from

---

[25] See the acknowledgment of this in the king's statement in 3.9: 'Who knows? God may repent and turn from *the burning of his nostrils.*'

[26] See BDB, p. 406, and various translations, e.g. NASB, NRSV, NIV.

a different angle.[27] Having just asked Jonah about his *anger* over the plant (4.9a), God ostensibly changes the subject to the issue of Jonah's *pity* for the plant (4.10). But has the subject really changed? God's words juxtapose the low merits of Jonah's feelings over the plant (4.10) with the high merits of God's own feelings for the city of Nineveh (4.11). In effect, God asks Jonah, 'Why shouldn't I have feelings for this great city?' with the obvious implication of: 'And why shouldn't you?' But then isn't it obvious that Jonah *does have feelings* for Nineveh, strong feelings, feelings that have been churning beneath the surface of the entire story from the beginning, although never once being explicitly acknowledged? Aren't these intense feelings precisely what God has taken aim at here in the last chapter by repeatedly quizzing Jonah about his anger? Jonah has admitted anger over the plant, but God has put his finger on the pity that lies hidden in the background.[28] Correspondingly, God has asked, why not pity for Nineveh? But doesn't this put the finger on the anger that surely lies hidden in the background?

Jonah has confessed his wish to die, but he hasn't yet confessed his desire to see Ninevites die (cf. 4.5). He has focused his anger on the compassion of God (4.2), but he hasn't yet expressed the deeper passion of his hatred for the Assyrians? And this, I would suggest, is what God's final question is aiming to provoke.

> Should not I have compassion upon Nineveh, the great city, in which there are more than a hundred and twenty thousand persons who cannot discern right from left, as well as numerous cattle? (4.11).

At the midpoint of Jonah's journey, God spoke to a fish to make it vomit. Here at the end he speaks to a prophet to make him spit out, to vomit, if you will, what has been lodged inside. And the final phrase, I would submit, far from being a frivolous addendum, is actually the very climax of the provocation. In drawing attention to the many cattle, is it for oxen that God is concerned? (cf. 1 Cor. 9.9). Notwithstanding the animal-rights-activist reading that would garner support in our day,[29] Jonah would scarcely have read Yahweh as valuing animals on par with people, but it is for certain that he would have been all too aware of an empire that treated people like animals, and valued both enough to send armies into their countries so that such 'valuables'

---

[27] Such is, of course, the same strategy God has used in moving from his direct question in 4.4 to his furtive actions in 4.6-8. Reason is committed to linear moves, but isn't it true that emotion characteristically answers to moves much more indirect?

[28] See Trible, *Rhetorical Criticism*, pp. 221-22, on how God's unveiling of Jonah's pity in 4.10 fits the pattern used elsewhere in the book of revealing information previously withheld (e.g. 4.2).

[29] Coming close to this is Trible, *Rhetorical Criticism*, p. 223: 'An ecology of theology embraces plant and animal, perhaps even a worm'.

could be confiscated and carried back to the great cities of the empire. We do not have to guess about this. It is engraved in stone. A quick glance at the Assyrian reliefs featured in James B. Pritchard's work, *The Ancient Near East in Pictures,*[30] can show us the plunderers' own snap-shots of their acts of deporting women and children, little ones who probably did not know their right from their left, *and also much cattle.* The concluding mention of Nineveh's many cattle, then, puts a sur-prising and piercing twist on God's final question, turning it from an incentive to pity into an incitement to rage.

God is not creating Jonah's anger. It has been there all along. God has insistently asked Jonah about it, but the prophet has been evasive. God is simply the *provocateur* who opens closed up passions.

The ultimate passion in the book of Jonah is pity. It comes at the end[31] because it *is* the end, the *telos* of Jonah. The book turns on God's move from wrath to pity,[32] but within this larger divine move we trace the journey of Jonah. When we get to the end of the book, Jonah has not yet reached God's destination. Jonah is stuck in his anger, stuck to the point that he proposes to make it *his end,* to be, in his words, 'an-gry unto death' (4.9b). Yet obviously God's pity includes Jonah, so God will not let it end there. Jonah is stuck in anger because anger is stuck in Jonah, and so out of pity God provokes.

This, then, is my proposal: that the end of Jonah points to the divine provocation and convergence of prophecy, prayer, and passion. In Pentecostal spirituality these have long been linked in the experience we have called 'praying through'. This is prayer that, not unlike the biblical laments, calls for pouring out all of our passions upon the altar

---

[30] The full title is *The Ancient Near East in Pictures Relating to the Old Testament* (2nd ed., Princeton, NJ: Princeton University Press, 1969). See p. 128. I gratefully acknowl-edge the help of my teaching assistant, Gregory Moder, in scouting out this reference and serving as a willing conversation partner while this work was in process. For biblical examples of the taking of cattle (בהמה, *behemah*) as military plunder, see Num. 31.9, 11; Josh. 8.2, 27.

[31] See Trible, *Rhetorical Criticism,* p. 221-23, for her compelling observations on how the narrative introduces the term *pity* (חוס, *khus*) in the last two verses. She points out that whereas the deliverance of Nineveh in ch. 3 is portrayed in terms of a *theology of repentance* (God repents when Nineveh repents, *quid pro quo*), the end of ch. 4 points beyond this to an unconditional *theology of pity.*

[32] Heschel, *Prophets,* II, p. 77, has some discerning comments on the larger biblical witness to this move: 'the pathos of anger is by no means regarded as an attribute, as a basic disposition, as a quality inherent in the nature of God. ... In both its origin and duration, anger is distinguished from mercy... The pathos of anger is a transient state. What is often proclaimed about love – "For the Lord is good, for His steadfast love en-dures for ever" (Jer. 33.11; Ps. 100.5; Ezra 3.11; I Chron. 16.34; II Chron. 5.13; 7.3) – is not said about anger... The normal and original pathos is love or mercy. Anger is pre-ceded as well as followed by compassion (Jer. 12.15; 33.26).'

of God. This is the experience and the tradition that Larry McQueen has identified and explicated in relation to his study of the book of Joel.[33] Here an ancient prophet and a contemporary Pentecostal come together in voicing 'the cry of a prophetic hermeneutic'.[34]

Jonah, unlike Joel, is not yet ready to cry. There are those times, especially for the victimized, when anger feels better than grief. Yet folks who know about 'praying through', praying through the *Sheols* of life and the private hatreds of our soul, know about a God who comes at us armed with questions. He wrestles with us and against us and for us through the night, and he does not relent until all of our passions are poured out before his relentless passions. No wonder the Psalms are so populated with laments, which are filled with complaints and even curses![35]

The relation of laments to psalms is very much to the point for the book of Jonah, which gives us the prophet's psalm (ch. 2) but ends up waiting for the lament that is not forthcoming,[36] at least not until we

---

[33] McQueen, *Joel and the Spirit,* pp. 76-82.

[34] McQueen, *Joel and the Spirit,* pp. 107-12.

[35] The vital function of the lament in relation to Psalms was first illuminated in modern scholarship by Claus Westermann, *Praise and Lament in the Psalms* (Atlanta, GA: John Knox Press, 1981), but some of the most insightful comment on that relation has come from Walter Brueggemann, *The Message of the Psalms* (Minneapolis, MN: Augsburg, 1984). Commenting on expressions of vengeance, which are found frequently in the Psalter, Brueggemann says, 'Psalmic prayer practices no cover-up. Real prayer is being open about the negativities and yielding them to God... What is clear is that they are never *yielded* unless they be fully *expressed*' (p. 66). Later, in reference to that most extreme expression of vengeance in Ps. 137, Brueggemann, with a question which would be fitting for Jonah, asks, 'Could it be that genuine forgiveness is possible only when there has been a genuine articulation of hatred?' (p. 77). A Pentecostal scholar who has recently stressed the importance of lament for church renewal is Michael K. Adams, 'Music that Makes Sense: Inclusiveness of the Lament May be the Key to Renewal in the Church', Paper Presented at the Twenty-third Annual Meeting of the Society for Pentecostal Studies, Guadalajara, Mexico, November 1993.

[36] Jonah, of course, initiates the lament form in his prayer in chapter 4 (see vv. 2-3; 9), but God's questions indicate that Jonah has stopped short of expressing his full lamentation, which, as I have argued, would entail the enunciation of hatred toward the Ninevites. Another bit of indirect evidence that Jonah has indeed been holding back this expression of hatred can be gleaned from Jonathan Magonet, *Form and Meaning: Studies in the Literary Techniques in the Book of Jonah* (Bible and Literature Series; Sheffield: Almond Press, 1983), pp. 44-47. He shows how Jonah's psalm in chap. 2 utilizes several quotations or partial quotations from the book of Psalms (e.g., Jon. 2.3a=Ps. 120.1; Jon. 2.4b=Ps.4.8b; Jon. 2.5a=Ps. 31.23; Jon. 2.7a=Ps. 142.4; Jon. 2.7b=Ps. 103.4), and among them there is the altered quotation of Ps. 31.7 in Jon. 2.9. Whereas the Psalmist here prays, 'I hate those who regard lying vanities', Jonah evades the expression of hatred altogether by praying, 'Those who regard lying vanities forsake their own mercy'. Magonet's explanation – that 'the speaker has come to a more tolerant, though still rather grudging view of idolaters' (p. 46) – is rather weak, but my view that Jonah is suppressing his wrathful passions fits the alteration of the quotation precisely!

come later to the prophet Nahum! Such lamentation carries us deeper into the pain, deeper than we may want to go, deeper until we must face the consuming passions of the One who meets us at the end of ourselves. Against such prospects we, like Jonah are ever inclined to flee toward spiritualities more cerebral and composed and toward hermeneutical methods more orderly and closed.

Yet the ending of Jonah is open, and it thereby *functions to open*. It denies closure not only to Jonah but also to the reader.[37] For what's a reader to do with a biblical book that ends like no other, with a question?[38]

[37] See the fine study by Walter B. Crouch, 'To Question an End, to End a Question: Opening the Closure of the Book of Jonah', *JSOT* 62 (1994), pp. 101-12, who astutely recognizes that 'the lack of closure at the end of the narrative is a literary device used to involve the reader' (p. 112).

[38] Jonah's ending is striking even alongside the other two biblical books that close with a question, Lamentations and Nahum, the latter of which, like Jonah, directly concerns Nineveh! Note the comment of Elie Wiesel, *Five Biblical Portraits* (Notre Dame, IN: University of Notre Dame Press, 1981), pp. 154-55: 'If indeed Jonah answered God's question, the answer has not been recorded. The book ends with God's word, which is only natural: God makes sure He has the last word, always. But, uniquely, the book ends on a question – and that is what leaves us astonished and deeply affected. How many other sacred and eternal, inspired and inspiring books are there in which the last sentence is neither affirmation nor injunction, nor even a statement, but quite simply, a question?' Wiesel's discerning insights, together with those of Heschel, which have been significant for me from the outset of this study, prompt me to underscore the profound connection that I continue to sense between Jewish approaches to interpretation and Pentecostal hermeneutical impulses. Yet I would finally mention the crucial role played by my own local Pentecostal community in my interpretive work. The origins of this paper, in fact, can be traced back to a rigorous, prayerful, and passionate study of Jonah that I shared with two students, Marcia Anderson and Joseph Perfidio, in a seminar at the Church of God Theological Seminary in Spring 1990. I gratefully acknowledge my students and colleagues, then and now, as among the richest sources for my research into the biblical text.

8

The Prophetic Path from Lament to Praise: Tracking the Burden of Habakkuk*

The entire corpus of the Hebrew prophets, not just Jeremiah, is extensively associated with lament (see e.g. Isa. 21; Joel 1; Mic. 1.8; Jon. 4). The prophets' lamentation largely corresponded with the disastrous downfall of their nation in the event known as the Exile. They wept because they faced the ending that their people refused to face. Their lamenting was mostly rejected by their people at the time as a breach of faith and hope for their nation. Yet significantly the prophets who led the way in lament became in the end the very ones who led their people beyond false hope and eventual despair to lasting praise. In so doing, the prophets of Israel played a pivotal role in discovering the integral relation of lament to praise – that lament is not, as is commonly assumed, a negation of praise, but it is ultimately the deep well from which the highest manifestation of praise springs forth.

The book of Habakkuk offers an especially clear and instructive example of the dynamic relation between lament and praise, tracking the prophet's move from the one to the other in the course of its three brief chapters.

Habakkuk's first chapter begins with a lament that is generalized to the point of functioning paradigmatically. The prophet is and for some time has been ('How long, O LORD?!' [1.2])[1] seeking divine help in the face of an outrage he has been witnessing among his people: 'destruction and violence ... the torah is ignored ... the wicked surround the righteous' (1.3-4). Ironically, Habakkuk is urgently presenting *to* the LORD a burden that the book's superscription has already intimated to be coming *from* the LORD (for the Hebrew term משא, *massa*, in 1.1 refers to a divinely given 'burden' or 'oracle'). Thus, God appears to be *the instigator of the lament*. Habakkuk comes close to this truth when he asks God in 1.3, 'Why do you make me see iniquity and cause me to look on wickedness?'

* First published in *The Living Pulpit* 11.4 (October–December 2002), pp. 26-27.
[1] In this study, translations from the Hebrew text are my own.

God promptly responds not by answering this question but by further provoking and intensifying it, indeed by proposing to make Habakkuk *see even more*, punctuating the point with two verbs of vision:
'*Look* among the nations ... (1.5); '*Behold*, I am raising up the Babylonians, that ruthless and impetuous nation that marches across the
earth...' (1.6). God then elaborates in 1.7-11 on the point that these
Babylonians 'all come for *violence*' (1.9), the featured term of Habakkuk's prior lament (cf. 1.2, 3) now expanded on the vast scale of Babylonian conquest. The cry for God to act against the parochial violence
within Israel is now answered with the announcement that God would
do so by sending imperial violence from beyond Israel. Obviously
there is now more to cry about than Habakkuk had seen. Thus God
shows himself here to be *the intensifier of the lament*.

And sure enough, Habakkuk resumes his lamentation to God with a
new and urgent focus in the light of God's radical and unexpected
response concerning the Babylonians. Granting that 'you, O LORD,
have appointed them to judge' (1.12), the prophet shifts the focal point
from what his eyes have been made to see to what God's eyes see:

> Eyes too pure to countenance evil,
> and to look on at oppression you are not able.
> Why then do you look on at those acting treacherously
> and keep silent when the wicked swallow up those more righteous
> than they?' (1.13).

In one sense this is the same question as before: Why is God not
stopping the wicked from harming, oppressing, and terrorizing others?
This is a universal lament that lurks in every one of us at one time or
another, from home life all the way to the level of international affairs.
However, God's response has pushed against Habakkuk's initial posing
of this question in such a way as to provoke some decisive differences
in the prophet's perspective and posture in this second posing of the
question. Specifically, we see the question introduced this second time,
not with testy complaint as before (cf. 1.2), but with a sense of reverence, the first signs of praise: 'Are you not from everlasting, O LORD,
my God, my Holy One? We shall not die' (1.12a). One can see in this
comment a different attitude not only toward God but also toward the
people of Israel – the national division of us versus them (righ-
teous/wicked), registered earlier, is now replaced with the 'we' of soli-
darity and advocacy.[2] Now that the whole nation is threatened,
Habakkuk can view his people altogether as 'those more righteous'
than the 'wicked' Babylonians (1.13). God's intervention has brought

---

[2] It is a bit like the coming together of America's Republicans and Democrats in the
immediate aftermath of 9-11.

about new discriminations and delineations of moral terms and social lines that redefine those that first ignited the lament.

Another decisive change in Habakkuk can be seen at the conclusion of his second round of lament. The prophet announces in 2.1, 'I will stand on my watchtower and station myself on the rampart; I will look to see what he will say to me'. At the beginning, Habakkuk had seen enough and had just about 'had enough' of waiting ('How long, O LORD?!'), but now he is ready and determined to watch and wait until God responds with an answer to his intensified question. Ironically and perhaps suggestive of his shaken perspective on God, Habakkuk stages his wait for God on the watchtower, the place from which one would watch for an approaching enemy! The lamenter, who has been moved to see others and himself differently, has now been opened to seeing God in a new way too. Could this be precisely the point of it all?

God's reply comes in the next verse (2.2); we do not have to wait for it. It entails commands to Habakkuk to record a vision that relates to an 'appointed time and hastens to the end' (2.2-3a). The prophet must wait for this, though God assures him that it will not delay (2.3b). Ironically, we the readers are not told at this point what, in fact, the vision is; the book makes us wait for this!

Although we are not here given the content of Habakkuk's vision, in the next verse we are invited to see what appears to Habakkuk in the light of this vision: 'Behold, the arrogant, his desire is not upright within him; but the righteous by his faithfulness will live' (2.4). This most famous verse of Habakkuk announces the way to wellbeing for those who had been of prime concern in the prophet's prior lamenta-tion – 'the righteous'. The way is defined here in terms of 'faithful-ness', one of the most important covenant virtues required for waiting upon, even lamenting one's way to, the vision of God.

Almost all of the rest of ch. 2 defines the alternate way of the arro-gant (2.5-19), largely cast in terms of what their victims will eventually say about them. Yet the last verse of the chapter calls for 'all the earth' to keep silence before the LORD who is in his holy temple (2.20). All human divisions, even those between conquerors and their victims, are finally muted in the face of a holy God.

This brings us to the third and final chapter, which is none other than a description of a revelation of *the face of God*, a *theophany*. This would seem to be the very vision that Habakkuk had been told to write down (cf. 2.2). The prophet sees the glory of the coming of the LORD. Beyond Habakkuk's plea to see the coming of national justice and beyond God's initial response to make him see the coming of the Babylonians, the prophet has been brought to the point of seeing an invasion much more decisive, terrifying, and ultimate: nothing less and nothing more (what could be more!) than *the coming of God*. It is enough to eclipse fear of Babylonians with the confession, 'O LORD, I heed your report; I am afraid' (3.2a). It is enough to eclipse the demand for justice with the plea for mercy, 'in wrath remember mercy' (3.2b). In fact the prophet sees that it is enough to eclipse all of creation (3.3-11) as well as human history (3.12-15) – a total eclipse. Indeed it is total to the point of bringing the prophet to awareness and confession of his own end: 'I heeded and my belly trembled; at the noise my lips quivered, rottenness enters into my bones and my steps totter beneath me' (3.16a). It is as if the prophet reaches the final step, the end of the trail, the end of the prophet.

However, the prophet comes to this final step, the end of himself, only to discover 'the LORD God is my strength; he makes my feet like deer's feet and makes me walk on my lofty hills' (3.19). Freshly revealed to his faithful lamenter, *God is the end of the lament*. Indeed, his self-revelation is the lament's *telos* and termination, as lament at last is replaced by praise: 'Though the fig tree may not bloom, nor fruit be on the vines, ... yet I will rejoice in the LORD. I will joy in the God of my salvation' (3.18).

Thus, the lament over oppressive life conditions, instigated and then intensified by God himself, becomes the course that, when followed with tenacious faithfulness to the end, indeed the end of ourselves, leads us to the revelation of God as the true end, highest joy and lasting praise of our life.

In this way, Habakkuk presents a prophet's succinct and self-revealing prayer journal that poignantly tracks the path from lament to praise. This path marked by Habakkuk may offer to us an important *re*course to the weary *dis*course in which we have gotten stuck in the face of the injustices and terror of our own day and time – a discourse of self-buttressing criticism that stagnates us in a de-sacralized zone that never plumbs as low as lament or reaches as high as praise. It is a zone that does not risk either the deeper criticisms to which solemn lament might lead us or the breath-taking implications that can appear when our 'eyes have seen the glory of the coming of the LORD'. When, since Martin Luther King Jr. or Abraham Lincoln, have we heard in our public discourse the solemn and risky use of this biblically and prophetically rooted language. Yet it is perhaps time to ask, will anything less than this language prove to be a match for our own situation in the end?

9

Futile Labor versus Fertile Labor:
Observing the Sabbath in Psalm 127[*]

The short psalm ascribed to Solomon in the 127th division of the Psalter offers a suggestive, if indirect, resource for observing the import of the Sabbath.

> Unless the LORD builds the house,
>   those who build it labor in vain.
> Unless the LORD watches over the city,
>   the watchman stays awake in vain.
> It is vain that you rise early and go late to rest,
>   eating the bread of anxious toil (vv. 1-2a, RSV)

The psalm begins with the subject of house building (v. 1a), then moves on to the matter of guarding what has been built (v. 1b), before arriving at a pointed statement that shifts address to the reader in asserting the vanity or futility of human toil (v. 2a). Building, toil, vanity – all are terms which certainly accord with the ascription to Solomon, reminding us of another portion of Hebrew Scripture associated with this regal high-achiever. Ecclesiastes' emphasis on the vanity of human toil, together with its subdued but persistent undercurrent of exhorting the enjoyment of one's present portion of life, have prompted some to see this heavy book, in the end, as making a rather strong, if indirect, argument for the merits of a Sabbath-oriented life.[1]

But where is the Sabbath in this psalm? It comes in the simple and certain acknowledgment at the end of v. 2:

> For He grants sleep to those He loves (v. 2b).

This statement is a rejoinder to the preceding conclusion about the futility of, as we call it, 'burning the candle at both ends'. When it comes to building projects, our conventional wisdom says, 'Work,

---

[*] First published in *The Living Pulpit* 7.2 (April–June 1998), pp. 24-25.
[1] See Robert K. Johnston, 'Confessions of a Workaholic: A Reappraisal of Qoheleth', *CBQ* 38 (January 1976), pp. 14-28.

work, work!' But this poem counters our anxious obsession for work with God's gift of rest. It is a gracious rebuke of our workaholism.

We put stock in our efforts and our initiatives as if our lives depended upon them, only to learn too late, perhaps like Solomon, that real life comes as a gift from a loving source. Life isn't made 'the old-fashioned way', as the investment firm's advertisement claims, 'because we earned it'. God's Sabbath calls our work to a halt in order to give us a chance to remember and to observe whence our life really and truly comes. Since God is the source, his portion of rest yields more than all of our toil.

The last half of the psalm, which has often been accused of changing the subject, actually serves to elaborate what the Sabbath-receiving life of the LORD produces.

> Children are a heritage from the LORD,
>   the fruit of the womb a reward (v. 3).

These are the beneficent terms of God's labor contract: in the place of vain labor, we are offered labor that brings forth children. Sons and daughters, far from representing a change of subject, constitute *the very house* that the LORD sets out to build. Just as we are prone to think *toil* when it comes to the activity of building, we are inclined to think of *a building* when it comes to the matter of a 'house'. But this poem again subverts our vain inclinations. For the house that the LORD is involved in building does not consist of bricks or lumber, but rather and precisely of sons and daughters. That's the kind of house that the LORD had in mind when He promised Solomon's father, David, 'I will build a house for you' (2 Sam. 7.11). How deeply the worldview of this psalm makes this connection can be seen in the fact that the Hebrew words for 'build' (בנה, *banah*), 'house' (בית, *bayith*), 'daughters' (בנות, *banoth*), and 'sons' (בנים, *banim*), all come from the same Hebrew root (בנה, *bnh*)! This psalm ingeniously works (or plays!) with words from the same root family in order to display *family* as the *supreme fruit of all work*.

The psalm has another important connection to make. In reference to guarding the city, the other human endeavor initially lifted up for consideration, the poem finally wants to insist that having children – not military strategy, not security systems, not insurance policies – *having children* is ultimately our best protection against the life threats that we so fear. Just as this psalm offers *rest* as the surprising answer to the futility of our self-grounded efforts at construction, it proposes *having children* as the surprising alternative to our vain efforts to secure and sustain ourselves.

In contrast to the unfortunate one who trusts in the 'watchman (who) stands guard in vain' (v. 1b) is the 'blessed one' whose house and years are filled with children.

> Like arrows in the hands of a warrior
>   are children born in one's youth.
> Blessed is the one whose quiver is full of them.
> They will not be put to shame
>   when they contend with their enemies in the gate (vv. 4-5).

The threat of a cursed life of vanity, which is introduced in the first verse of the psalm, is at last answered in the final verse by the promise of a blessed life. The blessed life, here, finally consists in nothing other than the plenitude of one's children, and what's more, the blessedness is secured and protected by nothing other than the children themselves!

It might seem odd that such wisdom, as this psalm offers, would be ascribed to Solomon. After all, this king is known for an excessive, not to mention oppressive, building program that led to a broken kingdom (if you follow 1 Kings) and to an epithet of utter futility (if you follow Ecclesiastes). Moreover, Solomon is known for perverting the blessing of procreation, through his presumptuous indulgence with a thousand women.

Conversely, this wisdom may suit Solomon a lot better than it suits us. For we live in a society that conditions us to take nothing as seriously as our work. Our *doing* is our *ground of being*. Our language, no less than the Hebrews' as noted ealier, reveals our worldview in this regard. And so when people ask, 'What do you do?' or 'What are you?' we tell them about our work. And as regards children, we are conditioned to experience them as dependants, minors (!) who depend upon our livelihood, more often than as blessings upon which our very life depends. Children who grow up as burdens rather than as blessings inherit the burden of their progenitors: they must 'make something of themselves'; they must *do* something significant if they are ever to *be* anything significant. So human *doings* become the source *and the end* of human *beings*. Human beings are left to become mere means. No wonder our Western society has developed such an aggressive work ethic and has worked its way to such amazing and efficient methods of, among other things, preventing conception and procreation. When the means (our children) impede our end (our work) we work out a way to stop them. But *nothing* remains to justify stopping our work.

Thus, we construct a world without Sabbath and (increasingly) without children, God's two holy witnesses against the vanity of our doing and the emptiness of our being. It is a world about which this psalm and Ecclesiastes both warn us, a world whose final epithet has already been written:

> Unless the LORD builds the world,
> Then for its builders, all is vanity.

Against this curse, Psalm 127 offers a blessed hope – one that would hopefully uplift us in the prospect that our final epithet, unlike Solomon's, has not yet been written.

A Home for the Alien: Worldly Wisdom and Covenantal Confession in Proverbs 30.1-9[*]

The passage introduced as 'the words of Agur,' found near the end of the book of Proverbs (30.1-9), is a strange text. Recent scholarly treatment of this passage has led to readings as different in their grasp of a single text as one could probably find anywhere in biblical interpretation. In an important article, which appeared in 1983, Paul Franklyn aptly characterized the debate on the Agur text in terms of two basic views, which see the passage as featuring either an uninterrupted confession of *piety* or a startling expression of theological *skepticism*.[1] This latter view, which was made prominent by R.B.Y. Scott, involves displacing the difficult MT reading of Agur's opening words with a reading which yields an outrageous theological negation unparalleled elsewhere in the canon, 'There is no God, there is no God, and I am powerless.'[2] Notwithstanding that this translation depends upon re-rendering this line alone as Aramaic or else emending the Hebrew with no less than five consonantal changes,[3] this view has attracted support from such prominent scholars of biblical wisdom as William McKane and James Crenshaw.[4]

---

[*] First published in *Zeitschrift für die alttestamentliche Wissenschaft* 106 (1994), pp. 96-107.

[1] Paul Franklyn, 'The Sayings of Agur in Proverbs 30: Piety or Skepticism?' *ZAW* 95 (1983), pp. 238-52.

[2] R.Y.B. Scott, *Proverbs, Ecclesiastes* (AncB; Garden City, NY: Doubleday, 1965), p. 176. Franklyn, 'Sayings of Agur,' p. 238, traces the view from E.J. Dillon, *The Skeptics of the Old Testament* (London: Ibister, 1895), p. 137.

[3] Scott retreated to this option in a later treatment (*The Way of Wisdom in the Old Testament* [New York: Macmillan, 1971], p. 168), conceding the unlikelihood of a single Aramaic phrase in an otherwise Hebrew text.

[4] McKane, *Proverbs: A New Approach* (OTL; Philadelphia, PA: Westminster, 1970), pp. 645-47; Crenshaw, *Old Testament Wisdom: An Introduction* (Atlanta: John Knox, 1981), p. 176; and more recently 'Clanging Symbols,' in *Justice and the Holy: Essays in Honor of Walter Harrelson*, edited by Douglas A. Knight and Peter J. Paris (Atlanta, GA: Scholars Press, 1989), pp. 51-64. It should be noted that Crenshaw here makes a case for viewing the Agur passage as extending

Against what has become a growing scholarly trend to so read the words of Agur as confessions of an atheist or skeptic that end abruptly at v. 3 or 4 and which are then followed in vv. 5-9 with some rather bland counterpoints by a pious editor, Franklyn has offered a meticulous analysis that defends the more traditional interpretation. While Franklyn's viewing of the entire passage in terms of a single orthodox expression is admittedly not new,[5] his effort represents a significant counter current to the more skeptical historical-critical trend, offering a fresh and credible case for reading the words of Agur as a coherent, orthodox confession of faith that discloses some profound and previously overlooked connections to Israelite belief.

I propose in this paper to build upon Franklyn's interpretation of the Agur text, reinforcing his insights on the internal workings of the passage with some broader contextual considerations, which not only support the more traditional reading but also point up its profound theological implications for the book of Proverbs and the Hebrew canon. I will first summarize Franklyn's treatment before offering my own.

In brief, Franklyn argues that the 'best and least damaging textual and grammatical decisions' for the Agur passage make possible a coherent reading of 'beautiful structural symmetry.' He sees an opening confession and a closing prayer surrounding a pair of quotations, which all converge upon the context of a humble man, near death, approaching his final covenantal oath before Yahweh. Franklyn points out how the initial confession, the concluding prayer, and the intervening quotations all begin with recognition of human ignorance and inadequacy and move toward concern for proper acknowledgement of God.

A key thread that seems to run through and open up this interpretation is the recognition of a striking confluence of sapiential and prophetic traditions. This begins in the superscription with the appearance of the words המשא (hamassa), 'the oracle,' and נאם (ne'um), 'declared,' both standard references to prophetic utterance and yet here attributed to man, הגבר (hageber), rather than, as normal, to Yahweh. Franklyn notes that נאם is so used in reference to humans only two other times in the Old Testament: in Numbers 24 in reference to Baalam's oracle and in 2 Samuel 23 in reference to David's last words, a non-coincidental parallel, one might suggest, to Agur's last words here. Most all commentators note the sapiential kinship between Agur's

through v. 14. See also Dermot Cox, *Proverbs* (Old Testament Message, 17; Wilmington, DE: Michael Glazier, 1982), pp. 237-43.

[5] Franklyn cites C.T. Fritsch, *The Book of Proverbs* (IB 4; Nashville, TN: Abingdon, 1955), pp. 946-49, as the last scholar before him explicitly to support this view.

rhetorical questions in verse 4 and God's rhetorical questions in Job 38, but Franklyn's article shows their form-critical relationship to the creation hymns in the prophecy of Amos (4.13; 5.8; 9.6). The correspondence between Agur's climactic question, 'What is his name?' and Amos' hymnic refrain, 'Yahweh of hosts is his name!' is noteworthy, especially if Crenshaw is right in his dissertation thesis that this refrain's setting concerns the determent to false oaths.[6] Franklyn argues that the concern to discourage false oaths is what motivated Agur not only in his concluding prayer in vv. 7-9, but also in his use in vv. 5 and 6 of a composite quotation from David's victory song in 2 Sam. 22.31 and Moses' sermon in Deut. 4.2, texts that respectively commend and exhort Israelites to acknowledge their God faithfully.

To build on Franklyn's observations, the fact that the 2 Samuel text borders on and is literarily linked[7] to the canonical presentation of David's last words, encountered earlier, while the Deuteronomy quotation comes from the canonical presentation of Moses' last words, may be even more determinative of Agur's agenda in choosing these texts than their topical connection to determent from false oaths. I would suggest moreover that Agur's use here of two quotations that are drawn directly from Israel's prophetic/covenantal canon and tradition, in distinction from the wisdom tradition in which Agur's entire expression finds its canonical placement, may have additional and decisive significance. In fact, I would even venture to suggest that this might have substantial import for the canonical placement of Agur's utterance near the end of the book of Proverbs, with suggestive implications for how wisdom was intended to be situated in Israel's canon.

Before moving to these wider implications, I should first set the stage with my own expository grasp of the given passage, building upon Franklyn's ably argued reading. I am aware, of course, that in the years since Franklyn's article appeared, the ground of interpretation in biblical studies has shifted dramatically from the text to the interpreter. One speaks now of readings instead of exegesis. Thus, Crenshaw's recent treatment of the Agur passage, though maintaining his earlier 'skeptical' view, is offered as one reading alongside others, where con-

---

[6] Crenshaw, *Hymnic Affirmation to Divine Justice: The Doxologies of Amos and Related Texts in the Old Testament* (SBLDS 24; Missoula, MT: Scholars Press, 1975), pp. 75-101.

[7] First to notice this linkage was Karl Budde, *Die Bücher Samuel* (Tübingen: J.C.B. Mohr, 1902), p. 304. Some additional and more refined judgments on the close redactional and literary linkage of David's song in 1 Sam 22 and his last words in 23.1-7 have been presented by R.A. Carlson, *David the Chosen King* (Stockholm: Almqvist & Wiksell, 1964), pp. 228-47.

sensus is neither expected nor pursued.[8] In this environment there is no longer an authoritative 'skeptical' interpretation of the Agur text to attempt to challenge,[9] unless one is prepared to challenge what might be regarded as the skeptical nature of interpretation itself, as it is now so widely being understood. I would only say here that the Agur passage would strike me as the worst place in the Hebrew Bible from which to launch such a challenge. Consider the infamous introductory phrase:

> To Ithiel, to Ithiel and Ucal (as pointed by MT).

or

> I am weary, O God; I am weary, O God, and I am spent (following NRSV, margin, or NEB).

The plethora of possible readings met when studying just this first verse alone[10] should be enough to lead any interpreter to the point of identifying and agreeing with Agur upon reaching the second verse:

> Surely I am too stupid to be human;
> > I do not have human understanding.
> I have not learned wisdom,
> > nor have I knowledge of the Holy One (NRSV, margin).

If this confession does not implicate all human interpretation, I think it would nevertheless serve well to preface my own reading of Prov. 30.1-9.

Agur, of whom scholars suspect a foreign identity (Patrick Skehan translates Agur, 'I am a sojourner' from the root גור, *gur*),[11] approaches the end of his life with the reverent desire to declare honestly the essence of his faith. As just noted, Agur begins with a confession of ignorance on the order of what we find in Ps. 73.22 ('I was stupid and ignorant; I was like a brute beast toward you'). He culminates this

---

[8] Crenshaw, 'Clanging Symbols,' p. 52.

[9] Perhaps we see something of this perspective already in Brevard S. Childs' comment on the Agur passage in his *Introduction to the Old Testament as Scripture* (Philadelphia: Fortress, 1979, p. 556: '[Agur] inquires after God's name, but despairs of learning because of God's hidden nature. Verses 5 and 6 offer an answer to this oracle – whether original or redactional is irrelevant in terms of the effect.'

[10] For a summary of proposals see Franklyn, 'Sayings of Agur', pp. 239-44; and McKane, *Proverbs*, pp. 643-46, who calls the difficulties in elucidation 'insuperable'.

[11] Skehan, *Studies in Israelite Poetry and Wisdom* (CBQMS 1; Washington DC: Catholic Biblical Association, 1971), p. 42. See also Crenshaw, 'Clanging Symbols,' p. 53.

confession in a couplet of intriguing ambiguity. The first line reads clearly, 'I have not learned wisdom (חכמה, *hokmah*).' The second line, with inverted parallel word order, could be read, 'and knowledge of the Holy One I do not know,' assuming the carry-over of the negative of the first line, or it could be read, 'but knowledge of the Holy One I shall know', seeing disjunction in the switch from the perfect tense in the first line to the imperfect in the second. In other words, Agur seems either to be saying, 'In myself I cannot claim wisdom and/or knowledge of the Holy One', or to be saying, 'I shall have knowledge of the Holy One, but not through the pursuit of wisdom.' A third possibility is that the ambiguity is at this point intended, and I would offer a way to capture it with an English infinitive:

> I have not learned wisdom,
> > knowledge of the Holy One to know (v. 3).

At any rate, knowledge of the Holy One seems to be the crucial issue, and for Agur, wisdom (הכמה, *hokmah*) does not hold an answer.
This point is pressed in the flurry of rhetorical questions that follow.

> Who has ascended to heaven and come down?
> Who has gathered the wind in the hollow of the hand?
> Who has wrapped up the waters in a garment?
> Who has established all the ends of the earth? (v. 4ab)

Agur thus turns first to the universal terms of the wisdom tradition, with which he, if a foreigner, would have been natively conversant, asking for wisdom's empirical, creation-oriented modes of knowledge to yield vital information about God. Agur culminates this series of questions with,

> What is his name or his son's name?
> > Surely you know! (v. 4c)

As in the book of Job when God chides out similar questions, there is here no answer. Is such knowledge too wonderful for this epistemology? A flurry of questions evokes no human words. However, in the absence of words of worldly wisdom there next appears a canonical quotation which concerns the word of God.

> Every word of God proves true;
> > he is a shield to those who take refuge in him (v. 5).

This verse does not offer the facile response one might expect, viz. 'Yahweh' or 'Yahweh is his name.'[12] In fact, the quotation's one pro-

---

[12] See Crenshaw, 'Clanging Symbols', p. 57, who acknowledges how the text here counters our expectations in not mentioning the divine name, though he offers an explanation different from my own. It is noteworthy that verse 5 alters

nounced alteration of the 2 Samuel text is the substitution of 'Eloah' (word of God) for 'Yahweh'. This would indicate that the quotation here is very conscious of the facile answer. However, the quote is being appropriated here, it would seem, in order to respond to the preceding comments in a deeper way, in a way that addresses not only the identification question, 'Who?,' but also the epistemological question which underlies it: 'How is the knowledge of the Holy One to be gained?' (cf. v. 3). In this light the appropriateness of this quotation from David's song (2 Sam. 22.31) comes into view. God's revelation ('*Every word of God*') yields what wisdom investigation by itself could not, viz. the identification of God, 'Eloah': 'He is a shield'. Whereas הכמה (*hokmah*) had no answer, an answer is now seen to be forthcoming from the word of God. What human investigation could not find, God's revelation makes manifest. We see here a decisive shift from wisdom tradition to covenantal canon, from investigation of nature to revelation in history, from looking for an abstract word, a conceptual knowledge, to testifying of an event-word (cf. דבר, *davar*), a relational/covenantal knowledge (cf. ידע, *yada*).[13] Vital truth is seen finally to be a matter not of human search but divine disclosure. Yet it is nevertheless disclosure that demands something. It is accessible only 'to those who take refuge' in God.

The next verse pushes the demands of this knowledge a step further. Agur follows David's divine word of promise concerning God's revelation with a divine word of prohibition from Moses,

> Do not add to his words (v. 6a),

to which Agur appends,

the wording of 2 Sam. 22.31 (=Ps 18.31) from 'Every word of Yahweh (יהוה, *Yahweh*)' to 'Every word of God (אלוה, *Eloah*)', avoiding the Tetragrammaton, as if to delay use of this more explicit identification until it finally appears in v. 9. The effect is to make a less abrupt transition from international wisdom categories to the categories of the Yahwistic covenantal tradition.

[13] For insight into Israel's covenantal concepts of revelation and knowledge, see Hans Walter Wolff, 'Wissen um Gott: bei Hosea als Urform von Theologie', *EvTh* 12 (1952/53), pp. 533-54; and his comment in his *Hosea: A Commentary on the Book of the Prophet Hosea* (Hermeneia; trans. Gary Stansell; Philadelphia, PA: Fortress, 1974), p. 79: 'The content of the knowledge of God in Hosea, in addition to divine law, is the basic deeds of salvation performed by Yahweh.' See also my study on 'Canon and Charisma in the Book of Deuteronomy,' presented in Chapter 2 of this volume; and Walter Brueggemann, 'The Epistemological Crisis of Israel's Two Histories (Jer 9.22-23)', in: *Israelite Wisdom: Festschrift for Samuel Terrien*, ed. John G. Gammie *et al.*, (Missoula, MT: Scholars Press, 1973), pp. 85-105, who traces the theme of the 'knowledge of God' through Jeremiah.

lest he rebuke you and you be proven a liar (v. 6b).

The statement's effect here, in the context of Agur's just having challenged the sufficiency of human wisdom, is to prohibit any move to
treat God's word as insufficient. God's word does not need to be com-
pensated by human wisdom. Moreover, in contrast to an empirical
epistemology that is accustomed to proving everything else, it seems as
if Agur wants to emphasize that it is *our word* and not God's that finally
must be proven.

Agur's final prayer reflects his own sense of vulnerability before the
prospect of divine proving. He goes beyond acknowledgment that he
is dependent upon God for the divine word. He confesses dependence
upon God for his own human words of faith as well.

> Two things I ask of you;
> > do not deny them to me before I die:
> Remove far from me falsehood and lying;
> > give me neither poverty nor riches;
> > feed me with the food that I need,
> or I shall be full and deny you,
> > and say, 'Who is Yahweh?'
> or I shall be poor, and steal,
> > and profane the name of my God (vv. 7-9).

In this prayer Agur finally comes to utter the divine name itself,
Yahweh, the confession which was earlier called for, the knowledge
which wisdom could not deliver. One final reference to God con-
summates Agur's covenant prayer, perhaps the quintessential covenantal address, 'my God'. Yet it is especially remarkable how this prayer
joins such 'heavenly' references to a down-to-earth, one might even
say an empirically oriented, realism. Divine intervention is balanced
with human responsibility here in a way that takes the empirical conditions of human life seriously. Whereas Agur earlier saw wisdom's need
to defer to covenantal revelation in answering life's ultimate questions,
this concluding prayer nevertheless shows that he continues to depend
upon the practical insights of wisdom in facing the prospects of everyday life.

In light of the foregoing reading, it would seem to be appropriate to
consider the implications that this reading of the Agur text has for the
book of Proverbs and even the larger canon. Brevard Childs has drawn
special attention to this text in discussing the canonical shape of the
book of Proverbs.[14] However, in contrast to what I have offered,
Childs sees the Agur text as intending not to set divine revelation over

---

[14] Childs, *Introduction*, pp. 556-57.

against human wisdom, but rather as functioning to *identify* wisdom *as* words from God. He says of the passage,

> It registers the point that the proverbs which originally derived from man's reflection on human experience of the world and society had become understood as divine words to man which functioned as sacred scripture along with the rest of Israel's received traditions.[15]

In this light, the Agur text only reinforces Childs's view of the canonical shaping that he derives from the superscription of Proverbs. By contextualizing the entire book under the reference, 'Solomon, son of David, king of Israel,' the canon, Childs argues, has presented Proverbs in terms of 'the "official" record of Solomon's place within Israel', which emphasizes his role in representing international wisdom (1 Kgs 3–10), not 'the sacred historical tradition of Israel'.[16] Thus Childs concludes,

> The superscription thus guards against forcing the proverbs into a context foreign to wisdom such as the Decalogue, which is the traditional theological move…The title serves canonically to preserve the uniqueness of the sapiential witness against the attempts to merge it with more dominant biblical themes.[17]

However, Childs's view of canonical shaping in Proverbs seems vulnerable at both ends of the book. As relates to the beginning of the book, what Childs takes to be 'the "official" record of Solomon's place within Israel', which he finds suggested in the superscription, cannot be extricated from the Deuteronomistic judgment on Solomon, which finally measures Solomon's wisdom against the claims of the covenantal tradition, as Walter Brueggemann and P. Kyle McCarter Jr. have recently pointed out.[18] As McCarter puts it, 'The tradition of royal wisdom has not been suppressed [in the Deuteronomistic History], but it is not shown to lead automatically to good results. The benefits of Solomon's wisdom avail him nothing in the end.'[19] In Brueggemann's words, 'Solomonic wisdom is characterized in ironic ways to show that it did not work.'[20] Shouldn't this too be seen as part of what Childs

---

[15] Childs, *Introduction*, p. 556.

[16] Childs, *Introduction*, p. 552

[17] Childs, *Introduction*, p. 552.

[18] Brueggemann, 'The Social Significance of Solomon as a Patron of Wisdom', in *The Sage in Israel and the Ancient Near East*, ed. John G. Gammie and Leo G. Perdue (Winona Lake, IN: Eisenbraun's, 1990), pp. 117-32; and McCarter, 'The Sage in the Deuteronomistic History,' in *The Sage in Israel*, pp. 289-93.

[19] McCarter, 'The Sage', p. 293.

[20] Brueggemann, 'Social Significance of Solomon', p. 128.

calls the 'official' record that stands behind the superscription of Proverbs? Consider how much differently Proverbs' superscription would register if it were to present the name of Hezekiah and not Solomon.

As relates to the end of the book of Proverbs, I am not the first to see canonical shaping differently than Childs. Recently Claudia Camp has argued impressively that the book's concluding poem on the woman of worth (31.10-31) combines with the introductory poems on Woman Wisdom in Prov. 1–9 to give the proverbs collection, that is, chs. 10–30, a new literary and thematic framework governed by female imagery.[21] Camp argues that this canonical shaping reflects the early post-exilic period when the authority structures and revelational locus of community life shifted to the province of the family, where 'Wisdom built up her house' (9.1), after the demise of royal authority structures and before Scripture took its eventual place as revelational norm.[22] Thus, in contrast to Childs' view of the definitive Solomonic cast of Proverbs, Camp seems to see the canonical framework of Proverbs pushing beyond the *royal* paradigm of wisdom to the point of standing in some tension with it. She concludes,

> Even if the book were used in an extra-familial instructional setting in the post-exilic period, those instructors had as one of their explicit goals the inculcation of family values as the basis for a workable social organization. This goal has taken complete precedence in the final composition over whatever diplomatic training for which the book may previously have been used, even though traces of the latter still remain.[23]

Like Camp, I am also suggesting that the end of the book of Proverbs yields evidence of canonical framing that offers a kind of critical recontextualization of the Solomonic tradition. However, I am suggesting this in relation to the Agur passage, which Camp's thesis largely overlooks or lumps together with the proverb collection of chs. 10–29.[24] I do not see how the Agur text can be easily ignored as a framing

---

[21] Camp, *Wisdom and the Feminine in the Book of Proverbs* (Bible and Literature Series; Sheffield: Almond/JSOT Press, 1985). A more modest thesis in the same vein, appearing the same year, is that of Thomas P. McCreesh, 'Wisdom as Wife: Proverbs 31.10-31', *RB* 92 (1985), pp. 25-46.

[22] Camp, *Wisdom and the Feminine*, pp. 233-54.

[23] Camp, *Wisdom and the Feminine*, pp. 251-52.

[24] Note how Camp, *Wisdom and the Feminine*, p. 151, refers to 'Prov 10-30' as 'the proverb collection', despite the fact that ch. 30 clearly constitutes an appendix to the proverb collection in its own right. Elsewhere Camp follows Patrick Skehan's numerical scheme for the compositional structure of Proverbs, which postulates an earlier version of the book that ended with the Agur passage. However, Camp speculates that the Agur text's original position as conclusion

theological appendix in its own right, with its own distinctive contribution to the final form of the book.

Doesn't it seem significant that a book, which begins with exuberant invitations to young men to pursue the promise of wisdom, winds down with reverent reflections of an old man pointing toward essentials that wisdom cannot give? Of course this latter theme finds many earlier antecedents in the book, such as (1) the maxims which contrast human proposal and divine disposal (e.g. 16.9; 21.31; 19.14), (2) the classic warning against depending upon one's own insight as opposed to acknowledging God in Prov. 3.5-7, and (3) especially the references throughout the book to the fear of Yahweh as the starting point and prime lodestar of the wisdom quest (e.g. 1.7; 9.10; 10.27; 14.27; 15.33; 19.23; 23.17). In all of these references the need to augment the wisdom search with reliance upon the covenantal tradition is implicit. Yet Agur makes this need explicit and presses the point further.

Agur's last words, as perhaps Agur himself, are rooted in and move from the international tradition of wisdom. However, Agur brings his own quest to rest in the last words of David and Moses, those individuals who represent Israel's two major covenant traditions. The quotations themselves serve well to represent not only these covenant traditions but also the other two canonical divisions, Prophets and Torah, from which the quotes are respectively drawn and to which their concern with divine revelation would seem naturally to point.[25] Agur's purpose, it would seem, is not merely to acknowledge these sources of revelation but to give them a sense of final priority in relation to the ultimate questions of mortal existence. And yet Agur does not take the next step with Sirach simply to collapse the wisdom tradition into

---

was due only to its function to fill remaining numerical gaps (p. 320 n. 7). She argues that the present MT and LXX arrangements, which place the woman of worth passage last, reveal a deliberate move to displace 'the words of an unknown man (Agur) and, even more importantly the instruction of a foreign queen [Lemuel's mother] ... when the monarchy was a more distant memory' (pp. 252-53).

[25] In quite a different way, Crawford H. Toy, *A Critical and Exegetical Commentary on the Book of Proverbs* (ICC; Edinburgh: T. & T. Clark, 1899), p. 523, suggests an allusion in this passage to the three major divisions of the Hebrew canon. He says, 'The *words* [mentioned in Prov. 30.6] are the written revelation, that is, the Law, and probably the Prophets, and also the Psalms, since one of these is quoted. The threefold division of the Jewish Scriptures (Law, Prophets, Writings) is first expressly mentioned in the Preface to Ben-Sira (132 BCE), and this paragraph may have been written not far from that time.'

scriptural revelation.[26] The wisdom tradition's empirical insight into human experience, seen in Agur's references to the proclivities of poverty and wealth, inform Agur's prayer for his remaining days as surely as the covenant tradition informs Agur's appeal to God's word in the face of life's final end. Agur, then, is not negating the wisdom tradition that Solomon represents. However, he is registering tension with the autonomous, covenant-negating way in which Solomon in the end represented it. The same tension can be felt, perhaps even more directly, in Agur's comments on wealth and poverty. For who better than Solomon represents the excess of wealth which tempts one to forget Yahweh?[27] Still the daily portion of wealth, like the everyday role of wisdom, is firmly endorsed and embraced by Agur as being vital to covenant faithfulness.

If, as Claudia Camp has argued, the book's concluding poem on the woman of worth gives culminating embodiment to the 'everyday,' common sense tradition of wisdom,[28] which Agur himself seems to appreciate, then perhaps the complementary function of the Agur text is to check the tendency to push beyond wisdom's common sense to more ultimate claims which end up undermining one's ultimate dependence on divine revelation.

Finally I would offer a comment on the larger canonical implications of this discussion. Harmut Gese once referred to wisdom literature as 'an alien body in the world of the Old Testament.'[29] While some might reject such a characterization as an improper challenge to wisdom's

---

[26] On this point see the perceptive comments of Childs, *Introduction*, pp. 558-59. Cf. also the careful discussion of Crenshaw's *Old Testament Wisdom*, pp. 149-58.

[27] Recent studies on the treatment of wealth and poverty in the book of Proverbs include R.N. Whybray, *Wealth and Poverty in the Book of Proverbs* (JSOTSup 99; Sheffield: JSOT Press, 1990); James L. Crenshaw, 'Poverty and Punishment in the Book of Proverbs', *Quarterly Review* 9/3 (1989), pp. 30-43; and G.H. Wittenberg, 'The Situational Context of Statements Concerning Poverty and Wealth in the Book of Proverbs', *Scriptura* 21 (1987), pp. 1-23. It is remarkable that there is such a dearth of attention in these studies to the canonical effect of this teaching in relation to the legendary wealth of Solomon, under whose name the entire book is presented.

[28] Camp, *Wisdom and the Feminine*, pp. 151-78, argues convincingly that proverbial wisdom functioned primarily as common sense in an original context of oral discourse where there was 'no inherent conflict between the kind of interpretive formulation provided by religious faith and that of "plain old common sense." Rather these two ways of looking at the world naturally co-exist and, indeed, support each other in any given cultural context' (p. 176).

[29] H. Gese, *Lehre und Wirklichkeit in der alten Weisheit* (Tübingen: J.B.C. Mohr, 1958), p. 2.

canonical status and compatibility with the rest of the canon,[30] others might find in it welcomed support for seeing the wisdom perspective as an independent, alternative epistemological option over against the rest of the canon. In terms of origins, it is true that wisdom thinking could be considered as something of a foreign immigrant to Israel (note how foreign wisdom is a positive standard of comparison for Israel in 1 Kgs 4.30-31). However, on the model of Israel's covenant provisions for incorporating the *actual* alien, I would suggest that it might be more accurate to think of the wisdom tradition as a *resident* alien in the Hebrew Bible. And Agur, whose name, as pointed out earlier, may mean 'I am a sojourner,' could be credited with playing a canonically strategic role in showing the way that the wisdom tradition could be brought to terms with Israel's covenantal tradition, showing 'the way home,' as it were.

I would offer one final observation on the canonical shaping of the book of Proverbs. Thomas McCreesh is another scholar who has recently emphasized the decisive importance of the woman of worth passage to the canonical shape of Proverbs.[31] He sees this concluding poem as constituting a coda for the entire book, tying together the book's major themes by using, as Camp has argued, the image of woman so prominent from the early chapters. In McCreesh's treatment, the earlier time of courtship (chs. 1, 8, 9) is seen to give way at the end to wisdom as a wife who represents fulfillment of the marriage covenant. The words of Agur might here again be seen as serving an important transitional role, making the move from pursuit to fulfillment, pointing toward the covenantal bonds that finally envelop not only the sojourning sage but also Woman Wisdom herself.[32]

[30] For a recent and extensive effort in this vein, see F.J. Steiert, *Die Weisheit Israels – ein Fremdkörper im Alten Testament?* (FthSt 143; Freiburg: Herder, 1990).

[31] McCreesh, 'Wisdom as Wife', p. 46.

[32] I wish to express my gratitude to my colleague, John Christopher Thomas, who stepped forward in my illness to present an earlier draft of this paper before the 1991 meeting of the Society of Biblical Literature, and also to those there who passed along helpful comments, especially Claudia Camp and my former teacher, James L. Crenshaw.

11

The Integrity of Job[*]

In research of the book of Job, the relationship between the prose narrative and the poetic dialogue has proven to be the most pivotal as well as the thorniest problem facing the interpreter. How one resolves this issue virtually controls how one understands the message of the book.[1] One can find widespread agreement among modern scholars with respect to what we might call the historical aspect of the prose-poetry relationship. The view that a preexistent, time-worn folk tale (the prose) was utilized as a framework for a subsequently created poetic dialogue, is a view that has attracted a large following.[2] While the evidence commending this view[3] is much too extensive to be rehashed here (and too familiar to need it), I would only point out that the ob-

---

[*] First published in *Catholic Biblical Quarterly* 45.1 (January 1983), pp. 17-31.

[1] One may challenge the assumption that the book has a single message. While it is true that the dialogue lends itself to the elaboration of a variety of views, the book cannot be treated simply as an eclectic display of viewpoints (so N. Tur-Sinai, *The Book of Job* [Jerusalem: Kiryath Sepher, 1967], pp. lviii), for the dialogue comes to rest in a climactic encounter that disallows such neutrality. This climax comes to a point and forces us to face the question, 'What is the point?' Cf. G. von Rad, *Old Testament Theology* (2 vols.; New York: Harper & Row, 1962), I, p. 416.

[2] This view can be traced from J. Wellhausen (in a review of A. Dillmann, *Das Buch Hiob*), *Jahrbücher für deutsche Theologie* 16 (1871), pp. 555-58 and K. Budde, *Beiträge zur Kritik des Buches Hiob* (Bonn: A. Marcus, 1876), pp. 29-62, who introduced the term *Volksbuch*. For a list of others holding this position, see S. Terrien, 'Job,' *Interpreter's Bible* (New York: Abingdon, 1954), vol. III, p. 885. Recognizing the *Volksbuch*-theory as the most common, H.H. Rowley (*Job* [Century Bible; Nashville, TN: Nelson, 1970], pp. 9-10) registers his opposition: 'On the basis of the tradition the author most probably wrote prologue, dialogue, and epilogue, and to him we owe this masterpiece as a whole.' Embracing this latter view are also F. Andersen, *Job* (Tyndale Commentary; London: InterVarsity, 1976), p. 55; and, less recently, E. Dhorme, *A Commentary on the Book of Job* (Nashville, TN: Nelson, 1967), p. lxxxv; and M. Buttenwieser, *The Book of Job* (New York: Macmillan, 1922), p. 7.

[3] One of the best presentations of the evidence (both pro and con) is given by Terrien, *Job*, pp. 884-88.

vious and drastic difference between the idyllic, stylized character of the narrative and the passionate, existential creativity of the poetry, places a heavy burden of proof upon anyone who would resist seeing evidence of two literary hands – indeed, of two literary worlds.

Even though most scholars agree on the historical priority of the prose story, agreement breaks off sharply when another aspect of the narrative's relationship to the poetry is considered. Has the dialogue been carefully fitted into the narrative framework to form an integrated, harmonious whole or has the dialogue been thrust over against the framework story in disjunctive fashion so as to call in question the tale's simple implications? In short, do the poetry and prose relate to one another in terms of thematic integration or thematic disjunction?

This fork in the road is not the end of disagreement. For whereas the argument for thematic disjunction leads basically in one direction (viz., belief that the poetry was written to challenge the message of the prose), the argument for thematic integration can go (and has gone) several ways. The thematic integration of the prologue, dialogue, and epilogue might readily suggest that the poet was sympathetic to the message of the original story and sought to reinforce, elaborate, and advance it,[4] but such integration would not preclude the possibility that a desire to supersede or totally contradict the former was at work.[5]

Which of these many roads should we take? Perhaps we might start by finding a point at which all roads intersect. All interpretations must admit that a thematic tension exists between the frame story and the dialogue. The fact that the issue of integration versus disjunction has asserted itself so prominently clearly testifies to the presence of that tension. It also seems obvious that thematic tension must center in one of three areas: (1) the depiction of the friends; (2) the depiction of God; or (3) the depiction of Job. To locate the center of tension is to make progress toward understanding the poet's intention and hence the message of the book, for the focal point of thematic tension between the prose and poetry should reveal what aspect of the frame story the poet sought to elaborate, supplement, supersede, or contradict.

Of the three possibilities, it seems safe to conclude that the center of thematic tension is not focused upon Job's three friends. To be sure,

---

[4] Cf. A.S. Peake, *Job* (Century Bible; New York: Henry Frowde, 1905); M. Pope, *Job* (AncB; Garden City, NY: Doubleday, 1979); M. Buttenwieser, *Book of Job*.

[5] This position is taken by D. Robertson, 'Book of Job: A Literary Study,' *Soundings* 56 (1973), pp. 446-84, and J.G. Williams, '"You Have not Spoken Truth of Me": Mystery and Irony in Job', *ZAW* 83 (1971), pp. 231-55, whose publication, though earlier, footnotes Robertson's then unpublished article.

God's angry condemnation of the trio in the epilogue seems a bit in-congruous with their deficient religiosity in the dialogue. There is good reason to think that God's stern judgment originally (in an earlier version of the dialogue) indicted the friends for encouraging Job to curse God, for their offense is categorized in the divine verdict by the same term (נבלה, *nebalah*, 'folly') that Job uses to categorize his wife's suggestion to curse God and die.[6] Notwithstanding this, the poetic presentation of the three friends does not leave us totally unprepared for so negative a put-down as we find in the epilogue. Their bigoted orthodoxy turns our sympathies completely against them. While ex-pounding 'flinty theology'[7] is a far cry from urging someone to curse God, the three friends fulfill the same kind of role either way. They are foils for the protagonist; they are bad comforters.[8] The condemnation of the friends does not clash with the poetry nearly so much as the commendation of Job, who is last seen repenting. The friends are not the center of thematic tension.

The possibility that the poet transformed Job's antagonists from he-retics to theologians is enough to make us consider whether the crux of thematic tension (and, hence, the poet's motive for adapting the prose) should be sought at the theological level. Not a few interpreters have viewed the narrative and the dialogue in terms of a theological polarity, the dialogue being seen as a polemic against the theology of retribution, the narrative being seen as an endorsement and exhibition of it.[9] Yet this contrast is a bit overdrawn. Within the prose tale, Job's plight is anything but an exhibition of the connection between mis-deed and misfortune. God is *not* represented as the predictable rewarder of virtue and punisher of vice. The prose story rather emphasizes that God, for reasons unknown to humankind, may cause evil to fall upon the good. Some would insist that while the scheme of retribution is suspended, the fact that it was done only for so exceptional a case as Job[10] and that he is doubly restored in the end serves finally to vindicate

---

[6] Cf. Pope, *Job*, pp. lxxx-lxxxi; also Peake, *Job*, p. 32, who points to the same evidence. The argument is not conclusive, however, since נבלה (*nebalah*) con-veys a wider range of activity than the counsel to curse God.

[7] This term is from Peake, *Job*, p. 12.

[8] For a more positive assessment of the role of the three friends, see G. von Rad, *Old Testament Theology*, I, p. 411.

[9] See especially the articles of Williams and Robertson cited above.

[10] That God admits to destroying Job 'without cause' might suggest that he is accustomed to doing such things when, but only when, human behavior calls for it. J.L. Crenshaw (in his article, 'The Two-Fold Search: A Response to Luis Alonso Schökel', *Semeia* 7 [1977], p. 64) points to the advice of Job's wife ('Curse God and die.') as an example of how the prologue breathes the spirit of retribution.

the deed-consequence nexus. However, Job's climactic response to his loathsome situation, 'Shall we receive good at the hand of God, and shall we not receive evil?' plainly reveals his (and the narrator's) willingness to embrace a theology in which that nexus is *not* maintained. The prose, then, represents not a defense or an endorsement of retribution theology but rather an abrogation of it.

We see, therefore, that the poetic dialogue, in its stand against a theology of retribution, is *not* pitted against the prose narrative, as many have maintained. This knocks the props out from under the 'ironic' interpretation of D. Robertson and J.G. Williams, which insists on seeing such a theological antithesis between narrative and dialogue. How could the poetry have been inserted to contradict the theological thrust of the prose (or rather to get it to contradict itself) when the latter does not present a theological picture with which an opponent of divine retribution would decisively have taken issue? To be sure, Job's depiction of God throughout the dialogue (as a God of caprice) evokes theological irony over against God's pronouncement in the epilogue that Job 'has spoken of me what is right'. Yet this is no revelation of the poet's prime intention, for the *same* theological irony is present *already within* the prose. God's verdict, by vindicating Job's words in the prologue, 'shall we not receive evil (from the hand of God)', already is an admission of capricious rule.

The idea of divine caprice is not the theological scandal for these ancient monotheistic writers[11] that it is for Robertson and Williams. It is clearly not a source, much less the center, of thematic tension between poetry and narrative. One might try to dispute this by pointing to the radical antithesis between Job's original attitude toward divine arbitrariness and his attitude in the dialogue. He moves from reverent acceptance to bitter revolt. However, this testifies not so much to a theological tension[12] as to a tension between the poetic and narrative portrayals of Job.

---

[11] Cf. the discussion of J.L. Crenshaw, *Prophetic Conflict* (BZAW 124; Berlin/New York: de Gruyter, 1971), pp. 77-81.

[12] Williams and Robertson, however, base their interpretation on the belief that focal theological tension is created and the poet's theological position is revealed in Job's rebellion. But if the poet's theological position is to be identified with his portrayal of Job's attitude, then Job's *repentance* as well as his rebellion must be taken into account. This is where the interpretations of Williams and Robertson fall short. Seeing the poet's theological position *only* in Job's rebellion leads them to an arbitrary dismissal of Job's repentance as insincere. (See the able criticism of E. Good, 'Job and the Literary Task: A Response', *Soundings* 56 [1973], p. 482, on this point.) Job's attitude toward deity, though different in poetry and prose, finally presents no significant theological tension,

It is difficult to resist the conclusion to which our analysis keeps pointing – Job is the center of thematic tension. This should not surprise us. The narrative is a story about him, moving from his life to his death. Job is a paradigm.[13] I would expect that a poet with something to add or subtract would, like the prose story, primarily be concerned with Job. I believe this to be the case. The poet has staged a dialogue, giving Job the first and last word, in order, primarily, to say something else about him.[14]

To identify more specifically the purpose of the poet, it would help to return to our earlier question. Has this 'something else about Job' been harmonized with the prose portrait of Job or has it rather been butted up against the latter in order to create a disjunctive contrast? Most of those who have tried to settle this question have turned to the juncture between poetry and prose at the end of the book. Here the writing moves from Job's repentance in the face of divine rebuke to divine confirmation of his integrity. It would seem natural to look for the poet's intention precisely where he joins his materials, for whether he intended harmonization or counterpoint, it is here we would expect to find either careful sutures or a glaring clash of colors.

The juxtaposition of Job's repentance and exoneration seems, on the surface at least, to present a clash. In agreement with a divine rebuke, Job says, 'I have been wrong,' whereupon God says, 'You have been right.' Yet the obvious tension here has not kept many, even most interpreters from trying to reconcile and harmonize these two items. Alleviating this tension has been attempted in a variety of ways. One view is that God's verdict of approval is consequent upon Job's repentance.[15] However, there is a problem with this view. In repenting, Job speaks what is true about himself, not, as God specifies, 'what is right concerning me'. Other scholars acknowledge the tension but feel the verdict can be harmonized with the poet's 'general intention to applaud Job.'[16] Another group sees the problem resolved in that God's rebuke and Job's confession refer only to Job's ignorance, while in

---

for virgin-faith in the prologue and humble repentance in the poetry both represent acceptance of an unpredictable God.

[13] While my interest here is not form-critical, I would note the attempt of H. Gese, *Lehre und Wirklichkeit in der alten Weisheit* (Tübingen: Mohr [Siebeck], 1958), pp. 74-78, to see the book of Job as a paradigm of an answered lament.

[14] I cannot, then, accept the view of Robertson, Williams, and others that the poet's primary purpose was to say something else about God.

[15] See Good, 'Job and the Literary Task', p. 482.

[16] Peake, *Job*, p. 33. See also N. Snaith, *The Book of Job: Its Origin and Purpose* (Naperville, IL: Allenson, 1968), p. 5; Terrien, *Job*, p. 902.

God's verdict Job's moral integrity is confirmed.[17] This view is not unrelated to another approach that seeks to maintain, through a different reading of the text, that Job does not actually repent.[18]

The attempt to reconcile Job's repentance and exoneration has been the crux of the effort to integrate the Job of the narrative with the Job of the dialogue and to harmonize the poetry with the prose. Yet the different ways of explaining the text at this point where prose and poetry meet are very troublesome and leave one desirous of more conclusive information. If I am right that the poet's intentions are most accessible at the point where he joins his materials, there is another natural place to look, viz. at the juncture between poetry and prose at the beginning of the book. I intend to show that the relationship between chapter three and the prologue possesses significant and unnoticed illumination for this contention. In ch. 3 we find, once again, a portrait of Job that is in tension with adjacent narrative material. Since it contains the poet's initial response, ch. 3 provides the best vantage point from which to treat the question, 'Has the poet accepted and built upon the narrator's Job or has he rejected the latter and introduced a new Job, completely incongruous with the earlier portrayal?'

With this question in view, I now proceed to an analysis of ch. 3 and its relationship to the prologue.

Chapter 3

The first two words of the poetic section, 'after this', signal both separation and connection with the preceding narrative. The same effect is achieved in the very next phrase, 'Job opened his mouth.' This marks a break from the seven-day silence of the preceding narrative but retains the narrator's focus upon the mouth of Job. The narrator's earlier observation, 'In all this Job did not sin with his lips' (2.10), leads directly into the episode in which these lips are clamped in silence.[19] When the poet begins, 'After this Job opened his mouth', the reader cannot help but lean forward to hear what will come forth from these, until now, sinless lips.

[17] See Pope, *Job*, p. lxxx; Dhorme, *Commentary on Job*, p. lxxxi; and Rowley, *Job*, p. 12.

[18] Buttenwieser (*Book of Job*, p. 29) renders Job's words: 'I am comforted for my lot of dust and ashes.' Recently D. Patrick ('The Translation of Job, XLII:VI', *VT* 26 [1976], pp. 369-71) has suggested the reading, 'I repent of dust and ashes,' i.e., 'I turn away or desist from being sorrowful.' L.J. Kaplan ('Maimonides, Dale Patrick and Job XLII:VI', *VT* 28 [1978], pp. 356-57) has shown that this is not a new view.

[19] Was Job biting his tongue? Perhaps the poet thought he should have been.

Anticipation turns into surprise when we hear that Job has 'cursed the day of his birth' (3.1). With this revelation, we once again get the feeling that the poet is maintaining direct and deliberate contact with the prologue while making a decisive departure. Cursing is the predominant motif of the prologue,[20] but every place it occurs in the narrative is aimed at pointing up Job's distance from such behavior. His scrupulous piety covers even the possibility that his children had 'cursed God in their hearts' (1.5). Satan's predictions that Job would curse God to his face (1.11; 2.5) put Job's integrity in bold relief, especially as he buries his face to bless the name of the Lord (1.21). Similarly, his wife's suggestion to curse God (2.9) only gives Job occasion to express his outrage at such a thought. The narrative presents a blessing Job and does not prepare us for the cursing Job introduced by the poet.

Yet to curse a day, many would insist, is not to curse God. While Job's discharge of bitterness may mark a shift, it does not constitute a contradiction of his former character. Sure, Job has released a little steam, but there is no reason to think that, underneath it all, he is not his old self, for he has remained unflinchingly consistent on the one essential issue, the issue on which he is being tested. Job has not cursed God openly. Such reasoning persuades certain scholars that the poet maintains the integrity of Job and that they, therefore, should maintain the thematic integrity of the book.[21]

Other scholars, however, insist that in cursing 'his day' Job is, in effect, cursing God.[22] Robertson reasons that Job's curse entails a curse against creation, so, indirectly, a curse against the creator. He finds confirmation for this view in the mythological allusion of v. 8, for to arouse Yam[23] or Leviathan is to threaten all of creation with being thrown back into chaos. Robertson, however, overstates his case a bit here. Job's target in v. 8 is not creation at large but only and quite specifically the day of his birth: 'Let them curse *it*,' he says. While he certainly solicits forces considered inimical to all creation – which is

---

[20] Robertson ('Book of Job', p. 448) rightly calls the prospect of Job cursing God the hinge of dramatic action.

[21] Proponents of this view include Peake, *Job*, p. 10, Rowley, *Job*, p. 10, and Terrien, *Job*, p. 898.

[22] See Robertson, 'Book of Job', pp. 449-51; M. Fishbane, 'Jeremiah IV 23-26 and Job III 3-13: A Recovered Use of the Creation Pattern', *VT* 21 (1971), pp. 151-67 (he explains Job 3.3-13 as a 'counter-cosmic incantation').

[23] The recognition that יוֹם (*yom*) conveys an allusion to the Canaanite sea-monster goes back to H. Gunkel, *Schöpfung und Chaos* (Göttingen: Vandenhoeck & Ruprecht, 1895); yet seeing a double entendre, 'day' and 'Sea' (so Fishbane, 'Jeremiah IV 23-26 and Job III 3-13', p. 161), seems even more probable.

nothing more than the kind of hyperbole common to all cursing, both ancient and modern – he is directing these wishes against only that one bad day.

One could argue that to curse any created thing is to curse, by implication, the creator. However, one who makes so much of the potency of the spoken word, as Robertson does,[24] should respect the implications of what is left unspoken. Job does not curse God any more than Jeremiah does when he curses the day of *his* birth. Jeremiah shows us that he is carefully avoiding more theologically dangerous curses. He does not curse his mother, as Lev. 20.9b prohibits, but rather the day she delivered him. He does not curse his father, also taboo according to Lev. 20.9a, but rather the messenger who conveyed to him the news of birth – a true demonstration of rhetorical brinkmanship! So we must respect the fact that Job does not take the ultimate step and curse God. There is, then, no irreconcilable contradiction between the Job of the prologue and the Job of ch. 3 on this score. Yet such does not in itself verify their congruity. We must turn from what Job does not say in his curse to what he does say.

Job decries life. The full implications of this have not been acknowledged because its thematic relationship to the prologue has not been fully appreciated. The prologue, no less than Job's poetic lament, is preoccupied with the issue of the value of life. The narrator at the outset conveys silent assumptions about life's value. When he sets out to describe the richness of Job's life, the list begins, 'There were born to him seven sons and three daughters' (1.2). A low point in the narrative is reached with the messenger's words to Job, 'They are dead' (1.19). With acts of extreme mourning Job reveals his sense of loss and his radical variance from Qoheleth's conviction that 'the day of death

---

[24] Robertson ('Book of Job', p. 461), in the tradition of J. Pedersen, emphasizes the self-fulfilling power of the spoken word, arguing that Job's self-imprecation of ch. 31 'forces' God's appearance. E. Good ('Job and the Literary Task', p. 475) in his response article endorses Robertson's magical view of curse and extends it, arguing that Satan's oath-language 'forces' God to test Job. The fact that Good in his earlier essay on Job (*Irony in the Old Testament* [Philadelphia, PA: Westminster, 1965], p. 239) calls the book of Job 'the quietus on magic' (referring to the magical connection between deed and consequence) is quite ironic in itself! We find more credible the view of H. C. Brichto (*The Problem of Curse in the Hebrew Bible* [SBLMS 13; Philadelphia, PA: Society of Biblical Literature, 1963]), who after a thorough linguistic and exegetical analysis concludes, 'the evidence for magical concepts underlying the biblical phenomena of curse (and of blessing) has been grossly overvalued' (p. 215).

(is better) than the day of birth' (Qoh 7.1).[25] For Job, life is precious, a gift from God (1.21).

Even Satan can acknowledge life's extreme value: 'All that a man has he will give for his life' (2.4). This statement might be an overstatement for a man whose loyalty to God is most precious, yet God's demand that Job's life be spared might indicate that Satan is not far from the truth! Can God fully trust any but one to say, 'Not my will but thine be done'? More easily seen in the words 'only spare his life,' though, is God's own testimony to the value of life. Life is worth hedging in, 'Behold, it is very good.'

Job's testimony to life's worth, however, is most important of all, for he more than anyone seems to be in a position to say whether life is worthy of unconditional affirmation. When life for Job has become tortuous, his wife holds before him the temptation to relinquish it.[26] 'Curse God and die,' she says. His words of response, 'Shall we receive good at the hand of God, and shall we not receive evil?' communicate more than an affirmation of loyalty to God; they convey an affirmation of life, the conviction that life should be embraced despite anything, unconditionally. Job is consistent with his earlier affirmation in which life is met with acceptance, 'Naked I came from my mother's womb, and naked shall I return,' and even with praise, 'blessed be the name of the Lord' (1.21).

It should now be clear that, even though the Job of ch. 3 may not curse God, when he curses life, he stands in diametric opposition to the Job of the narrative. Rejection of life is set over against acceptance of life. Job's lament does not represent a mere shift in attitude or fluctuation in mood but rather a complete reversal of the narrative Job. Literary evidence convinces me, furthermore, that this reversal is not incidental but rather the deliberate and determinative design of the poet.

In ch. 3 the poet presents an easily identifiable thematic structure.[27] In the opening section (vv. 1-10) Job denigrates the womb; in a second

---

[25] A thorough discussion of Qoheleth's view of death is provided by J.L. Crenshaw, 'The Shadow of Death in Qoheleth', in *Israelite Wisdom: Essays in Honor of Samuel Terrien* (ed. J.G. Gammie et al.; Missoula, MT: Scholars Press, 1976), pp. 205-16.

[26] S. Terrien (*Job: Poet of Existence* [New York: Bobbs-Merrill, 1957], p. 42) calls the suggested action of Job's wife 'a theological method of euthanasia'. Helpful is the paraphrase offered by Crenshaw ('The Two-fold Search', p. 64): 'Do something heinous', she urges her husband, 'so God will punish you by sending relief in the form of death.'

[27] D.N. Freedman, ('Structure of Job 3', *Bib* 49 [1969], pp. 503-508) acknowledges the same three-unit structure here observed, finding support in strophic and metrical patterns. He accepts the *MT* verse-arrangement, seeing v.

(vv. 11-19) he celebrates the tomb. The final section falls into two divisions: the first (vv. 20-23) presents an indirect interrogation of the *giver* of life, 'Why is light given?' In the last (vv. 24-26) Job bemoans his present state, presenting a lamentation of self. The thematic structure of this chapter bears a striking correspondence to the progression of thought in the opening utterance of Job in the narrative (1.21). In the same order, this most crucial utterance speaks of the womb, the tomb, and the giver of life. This registers unmistakable evidence that the poetic lament of Job 3 is a step-by-step rebuttal of Job's manifesto of faith in 1.21. The opening soliloquy of the poetic Job has been written to confute the opening soliloquy of the narrative Job.[28] The following diagram should help illustrate this.

Job 1.21	*Job 3*
1.21a	3.1-10
A. Reverent acceptance of the womb: 'Naked I came from my mother's womb'	Job denigrates the womb: 'It did not shut the door of the womb'
1.21b	3.11-19
B. Reverent acceptance of the tomb: 'and naked shall I return'	Job regrets delay of the tomb: 'I should have been at rest'
1.21c	3.20-23
C. Reverent acceptance of deity: 'The LORD gives and the LORD takes away'	Indirect questioning of deity: 'Why is light given to him that is in misery?'
1.21d	3.24-26
D. Theocentric praise: 'Blessed be the name of the LORD.'	Egocentric lament: 'The thing I fear comes upon me.'

For the poet, 1.21 has triggered a counterblast; a positive affirmation has elicited a negative commentary. A blessing has been answered with a curse. A portrait of pious passivity has been countered with a depiction of raucous revolt. The poet has not attempted to develop the character of the traditional Job; he has contradicted it. Thus, the poet, unlike those who want to harmonize and integrate the traditional Job

---

16 not as a displacement but an intentional poetic device to reiterate the main theme of the section, much as vv. 7-8 function in the first section and v. 23 in the third.

[28] The view that 3.3-13 was structured according to the creation narrative of Gen. 1 (Fishbane) is not persuasive. Fishbane, like Robertson, makes the mistake of reading into the poem a death wish for 'the entire creation'. His view, moreover, fails to recognize the thematic break of the poem after v. 10.

with the poetic Job, has no stake in opening the dialogue with the assumption of his fundamental integrity. It does not surprise us, then, but only lends further support to this interpretation, when clear signs of the questionableness of Job's integrity appear in the first speech of the dialogue. Such can be seen in each section of the speech.

A. 3.1-10 'I loathe my life.'

Samuel Terrien sees as the theme of this first section the hatred of life, which gives way in the second section to the love of death.[29] Together these themes mark the first of three stages through which Terrien sees Job passing in his thinking on death. In 6.8-13 the idea of death as escape is replaced by the idea of death as a way to preserve faith in God.[30] A final stage is reached in 7.1-21, thinks Terrien, when the 'fascination of death has been swallowed up by its fear'.[31] Interpreting Job in terms of development is compatible with Terrien's desire to maintain continuity between the Job of the narrative and the Job of the poetry. The developmental interpretation is essential to Terrien's view that the dialogue begins with the 'poet's endorsement' of Job's integrity and only thereafter traces 'the "disintegration" of this fabulous integrity'.[32] Terrien credits Job's psychological struggle with death with spurring this moral disintegration,[33] driving him to a 'brand of egocentricity' where he could fashion himself as a god-like antagonist of God: 'Am I the sea or a sea monster?' (7.12).

Terrien's developmental interpretation of Job is a bit forced. Not treated in his discussion is Job's reflection on death in ch. 10, which begins with his words, 'I hate my life.' Job moves toward a climax at v. 18, where he returns to the precise thoughts of ch. 3: 'Why did you bring me forth from the womb? Would that I had died before any eye had seen me.' Death, once again, is seen as something to be hastened. Are we to think Job has returned to square one?

It is more defensible to maintain that the poet had no interest in presenting Job in terms of some psychological or moral regression. We would argue that the poetic Job's reflections on life and death, which

---

[29] Terrien, *Poet of Existence*, p. 46.

[30] Terrien, *Poet of Existence*, p. 55.

[31] Terrien, *Poet of Existence*, p. 60.

[32] Terrien, *Job*, p. 898.

[33] Terrien, *Poet of Existence*, pp. 62-63. Peake (*Job*, p. 12) also sees a gradual moral disintegration, but he sees the friends as responsible.

show vacillation rather than development,[34] call Job's integrity in question from the start.

Job's curse of life in ch. 3 registers a feeling expressed repeatedly throughout the poetry with the phrase, 'I loathe my life'. We have already mentioned the occurrence of this phrase in ch. 10 and how it leads to a death wish similar to the lament of ch. 3. In 7.16, immediately after a similar expression of the desirability of death, Job again starkly expresses hatred for life – this time with the verb מאס (*ma'as*), 'to reject, despise,' without an object. The context would indicate that 'life' is the implied object. 'I reject life' corresponds to the immediately preceding 'I choose death'.[35] In 9.21 Job again uses the verb *ma'as* to express the same thought – this time with the object: 'I despise my life'. But notice the context of this statement. The entire verse reads, 'I am blameless (תם, *tam*), I regard not myself, I despise my life.' In the face of his hatred for life, Job affirms his integrity. But should we? J. Crenshaw has refused to accept Job's second claim – that he does not regard himself: 'Job seeks vindication, his version of the highest good. Self interest gives birth to his titanic challenge of God.'[36] I would concur and would also reject Job's claim that his integrity remains intact. For support I point to 42.6, the final use of the verb *ma'as*. As in 7.16 the object is missing. I suggest that 42.6 is an echo of 7.16, 'I despise my life'.[37] Yet in the context of repentance, this final use takes on an altogether different connotation. In despising his life, Job is despising his guilt. The hatred of life with which Job commenced the dialogue now brings him around at the end to the hatred of his own wretchedness. With a new twist on the word *ma'as*, Job repents of his hatred for life.

---

[34] In 10.18-22, right after Job registers his wish that death had already visited him, he speaks as if he wished that death could be staved off.

[35] J.B. Curtis ('On Job's Response to Yahweh', *JBL* 98 [1979], pp. 503-504) discusses the various suggested interpretations of the implied object, defending his view that God is the object. On Curtis's view, see n. 37 below.

[36] Crenshaw, 'The Two-Fold Search', p. 64.

[37] Curtis concludes that the missing object of the verb in 42.6 is God and that the context presents not repentance, but a rejection of Yahweh. I am not convinced by Curtis's argument and would insist that, if the poem had been as theologically outrageous as Curtis contends, no editor would have been tempted to bring it into the service of the mild prose version of Job, as Curtis contends. It seems that Curtis's interpretation is based largely on silence – the missing objects of *ma'as*, which he thinks were deleted by some editor trying to defuse the heretical potency of the poem. Yet if this were so, why did not this hypothetical editor insert new objects to keep later interpreter's like Curtis from figuring out what the poet had really said?

B. 3.11-19 םת *(tam) or* תמ *(mot)*

Having considered whether integrity is compatible with hatred for life, we now view the same question from a different angle. Is integrity compatible with a death wish?

It may not be irrelevant to be reminded of the connotations alive in the ancient notion of integrity. םת *(tam)* is an adjective that conveys the idea of completeness and wholeness. Terrien, following Pedersen, sees integrity manifested in 'the personality that is integrated within itself and within its environment.'[38] The ideas of right relations and mental wellbeing[39] are not far away. A contemporary counterpart of this idea of integrity might be found in the idea of being 'well adjusted'. In view of this, it is interesting that a modern psychologist, applying behavioral analysis to Job 3, has concluded that Job manifests the symptoms of a psychological condition termed 'learned helplessness', common among institutionalized psychotics.[40] I, of course, am interested in a more exegetical diagnosis of Job's condition. Yet, then again, the fact that one would have profound difficulty picturing a well-integrated person giving vent to a death wish may not be entirely beside the point.

Within the text the notions of death and integrity are brought together in a significant way in the diabolical utterance of Job's wife.

> Do you still hold fast you integrity (םת, *tam*)?
> Curse God and die (תמ, *mot*). (2.9)

In the narrative, Job responds by embracing integrity. This choice involves not only a rejection of a God-curse but also a rejection of a death wish. We recognized earlier that Job's response affirms life. In choosing םת, Job rejects תמ. Chapter 3 conveys a very different response. Here the protagonist embraces the death wish that was earlier refused. Even if this life-curser manages to avoid cursing God, in light of the connection made by Job's wife, the question automatically reasserts itself: 'Do you still hold fast your integrity?'

C. 3.20-23 The Giver of Life

If integrity implies right relationships and especially a right relationship to God, then we must wonder about Job's integrity when he turns

---

[38] Terrien, *Job*, p. 898 (tense altered for stylistic purposes).
[39] Terrien, *Job*, p. 909.
[40] J.H. Reynierse, 'A Behavioristic Analysis of the Book of Job', *Journal of Psychology and Theology* 3 (1975), pp. 75-81.

suspicious eyes heavenward to ask, 'Why is light given?' This question, as I have shown, is the poet's response to the unquestioning reverence of the earlier 'answer', 'the Lord gives and the Lord takes' (1.21). If God's gift of life is a curse not a blessing, says Job, then why does God bother?

In this section Job is direct in referring both to God and himself. With v. 23, however, he becomes a bit more explicit, making direct reference to God and unmistakable reference to self: 'Why is light given to a man whose way is hid, whom God has hedged in?'[41] Job is not pleading the 'lot of aching humanity',[42] but rather grinding his own axe, with which he intends to fell deity.

The question that Job puts to God in this section reflects suspicion of God's creative work. While Job is immediately concerned with why God created *his* life, his language easily expands to the wider dimensions of God's creative activity. The 'light' Job rejects and the 'womb' he rejects find ultimate reference in the creative performance of God, who later will acknowledge himself as light's source (38.19, 24) and symbolize himself as creation's womb (38.29). Job's self-oriented questions here in his opening speech grow into a wider assault upon the creative and providential work of God.

Job's assault on God brings God's counter-assault on him. If Job wants to talk creation, God will oblige. God's 'How?' overwhelms Job's 'Why?' Job is rebuked for the line of questioning initiated by the theological suspicions of ch. 3. These suspicions rightly raise our own suspicions about Job's integrity.

D. 3.24-26 The Center of the Circle

In this final section, Job's lament of self provides a counterpoint to the traditional Job's praise of God in 1.21. Implied by the poetic response is the thought, 'Yahweh may be blessed, but I am cursed.' Theocentrism shifts to egocentrism. Three short verses contain all of ten references to self. The climactic statement of the section may hold an additional clue to the contrast. When Job cries, 'What I fear comes upon me', could he be making a veiled reference to God? The God-centered life of the traditional Job was epitomized in his fear of God (1.1). Now morbid fear replaces reverential fear, and self, not God, forms the center of attention.

---

[41] God's protective hedge – 'spare his life' – has become a prison wall.
[42] So Terrien, *Poet of Existence*, p. 50.

That God's speech from the whirlwind is aimed at showing Job he is not the center of the universe, hardly needs to be argued.[43] Throughout the dialogue Job's vision of self is magnified beyond all proportion, but a theophany readjusts Job's vision: 'Behold, I am small' (40.4).

David Robertson compares integrity to a circle.[44] Job finally discovers that God can be the only center of that circle.

Conclusion

The interpretation of the book of Job pivots on the issue of integrity. First comes the question, 'Do the prose and poetry comprise an integrated whole?' We saw that this question boils down to the question, 'Is the Job of the poetry integrated with the Job of the narrative?' I have suggested that ch. 3, because it is the place where the poet initiates his work and joins his materials, is the most promising place to look for an answer. My analysis of this chapter and its relation to the prologue has convinced me that the poet, in presenting Job, has not sought thematic continuity with the narrative but rather thematic disjunction. Job 3 is a negative commentary upon Job 1.21. The opening soliloquy of the poetic Job has been written to rebut the opening soliloquy of the narrative Job. The latter expresses reverent acceptance of life and the giver of life; the former, in unmistakable reference to the latter, conveys irreverent rejection of both. Those who try to salvage Job's former integrity in the face of his curse miss the point of the poetry. The poet has denied integrity to his character, and we should deny thematic integrity to the book.

There is another kind of integrity, however, that the poet has *not* denied to his character, the kind of integrity we call honesty. The traditional prose story presented an ideal paradigm, a model of innocent suffering. But it was a paradigm stylized, removed from commonplace reality. The poet sought to present a new paradigm, one with which people could identify, one that would express the fears, the anger, the hope, and the frustration of existential experience. If the poet's paradigm is less faithful to God, it is more faithful to human experience. Existential honesty receives a deity's rebuke, but it also receives a poet's sympathy – even God thinks enough to pay a visit to that kind of integrity.

Yet there is still another level at which the question of integrity can and, I think, must be viewed. The canon has forever bound together the words of a narrator and a poet. This canonical context suggests an

---

[43] Terrien (*Poet of Existence*, pp. 236-37) provides an excellent discussion.
[44] Robertson, 'Book of Job', pp. 446-84.

integrity that transcends the discontinuity I have heretofore delineated. Framed by a narrative that is expressive of an idealistic theological hope, the poet's message is itself changed, even as it changes the message of the narrative. The resulting dialectic between the real and the ideal can be seen as something quite at home in the Hebrew canon and in the faith that springs from it. The realization of suffering in this world is encompassed by an expression of ultimate hope – a hope that concerns not only what we shall have but also what we shall be. On this canonical, theological level we can at last affirm the integrity of Job. [45]

[45] It has been a number of years since I first published this study, and now, following my concluding comment on Job's epilogue, I would like to add something of a brief epilogue of my own. My foregoing argument pressed for a disjunction between the narrative and poetic depictions of Job in such a way as to support the idea of a compositional sequence and disjunction between two different writers – a poet writing in counterpoint to a narrator. While I argued for diametric opposition in the compositional process, I finally saw dialectical integration in the composite product. I would now not be so quick to ascribe this dialectical effect to the unintended outcome of canonization rather than to the literary intentionality of a poet or even a single poet-narrator. My change in perspective comes from having learned much through the years about the dialectical sophistication of ancient Hebrew writing and also from having recognized more and more my need to *un*learn many of my modern Western tendencies to see diametrical opposites in the dialectical tensions of ancient Near Eastern texts. Yet perhaps even more determinative than this has been what I have learned and had to unlearn about myself through my life experiences of faith and pain and struggle with God. I can honestly say that coming to see the stark disjunctions of my own life, in praise and lament, has made it much easier to see the integrity of Job, and vice versa.

12

Raw Prayer and Refined Theology: 'You Have Not Spoken Straight to Me, as My Servant Job Has'*

The following study on the book of Job is offered in honor of Donald N. Bowdle. This opportunity to honor my former teacher is indeed an honor for me. Twenty-five years ago I sat as one of his students in a course on Old Testament wisdom literature. There he opened our minds to an appreciation of the ancient wisdom tradition by using the resources of its primary modern counterpart, academic scholarship. Yet Donald Bowdle utilized more than scholarship, even as he aimed for more than just our minds. He modeled for us a blending of scholarship and spirituality, indeed of mind and Spirit. In his own way, he strove to keep the two together against the powerful forces which ever tend to drive the two apart. And so he informed *and inspired* many of us along this same course.

For me, this life-long course included pursuing (at his particular encouragement) advanced study in the OT, to include its wisdom literature. In this endeavor I had to face for myself those powerful forces that threaten to divorce spirituality from scholarship, criticism from confession, piety from theology, wisdom from prayer, talking *about* God from talking *to* God. I found these divisive propensities at work not only around me, but also *within* me. Yet more than that, I came to find these clashing forces not just in my own contemporary context but also in the ancient biblical text, particularly in OT wisdom literature,[1] and especially in the book of Job.[2] What I have found there has been extremely helpful to me in coming to my own integration of scholarship and spirituality, of mind and Spirit. I offer a small but representative example of my discoveries here as a tribute to my former

* First published in Terry L. Cross and Emerson B. Powery, eds., *The Spirit and the Mind: Essays in Informed Pentecostalism* (In Honor of Donal N. Bowdle) (Lanham, MD: University Press of America, 2000), pp 35-48.
[1] See my study, 'A Home for the Alien: Worldly Wisdom and Covenantal Confession in Proverbs 30.1-9', presented in Chapter 10 of this volume.

[2] See my study, 'The Integrity of Job', presented in Chapter 11 of this volume.

teacher in the hope of contributing in some small way to the pursuit of inspired wisdom, such as Donald Bowdle has encouraged in so many of us.

Translating Job 42.7
This paper focuses on a single verse at the end of the book of Job. With wording similar to most English translations, the New International Version renders it:

> After the LORD had said these things to Job, he said to Eliphaz the Temanite, 'I am angry with you and your two friends, because you have not spoken of me what is right, as my servant Job has' (42.7).

Obviously, this verse is crucial to the meaning of the book of Job, because it registers the crux of God's judgment on the entire proceedings between Job and his friends – an exchange covering most of the book, more than three dozen chapters. Even though God confronts Job before this verse with a lengthy discourse (chs. 38–41) that reduces Job to humble confession and contrition (42.1-6), the bottom line of God's judgment is this succinct verdict in 42.7, which draws a sharp contrast between Job and his friends on the matter of what they had not, but Job had, done.[3]

The friends receive condemnation; Job receives commendation. But what exactly had Job done that his friends had not done? Clearly it has to do with speaking. The second-person plural perfect of the common verb דבר (*davar*) has left no doubt about this. The only fuss for most translators and commentators has been over how to read the term, נכונה (*nekonah*, 'what is right'), which comes after the immediately following prepositional phrase, אלי (*elay*, 'of me'). The term נכונה (*nekonah*) belongs to the root כון, which has to do with being firm, established, right, upright, straight.[4] The root yields such common vocabulary as the adjective כן (*ken*, 'right/honest', also used adverbially), the noun מכון (*makon*, 'place'), and the noun מכונה (*mekonah*, 'base/pedestal'). The not-so-common feminine, singular participial form found in Job 42.7 has here been translated against this background. It has been taken either as an object[5] or an adverbial modifier[6] of the

---

[3] The crucial phrase is repeated in the following verse, 42.8.

[4] BDB, s.v.; *Lexicon Veteris Testamenti Libros*, ed. L. Koehler and W. Baumgartner (Leiden: E.J. Brill, 1958), s.v.; and *The Dictionary of Classical Hebrew*, vol. IV, ed. D.J.A. Clines (Sheffield: Sheffield Academic Press, 1998), s.v.

[5] Both KJV and JPS render it 'the thing that is right'; NIV, RSV, NRSV, and NASB all render it 'what is right'; and NJPS renders it 'the truth'.

verb דבר (*davar*), but either way the renderings produce the sense that what separates Job and his friends is the matter of the *rightness of their speech about God,* in other words, the *correctness of their theology.*[7]

Much comment has been generated, however, by the felt need to explain how Job's speech about God could be right and that of his friends not right. Throughout their debate it is the friends' theology, not Job's, that is hard to fault. They vigorously defend the orthodox doctrines of theology, while Job defiantly questions and even denies the justness of God.[8]

The conventional way to get 42.7 to square with this fact has been to explain that Job had been more accurate in addressing the overall theological scope of the issue at hand, as he challenged an overly narrow and rigid application of divine retribution.[9] This scholarly view trades heavily on how the friends had been *wrong about Job.* Yet 42.7, according to the accepted translation, specifies that it was *'about God'* that the friends had been wrong.[10] And so the specificity on this point

---

[6] BDB, p. 373, proposes reading it 'correctly', citing Sirach 5:11 as a parallel adverbial use of the feminine participle. Translations following an adverbial reading are NAB ('rightly') and NEB ('as you ought').

[7] On this sense for 42.7, then, there is a wide consensus, despite the expected minor variations in wording of translations.

[8] Of course, for many this dissonance contributes to the historical-critical conclusion that the poetic dialogue does not cohere with the prose narrative and that the two have been artifically combined in a way that has fallen short of reconciling the dissonance. See e.g. N.H. Tur-Sinai, *The Book of Job* (Jerusalem: Kiryat Sefer, 1967), p. 579; M.H. Pope, *Job* (AncB; Garden City, NY: Doubleday, 1965), p. 350.

[9] Advocates of this view, which are too numerous to enumerate, include H.H. Rowley, *Job* (New Century Bible; London: Marshall, Morgan & Scott), p. 267; R. Gordis, *The Book of Job* (New York: Jewish Theological Seminary, 1978), p. 494; N.C. Habel, *The Book of Job* (OTL; Philadelphia, PA: Westminster, 1985), p. 583; J.E. Hartley, *The Book of Job* (NICOT; Grand Rapids, MI: Eerdmans, 1988), p. 539. Recently this conventional approach has been taken up in a fresh and expanded way by famed Latin American theologian Gustavo Gutiérrez, *On Job: God-Talk and the Suffering of the Innocent* (trans. M.T. O'Connell; New York: Orbis, 1987). In his words, 'God's approval evidently refers to Job's speeches as a whole, to the entire way he has followed' (p. 11). On the basis of 42.7 he sees 'correct language about God' to be the pivotal issue of the book, and he sees Job modeling it in the way he, unlike his friends, insists on 'God-talk' that is not separated from the human experience of innocent suffering, moving from his own experience to the plight of innocent sufferers everywhere. He calls this the 'language of prophecy', and he sees it leading forward in Job to another level of discourse, which he calls 'the language of contemplation', which is all about 'living encounter with God'. He sees these two kinds of language in Job as making up 'correct language about God' (see pp. 11-17). In discussing Job's 'language of contemplation' (pp. 51-103) he approaches, as we shall see, my own thesis that prayer is pivotal in defining the difference between Job and his friends, although Gutiérrez does not see, as I will show, the explicit reference to prayer in 42.7.

[10] This also undercuts the attempt by a few scholars (e.g. C.H. Mackintosh, *Job and His Friends* [New York: Loizeau, n.d.], pp. 66-67), to argue that Job's right speech about God

strains against the theological generality of the conventional explanation.

An ancient way of alleviating this strain, it appears, shows up in a variant reading of 42.7 found in several Hebrew manuscripts, which has God faulting the friends for speaking 'against my servant (בעבדי, *be'evedî*) Job'.[11] As an apparent move to avoid the more difficult reading of the Masoretic Text, this variant has little to commend it.

One modern way of addressing the strain of 42.7 has appeared in the form of an 'ironic' interpretation of the book of Job that is found to hinge on this verse.[12] This view assumes that the poetic dialogue between Job and his friends was inserted into an older prose story (now the prologue and epilogue) not to augment it, as the common historical-critical approach has maintained,[13] but to impose on it an ironic twist. According to this 'ironic' approach, God's verdict in the prose epilogue had originally commended the pious speech of Job as depicted in the prologue ('In all this Job neither sinned nor charged God foolishly', 1.22). But now a poet, so goes the argument, has inserted a dialogue, in which Job has repeatedly charged God with being unjust, so that God's final verdict in the prose epilogue now ironically vindicates Job's charges against him! In effect, this view has God saying, 'Job has spoken *right* about *my* being *wrong!*'

This interpretation, though clever, nevertheless falters. It presupposes that the poet's irony is motivated by a desire to undermine a simplistic and rigid doctrine of retribution in the prose story – a doctrinal position that is simply not to be found there upon closer examination. There is nothing simplistic and rigid in this way, for instance, in Job's words, 'Shall we receive good from the hand of God and not receive

refers only to Job's confession in 42.1-6 and not to anything said earlier, despite the fact that, in his confession, it is *about himself, not God,* that Job speaks in a new way. For other evidence against this view, see the keen comments of E. Good, *In Turns of Tempest: A Reading of Job* (Stanford, CA: Stanford University Press, 1990), pp. 380-82, who points out that God's verdict in 42.7 is introduced with the words, 'after the LORD had spoken these words to Job', as if to bypass any reference to what Job had just spoken in 42.1-6.

[11] See the textual note in *Biblia Hebraica Stuttgartensia* and also Gordis, *The Book of Job,* p. 494.

[12] See D. Robertson, 'The Book of Job: A Literary Study', *Soundings* 56 (1973), pp. 446-84, and J.G. Williams, 'You Have not Spoken Truth of Me: Mystery and Irony in Job', *ZAW* 83 (1971), pp. 231-55, whose publication, though earlier, cites Robertson's article, which had not yet been published.

[13] This now common historical-critical view (cf. n. 8 above) that the poetic dialogue between Job and his friends was inserted into a much older prose 'folk tale' can be traced from J. Wellhausen (in a review of A. Dillman, *Das Buch Hiob*), *Jahrbücher für deutsche Theologie* 16 (1871), pp. 555-58. For a list of a number of others who have supported this position, see S. Terrien, 'Job,' *Interpreter's Bible*, vol. III (New York: Abingdon, 1954), p. 885.

evil?' (2.10).[14] There seems to be enough literary and theological depth
in the prose materials[15] that, if a poet had indeed so appropriated irony
to subvert the theological intent of the prose, the prose narrative,
through centuries of interpretation, must be credited with combining
with the poetry in a way that, *even more ironically,* subverts recognition
of the poet's irony! Yet even if there is too much irony here to be
believed, the 'ironic' reading of Job nevertheless sharply poses the
problematic nature of God's words in 42.7 with respect to the dialogue
of Job.

A striking solution to the foregoing difficulties encountered in the
interpretation of Job 42.7 can be found by following another rendering
of the verse – one which modern scholarship has scarcely considered.
It entails an alternative reading of the prepositional phrase אֵלַי (*'elay*).
The modern consensus, as noted earlier, has been to translate it
'of/about me' or 'concerning me',[16] so that the entire phrase yields
something like, 'you have not spoken right *about me*'. However, the
simplest rendering of this very common preposition with pronominal
suffix, as any first-year Hebrew student knows, is not '*about* me' but
rather '*to* me', as indeed it *is* rendered in most of its approximately 300
occurrences in Hebrew Scripture.[17] The Hebrew preposition that
would be typical for yielding 'about' or 'concerning' is עַל (*'al*).[18]
Granted, it is grammatically possible for אֶל (*'el*), to be used in this
sense, 'equivalent to עַל (*'al*)'.[19] However, it is only context that would
demand opting for this secondary sense of אֵלַי (*'elay*) over the primary
sense, 'to me'.

Interestingly, although modern scholarship has assumed this contextual demand, it has not always been taken for granted. In the ancient
versions one finds renderings of this prepositional phrase that make
room for its primary sense. The Septuagint reads ἐνώπιον μου (*enópion
mou*), 'before me'. The Syriac and Vulgate follow suit. The Aramaic

---

[14] See my discussion on this point in my study, 'The Integrity of Job', presented in the
previous chapter of this volume.

[15] On this see D.J.A. Clines, 'False Naivety in the Prologue to Job', *Hebrew Annual
Review* 9 (1985), pp. 127-36.

[16] So all of the translations mentioned in nn. 5 and 6.

[17] See S. Mandelkern, *Veteris Testamenti Concordantiae Hebraicae Atque Chaldaicae* (Tel
Aviv: Schocken, 1978), pp. 80-81; BDB, pp. 39-41.

[18] See BDB, p. 754; R.J. Williams, *Hebrew Syntax: An Outline* (2nd ed., Toronto:
University of Toronto Press, 1976), p. 51.

[19] Williams, *Hebrew Syntax,* p. 53. He lists as examples: 1 Sam. 4.19; 15.35; 2 Sam.
24.16. See also BDB p. 41, where it is noted that the use of אֶל (*'el*) in the sense of עַל
(*'al*), although not plentiful anywhere, shows up more in the following books: Samuel,
Kings, Jeremiah, and Ezekiel.

Targum of Job reads לוֹתִי (*lothi*), 'with me'.[20] In all these cases, the phrase and (consequently) the verse are translated in a way that points to the issue of speaking not merely *about* God but *to* God.[21] Conversely, among modern translators and commentators I have found only two scholars – and only one in this century – who has advocated the primary sense for אֵלַי ('*elay*) in Job 42.7.[22]

---

[20] These versional readings are noted and dismissed without argument in S.R. Driver and G.B. Gray, *The Book of Job* (ICC; Edinburgh: T. & T. Clark, 1921), p. 348. See also E. Dhorme, *A Commentary on the Book of Job* (trans. H. Knight; Nashville, TN: Nelson, 1984), p. 648.

[21] The Targum's 'with me' obviously conveys this more directly, whereas 'before me' in the Septuagint textual tradition readily includes the sense of speaking *to* God but not necessarily so. Its rendering could be taken to indicate *speaking in God's presence* without necessarily speaking directly *to* God. It is difficult to explain how the Septuagint would have come to translate אֵלַי ('*elay*) as 'before me', since this translation lacks the grammatical precedence one can find for 'about me'. The Hebrew לִפְנֵי (*liphne*) would be the expected source for 'before me', and in the absence of any Hebrew manuscript basis for this, one wonders whether the Septuagint here may have been representing a Greek impulse to make more room (in the book as well as the verse) for the sense of speaking *about* God vs. speaking *to* God – an impulse which modern scholarship has followed to the point of excluding *any* room for the sense of speaking *to* God. Another pre-modern scholar who observed the plain reading of the Hebrew, 'to me', in Job 42.7 is Saadiah Gaon, the famous Jewish philosopher who lived in Babylonia in the eighth century CE. However, he departs slightly from the primary sense of the following phrase to get: 'as to my servant Job'. See *The Book of Theodicy: Translation and Commentary on the Book of Job by Saadiah Ben Joseph Al-Fayumi* (trans. from Arabic L.E. Goodman; New Haven, CT: Yale University Press, 1988), p. 412.

[22] K.F.R. Budde, *Das Buch Hiob* (Göttingen: Vandenhoeck & Ruprecht, 1896), s.v., whose translation, *zu mir*, is acknowledged by Driver and Gray, *Book of Job,* p. 348, only for the purpose of summarily dismissing it along with Budde's defense that 'all human speech has God for its hearer, and is directed towards Him.' The other scholar is Eugene Peterson in his 'dynamic equivalence' translation, *The Message: The Wisdom Books* (Colorado Springs, CO: NavPress, 1996), whose rendering encompasses both of the given senses of אֵלַי ('*elay*): 'You haven't been honest either with me or about me – not the way my friend Job has.' Several years after first publishing this study I was made aware of the recent article of Pierre van Hecke, 'From Conversation about God to Conversation with God: The Case of Job', in J. Haers and P. De Mey (eds.), *Theology and Conversation: Towards a Relational Theology* (Leuven: Leuven University Press, 2003), pp. 115-24. Van Hecke's study, which independently arrives at the same conclusion as mine on the translation 'to me' in Job 42.7, along lines of argument that complement my own, although being unaware of the prior publication of my study, cites one other scholar who follows this translation in an article published the same year in which my study was first published: Manfred Oeming, '"Ihr habt nicht recht von mir geredet wie mein Knecht Hiob": Gottes Schlusswort als Schlüssel zur Interpretation des Hiobbuchs und als kritische Anfrage an die moderne Theologie', *EvTh* 60 (2000), pp. 103-16. Both Van Hecke and Oeming argue for the translation 'to me' on the basis of how the book of Job elsewhere translates this preposition in tandem with verbs of speaking (דבר [*davar*] in 2.13, 13.3, 40.27, 42.7 & 9; and אמר [*'amar*] in 1.7, 8, & 12, 2.2, 3, 6, & 10, 9.12, 10.2, 34.31). Determinative for Van Hecke, though, is Job 13.3, where there is not only the same verb and preposition, but also the same indirect object or addressee, *viz.* 'God', and

When the actual context of the book of Job is considered in relation to the translation 'to me' in Job 42.7, one can find some striking correspondence. This translation, of course, has God making an explicit reference to prayer. It is clearly the case that Job prays repeatedly during the course of his interaction with his friends, while they, on the other hand, are never seen addressing God a single time.[23] They speak profusely *about* God, and they even speak *about speaking to God,*[24] but only Job breaks out beyond the boundaries of inter-human dialogue to address God directly. In fact, Job is *too direct,* in another sense of the term, for the theological sensibilities of his friends. Indeed, this seems to be what sparks their dispute with Job in the first place. Job's lament in ch. 3 boldly challenges God, and this brings an end to the comforters' seven days of silence (and comfort!) and a beginning to their counter-challenge of Job.[25] Thus, in the dialogue, Job is distinct from his friends not only in that he speaks to God and they do not, but also in that he dares to speak to God with a bold, confrontive and challenging directness which they reject on theological principle. The words of God in Job 42.7 can thus be seen to fit this contrast between Job and his friends *perfectly.* The friends 'have not spoken *to* God', as Job has, neither have they, like Job, spoken to him '*firmly*' (following the most basic nuance of the root כון, *kun*)[26] or '*straight*' (to use a contemporary

where the surrounding context features Job's emphasizing the point, contra his friends, that he is committed to speaking forthrightly to God. My colleague Lee Roy Martin, before learning of Van Hecke's article, suggested to me a support for my translation of 42.7 in the very explicit and emphatic statement Job makes in a verse from ch. 13 that Van Hecke's article does not treat, 13.15: 'but I will argue my ways *to his face*' (אל־לפני, *'el-liphne*). Thus, God's reference to Job's speaking 'to me' in 42.7 can be seen making not just general reference to Job's prior address, but also specific reference to what Job had explicitly announced as his intention.

[23] This is carefully observed, detailed, and discussed by Dale Patrick, 'Job's Address of God', *ZAW* 91 (1979), pp. 268-282. After noting that 'Job's three companions never address God,' he proceeds to note Job's direct address of God in the following verses: 7.7, 8, 12-14, 16, 17-21; 9.27-28, 30-31; 10.2-14, 16-17, 18,20; 13.19, 20-27; 14.3, 5-6, 13, 15-17, 19-20; 16.7, 8; 17.3, 4; 30.20-23.

[24] See 5.8; 8.5; 11.13; 15.4; 22.27. In each of these cases the friends speak condescendingly to Job about how he should speak to God.

[25] See my discussion in the previous chapter.

[26] Again, see BDB, p. 465. Lamontte Luker, a friend and OT colleague, first suggested such a translation of this verse to me in a personal letter in March 1985. He proposed, 'For you have not spoken firmly to me as my servant, Job.' Although it was a long time before I took up this proposal and began to see its striking relevance for the whole book, I gratefully acknowledge Monte Luker's responsibility for planting the seed which grew into the thesis of this study.

colloquialism[27] of a term also identified as a basic nuance of (כון).[28] God's verdict, on both counts, is thus aptly expressed: 'you have not spoken straight to me, as my servant Job has'.[29]

Seeing 'right prayer' as the decisive issue here fits well with the immediate context of 42.7, for in the very next verse and in consequence to what God has just said, God tells Eliphaz and his friends to go with sacrificial offerings and 'let my servant Job pray for you.' The consequential relation between the two verses, then, is that, since only Job has prayed right and they haven't, they now need Job to pray for them. The rest of verse eight includes a repeating of God's words in verse seven, as if to underscore the tight consequential connection: 'for to him (*viz.* Job when he prays) I will show favor and not deal with you according to your folly, since you have not spoken straight to me, as my servant Job has.' The immediate context of 42.7 thus reinforces what we saw in the larger context of the book: The friends' 'straight'[30] God-talk has separated them from talking *straight to* God.

There is even more to be said for how a reference to prayer in 42.7 relates strategically to the entire book of Job. This comes into view in the light of the important work of Claus Westermann on the structure of the book of Job – a work first published three decades ago.[31] In this form-critical study, Westermann points out how lament is structurally the controlling genre of the book.[32] He observes that the dialogue be-

---

[27] See *The Oxford Encyclopedic English Dictionary* (3rd ed.; New York: Oxford University Press, 1996), s.v., which notes this usage of 'straight': '(of a verbal attack) delivered in a frank or direct manner.'

[28] See *Lexicon Veteris Testamenti Libros*, p. 426.

[29] I am not choosing this nuance of 'straight' in a way that intends to rule out the sense of 'correct' or 'right'. Job's 'straight' speaking to God, as it was characterized by the drama of the dialogue, is now characterized by a single term which confirms it as 'right'. What could keep the ambiguity and possiblities that are alive in the Hebrew term from functioning in this way?: Job's 'straight' speaking is finally declared to have been 'right', and his speaking that all along had been 'right' is acknowledged to have been 'straight'. Thus the term can at once convey that the *straight* speaking was *right,* and the *right* speaking was *straight.*

[30] I use 'straight' here with *double entendre*, in the sense of both 'straight down the line of established dogma' and 'straight without deviation,' (i.e. uninterrupted talking *about* God without ever talking *to* God). Again, I am playing on the ambiguity of the English word in a way that I do not take to be irrelevant to the characterization of the discourse of the friends in the book of Job.

[31] *Der Aufbau des Buches Hiob* (Stuttgart: Calwer Verlag, 1977), translated as *The Structure of the Book of Job: A Form-Critical Analysis* (trans. C.A. Muenchow; Philadelphia, PA: Fortress, 1981).

[32] *Structure of Job,* pp. 1-15. Even before Westermann, the argument that Job should be viewed as a paradigm for an answered lament was advanced by H. Gese, *Lehre und Wirklichkeit in der alten Weisheit: Studien zu den Sprüchen Salomos und zu dem Buche Hiob* (Tübingen: J.C.B. Mohr, 1958), pp. 63-78. Westermann mentions a number of others

tween Job and his friends (chs. 4–27) is framed by laments of Job (chs. 3; 29–31), 'which stand outside the disputation and are strictly laments, lacking any sort of address to the friends.'[33] For Westermann, 'this means that the dialogue stands *within* the lament. The lament has both the first and the last word.'[34] Job's lament turns away from the friends and opens up to direct address of God.[35] In fact, the last word of Job's lament (chs. 29–31), so Westermann notes, 'leads up to a summoning of God' (31.35-37).[36] Yet more than this, Westermann observes that 'this divine-human interaction is never totally interrupted in the middle section (chs. 4–27) but rather is continued in Job's laments, which are components of his speech in the dialogue section.'[37] On this basis, Westermann is able to conclude that 'there is only one way to see the whole of the book of Job: the encompassing confrontation is that between Job and God, while within this confrontation stands the one between the friends and Job.'[38]

One could even add to Westermann's observation on how Job's laments frame the dialogue, that these laments are themselves framed by a prose narrative that features intercession for his children as Job's first action (1.5) and prayer for his friends as his last (42.9-10). Indeed, prayer is primary from beginning to end.

Westermann's observations set in sharp relief the fact that the disputation initiated (ch. 4) and carried forward by Job's friends, appears (in the context of the entire dialogue section) as something of an interruption or an intrusion upon a more primary dialogue between Job and God. In fact, the friends' disputation is more than intrusion; it is intentional opposition prompted by and targeted against Job's course of prayer. Job, from beginning to end, seeks a hearing with God; he calls for it explicitly again and again.[39] However, the dispute of his friends forces Job to have to press his cry to God against and through their decrying objections. Their *refined theology* is pitted not only against the

who have also emphasized the importance of the lament form as a dominating feature of the book of Job (pp. 13-14).

[33] *Structure of Job*, p. 4.

[34] *Structure of Job*, p. 4 (emphasis Westermann's).

[35] It could be argued that Job's lament of ch. 3 cannot be regarded as direct speech to God, since Job here speaks *about* God (vv. 4, 23). However, the discourse of curse constitutes an appeal to supernatural power in a way that registers, at the very least, an indirect addressing of God.

[36] Westermann, *Structure of Job*, p. 6.

[37] Westermann, *Structure of Job*, p. 6. All of this is detailed in Patrick, 'Job's Address of God', pp. 268-72. See biblical references in the previous citation of Patrick's article above.

[38] Westermann, *Structure of Job*, p. 5.

[39] See 10.2; 12.4; 13.3, 15, 22-24; 14.15; 16.19-21; 19.25-27; 23.3-10; 30.20; 31.35-37.

daring content of Job's theology but, even more essentially, against the form it takes in *raw prayer to God*.

Westermann's study helps us see the *decisive place of prayer* in the genre and structure of the book of Job and the *decisive struggle over prayer* in the dramatic unfolding of the book. Yet Westermann does not connect this with or even notice the *decisive reference to prayer* at the end of the book.[40] We can see, however, that a reference to prayer in Job 42.7 is not only permitted by the grammar of the verse, it is also favored by the context of the book. Indeed, it speaks for the whole message of the book with summarizing decisiveness.

Broader Implications and Conclusions

The reference to prayer in Job 42.7 and its relationship to the book of Job, as illuminated in this study, have even broader implications. These are not unrelated to implications that Westermann saw for his study. He acknowledged that his findings on the dominance of lament in the book of Job had significant import for the question of its common classification as wisdom literature. He noted that the wisdom classification of Job 'has clearly exerted a pervasive, perhaps even controlling influence upon nineteenth- and twentieth-century exegesis',[41] particularly in the way it has predisposed 'most modern interpretations [to] proceed on the assumption that the Book of Job deals with a "problem".'[42] Westermann meant by this that these modern scholars have viewed the book in terms of a discussion of 'theoretical' rather than 'existential' character,[43] or, as he went on to express it, an 'inquiry' that treats 'suffering, or more precisely, the suffering of a just man [as an] object of thought.'[44] Westermann noticed how this has obscured the fact that more 'fundamentally the book treats an existential question' primarily by means of the 'existential process' of lament.[45]

To Westermann's observations I would have some of my own to add. His apt characterization of modern scholarship's dominant way of approaching the book of Job corresponds strikingly to the friends' approach to the problem of Job. Specifically, modern scholars approach the book as a theoretical 'discussion of a problem', without giving weight to the claims of particular, existential experience; and that is

---

[40] The same is true for the other scholars, previously noted (Gutiérrez, Patrick, and Gese), who have drawn attention in significant ways to the prime role of prayer in the book of Job.

[41] Westermann, *Structure of Job*, p. 1.

[42] Westermann, *Structure of Job*, p. 1.

[43] Westermann, *Structure of Job*, p. 2.

[44] Westermann, *Structure of Job*, p. 2.

[45] Westermann, *Structure of Job*, pp. 2-3. And the book does this, Westermann further emphasized, by depicting a particular event of a particular person (pp. 6-8).

how the friends press their disputation against Job. Again, modern scholars look right past the pronounced emphasis on lament; and the friends do likewise with respect to Job. Such correspondence could be explained in terms of the 'controlling influence' of the 'wisdom' categorization on both modern interpretation (as Westermann noted) and the friends' interpretation of the problem of Job (as I have just indicated). However, I do not believe this explanation goes deep enough with respect to modern interpretation. Which is the more fundamental truth?: (1) that the wisdom categorization of Job has influenced its modern interpretation, or rather (2) that modern interpretation has influenced the wisdom categorization of Job? I submit it is the latter. Modern scholarship has interpreted the book the way the friends interpret Job's problem because of the bent of the former's *own* 'wisdom' tradition. What Westermann regards as issuing from modern interpretation's wisdom classification of Job (*viz.* elevating theoretical inquiry over existential experience and raising discourse that treats reality as an 'object of thought' over discourse that addresses the particularity and concreteness of human experience) can be seen to issue *from modern interpretation itself,* that is, *from its very mode of interpreting* – one that is in obvious ways parallel to the ancient wisdom tradition represented by Job's friends.

This leads to an important implication. The modern criticism of the book of Job and its underlying hermeneutic, which thus have lined up with the friends' criticism of Job, cannot escape the counter-criticism that the end of the book delivers against the friends and the wisdom tradition they represent! The statement, 'you have not spoken right,' indicts the friends' refined theological discourse, but it also, by extention, implicates the modern scholarly discourse which has followed suit by downplaying and looking past the lament of Job. It has done this, I would submit, even to the point of *translating it out* of God's final verdict in Job 42.7.[46] However, the point of the verse and the book is finally inescapable: not speaking 'right *about* [God]' has to do with not speaking '"straight" *to* [God]' – something that both ancient wisdom and modern criticism have tended to crowd out of their purviews.[47]

My point has been to challenge modern scholarship's translation of a verse and thereby extend Westermann's challenge against 'most mod-

---

[46] Earlier I raised the question about the contextual demand for translating אֵלַי (*'elay*) 'about me' rather than its primary sense 'to me'. I submit that the contextual demand, which modern scholarship has routinely assumed, turns out to be the demand of modern scholarship's own conceptual context imposed on the text.

[47] On the limited place of prayer in OT wisdom literature, see J.L. Crenshaw, 'The Restraint of Reason, the Humility of Prayer', in ch. 9 of his *Urgent Advice and Probing Questions: Collected Writings on Old Testament Wisdom* (Macon, GA: Mercer, 1995), pp. 206-21.

ern interpretations' of the book of Job. Yet in so doing, I have come to the point of showing how the book and the given verse themselves pose a challenge to modern criticism itself, particularly as the latter is applied to theological discourse. Gustavo Gutiérrez has recently done something similar in his book, *On Job*.[48] Focusing like myself on Job 42.7, but following modern scholarship's translation of it, he argues that this verse identifies 'speaking correctly about God' as the key issue of the book[49] and 'talk about God' or 'God-talk' as what theology is.[50] By these terms, Gutiérrez places Job's example of right God-talk over against modern theology.[51] Job's experience reveals, as Gutiérrez points out, that language about God cannot be valid if it becomes separated from that which speaks from and for the experience of those suffering unjustly or innocently – what Gutiérrez calls 'the language of prophecy.'[52] Gutiérrez goes on to argue from Job's example that language about God that succeeds on this count will inevitably lead to what he calls 'the language of contemplation' or speech that entails the experience of worship and encounter with God.[53] He specifically mentions speaking *to* God in contrast to speaking merely *about* God,[54] although he never notices how Job 42.7 speaks directly to this point. On both counts Job's right God-talk, as brought forward by Gutiérrez's rich liberationist perspective, delivers a profound critique and challenge against modern theology.

My own perspective as a Pentecostal leads me to resonate deeply with Gutiérrez's liberating study, *On Job*. Pentecostalism, which itself has become so prominent in Latin America, undoubtedly has become so because of its deep lineage in the discourse of the oppressed.[55] Especially prominent in this discourse has been lament – the focus of the present study and something that my Pentecostal experience certainly has given me deep resources for seeing in Job.

Larry McQueen has recently shown the originating, generative role of lament in the Pentecostal movement and faith experience.[56] My

---

[48] Cited in n. 9.

[49] Gutiérrez, *On Job*, p. 11.

[50] Gutiérrez, *On Job*, p. xi.

[51] Gutiérrez, *On Job*, pp. xvii-xix.

[52] Gutiérrez, *On Job*, pp. 16, 19-49.

[53] Gutiérrez, *On Job*, pp. 16, 51-103.

[54] Gutiérrez, *On Job*, p. 54; here Gutiérrez cites the observation of Patrick, 'Job's Address of God', p. 269, that the friends never speak *to* God, as Job does, but only *about* him.

[55] See Cheryl Bridges Johns, *Pentecostal Formation: A Pedagogy among the Oppressed* (JPTSup 2; Sheffield: Sheffield Academic Press, 1993), esp. pp. 119-29.

[56] Larry R. McQueen, *Joel and the Spirit: The Cry of a Prophetic Hermeneutic* (JPTSup 8; Sheffield: Sheffield Academic Press, 1995), pp. 76-82.

attestation of this leads me to take issue with Gutiérrez's inclination to view prayer ('the language of contemplation') in terms of a 'second stage' to which right language *about* God will eventually lead.[57] This view stops short of what I see in Job – a man for whom prayer is both the beginning and end of all God-talk,[58] (1) so that talking *about* God takes place *within* the experience of talking *to* God and not apart from it; (2) so that talking to God is not rendered subsequent and secondary to theology, but it is primary, unto the point of challenging the very formulation (endorsed by Gutiérrez), which defines theology as 'talk *about* God';[59] (3) so that theology becomes embedded in worship, thus becoming worship once again;[60] (4) so that talking *about* God and talking *to* God come together so intimately that a single term (like אֵלַי ['*elay* in the Hebrew!) could refer to them both at the same time!

This is the way it was with Job, for whom the fear of the LORD[61] was the beginning (Job 1.1) as well as the end (Job 28.28; 42.5-6) of wisdom, and also for the apostle Paul and a long line of early theologians, for whom such integration was not so unusual, prior to the refashioning of theology in the image and form of Greek metaphysics.[62]

Yet forms, formulas, and formulations of refined theology perennially get raised up in ways that threaten to shut down prayer. The book of Job shows that this is not just a modern problem. Job also shows that it is a problem that can become the provoking catalyst for the form-

---

[57] See Gutiérrez, *On Job*, p. 88. At one point Gutiérrez says, 'Talk about God presupposes and, at the same time, leads to a living encounter with God' (p. 17), but overall his study emphasizes the 'gradual maturation [of God-talk] as the book moves along' (p. 17) especially in terms of the 'shift' from 'the language of prophecy' to the 'language of contemplation' (see esp. pp. 16, 88).

[58] Again, cf. Westermann, *Structure of Job*, p. 4.

[59] Gutiérrez, *On Job*, p. xi (emphasis mine).

[60] I am indebted here to my teacher and colleague R. Hollis Gause, who has richly expounded this definition and approach to theology for many years at the Church of God Theological Seminary.

[61] Deuteronomy grounds the OT experience of fear of the LORD in the theophanic encounter of Israel at Horeb or Sinai (Deut. 5, esp. 5.20-26). Fear of the LORD is widely accepted as the quintessential response of Hebrew worship.

[62] The role of Thomas Aquinas in this was undoubtedly major and set the stage for modern theology's commitment and attachment to Greek metaphysics. Interestingly, Aquinas's commentary on the book of Job, and Job 42.7 in particular, reflects both his philosophical orientation in relation to this larger role and also his direct influence on reading Job 42.7 in terms of a reference to theology rather than prayer. His commentary on the Latin text at this point reads: 'you have not spoken what is right before Me, *that is, faithful dogmas*, as has My servant Job' (*Thomas Aquinas: The Literal Exposition on Job, A Scriptural Commentary Concerning Providence* [trans. A. Damico; ed. M.D. Yaffe; Atlanta, GA: Scholars Press, 1989], p. 471).

shattering, breakthrough experience of lament[63] – what Pentecostals have long called 'praying through.'[64]

Job prays through. It takes God-talk that is straight and firm – firm enough to break through our forms and speak to the One who is no form,[65] the One who breaks all forms,[66] the One who breaks us. Yet the One who has broken me is the One who has spoken to me, revealing that I have spoken *straight to Him.*

> Let the words of my mouth
> and the meditation of my heart
> be acceptable before your face,
> O Lord, my strength and my redeemer.
> (Ps. 19.15)[67]

---

[63] See the recent study of Job by K.J. Dell, *The Book of Job as Skeptical Literature* (BZAW; Berlin: de Gruyter, 1991), who advances the compelling thesis that inherent in the very form of Job is an intentional pattern and programmatic effort to alter, parody, or deconstruct established literary forms in order to contest their claims. Dell takes note of my study 'Integrity of Job' (now presented in the previous chapter) and its argument that Job's lament of ch. 3 is a direct counterpoint of his confession of faith in 1.21. This study and more recent spadework in the book of Psalms, as it has been informed by my Pentecostal experience, have convinced me that breaking conventional language forms is a key element in the nature and dynamic of lament.

[64] McQueen, *Joel and the Spirit,* pp. 76-77.

[65] As Deut. 4.15 says, 'Therefore take good heed to yourselves. Since you saw no form on the day that the LORD spoke to you at Horeb out of the midst of the fire' (RSV).

[66] Immediately after highlighting the prohibition against making 'a graven image in the form of anything', Deut. 4.24 says, 'For the LORD your God is a devouring fire, a jealous God' (RSV).

[67] I am grateful to my colleague John Christopher Thomas for his dialogue and encouragement during the writing of this article, also for his reading of the manuscript and helping me to settle on the title.

Index of Authors

Index of Biblical References

Journal of Pentecostal Theology
Supplement Series

1. Steven J. Land, *Pentecostal Spirituality: A Passion for the Kingdom*. ISBN 1 85075 442 X.
2. Cheryl Bridges Johns, *Pentecostal Formation: A Pedagogy among the Oppressed*. ISBN 1 85075 438 1.
3. ** Jon Ruthven, *On the Cessation of the Charismata: The Protestant Polemic on Miracles*. ISBN 1 85075 405 5. ** Out of print. NEW EDITION: see no. 33.
4. Harold D. Hunter & Peter D. Hocken (eds.), *All Together in One Place: Theological Papers from the Brighton Conference on World Evangelization*. ISBN 1 85075 406 3.
5. Mark Wilson (ed.), *Spirit and Renewal: Essays in Honor of J. Rodman Williams*. ISBN 1 85075 471 3.
6. Robert P. Menzies, *Empowered for Witness: The Spirit in Luke-Acts*. ISBN 1 85075 721 6.
7. Stephen E. Parker, *Led by the Spirit: Toward a Practical Theology of Pentecostal Discernment and Decision Making*. ISBN 1 85075 746 1.
8. Larry R. McQueen, *Joel and the Spirit: The Cry of a Prophetic Hermeneutic*. ISBN 1 85075 736 4.
9. Max Turner, *Power from on High: The Spirit in Israel's Restoration and Witness in Luke-Acts*. ISBN 1 85075 756 9.
10. ** D. William Faupel, *The Everlasting Gospel: The Significance of Eschatology in the Development of Pentecostal Thought*. ISBN 1 85075 761 5. ** REPRINT by DEO
11. Wonsuk Ma & Robert P. Menzies, *Pentecostalism in Context: Essays in Honor of William W. Menzies*. ISBN 1 85075 803 4.
12. John Michael Penny, *The Missionary Emphasis of Lukan Pneumatology*. ISBN 1 85075 800 X.
13. John Christopher Thomas, *The Devil, Disease, and Deliverance: Origins of Illness in New Testament Thought*. ISBN 1 85075 869 7.
14. Samuel Solivan, *The Spirit, Pathos and Liberation: Toward an Hispanic Pentecostal Theology*. ISBN 1 85075 942 1.
15. Allan H. Anderson & Walter J. Hollenweger, *Pentecostals after a Century: Global Perspectives on a Movement in Transition*. ISBN 1 84127 006 7.
16. Roger Stronstad, *The Prophethood of All Believers: A Study in Luke's Charismatic Theology*. ISBN 1 84127 005 9.
17. Daniel E. Albrecht, *Rites in the Spirit: A Ritual Approach to Pentecostal/Charismatic Spirituality*. ISBN 1 84127 017 2.
18. Blaine Charette, *Restoring Presence: The Spirit in Matthew's Gospel*. ISBN 1 84127 059 8.
19. Matthias Wenk, *Community Forming Power: The Socio-Ethical Role of the Spirit in Luke-Acts*. ISBN 1 84127 125 X.

20. Amos Yong, *Discerning the Spirit(s): A Pentecostal-Charismatic Contribution to Christian Theology of Religions*. ISBN 1 84127 133 0.

21. Simon Chan, *Pentecostal Theology and the Christian Spiritual Tradition*. ISBN 1 84127 144 6.

22. Gerald Hovenden, *Speaking in Tongues: The New Testament Evidence in Context*. ISBN 1 84127 307 6.

23. Lynne Price, *Theology out of Place: A Theological Biography of Walter J. Hollenweger*. ISBN 0 82646 028 3.

24. Wonsuk Ma & Robert P. Menzies, *The Spirit and Spirituality: Essays in Honour of Russell P. Spittler*. ISBN 0 56708 167 2.

25. Peter Althouse, *Spirit of the Last Days: Pentecostal Eschatology in Conversation with Jürgen Moltmann*. ISBN 0 82647 162 5.

26. Martin William Mittelstadt, *The Spirit and Suffering in Luke-Acts: Implications for a Pentecostal Pneumatology*. ISBN 0 82647 164 1.

27. S. David Moore, *The Shepherding Movement: Controversy and Charismatic Ecclesiology*. ISBN 0 82647 160 9.

28. Kenneth J. Archer, *A Pentecostal Hermeneutic for the Twenty-First Century: Spirit, Scripture and Community*. ISBN 0 56708 367 5.

Volumes 1-28 were originally published by Sheffield Academic Press/Continuum. Subsequent titles are published by Deo Publishing under ISSN 0966 7393:

29. Kimberly Ervin Alexander, *Pentecostal Healing: Models in Theology and Practice*. ISBN 90 5854 031 6 / 978 90 5854 031 7.

30. Robby Waddell, *The Spirit of the Book of Revelation*. ISBN 90 5854 030 8 / 978 90 5854 030 0.

31. David Reed, *"In Jesus' Name": The History and Beliefs of Oneness Pentecostals*. ISBN 978 1 905679 01 0.

32. Lee Roy Martin, *The Unheard Voice of God. A Pentecostal Hearing of the Book of Judges*. ISBN 978 1 905679 07 2.

33. Jon Ruthven, *On the Cessation of the Charismata: The Protestant Polemic on Post-biblical Miracles*. Revised edition of no. 3. ISBN 978 1 905679 04 1.

34. Opoku Onyinah, *Pentecostal Exorcism: Witchcraft and Demonology in Ghana*. ISBN 978 1 905679 06 5.

35. Rickie D. Moore, *The Spirit of the Old Testament*. ISBN 978 1 905679 11 9.

36. Stephen J. Land, Rickie D. Moore, and John Christopher Thomas, eds., *Passover, Pentecost, and Parousia: Studies in Celebration of the Life and Ministry of R. Hollis Gause*. ISBN 978 1 905679 12 6.

37. Matthew K. Thompson, *Kingdom Come: Revisioning Pentecostal Eschatology*. ISBN 978 1 905679 14 0.

38. Simon Chan, *Pentecostal Ecclesiology*. ISBN 978 1 905679 15 7.

Note: Pentecostal Commentary series titles are now also published by Deo Publishing.